REVOLUTIONARY SUICIDE

AND OTHER DESPERATE MEASURES

D1564078

REVOLUTIONARY SUICIDE

AND OTHER DESPERATE MEASURES

Narratives of Youth and Violence from Japan and the United States

Adrienne Carey Hurley

DUKE UNIVERSITY PRESS   DURHAM & LONDON   2011

© 2011 Duke University Press
All rights reserved
Printed in the United States
of America on acid-free paper ∞
Designed by Amy Ruth Buchanan
Typeset in Quadraat by Keystone
Typesetting, Inc.
Library of Congress Cataloging-in-
Publication Data appear on the last
printed page of this book.

To Jimmy

CONTENTS

ACKNOWLEDGMENTS

I benefited from the support and guidance of many people while working on this project. First and foremost, I thank my teacher and dear friend James A. Fujii of the University of California, Irvine (UCI). His intellectual flexibility and commitment to making common cause with oppressed human and non-human animals made it possible for me to pursue this kind of work, and his encouragement has sustained me every step of the way. Jim has modeled for me ways to be honest about the relationships between the study of literature and the people and movements producing the knowledge that underwrites our scholarship. His politically engaged scholarship prepares us for the challenges ahead, and I am proud to be his student. Dana Bryon Staub of the Institute for Contemporary Psychoanalysis also contributed to this book in innumerable ways. She introduced me to the writings of Sándor Ferenczi and forever broadened my understanding of fiction's power in our daily lives. While the limits and failings of this work are my own, its greatest strengths I attribute to what I have learned from Jim and Dana.

I am also deeply grateful to two very astute and thoughtful anonymous reviewers whose detailed feedback was at once challenging and validating. They appreciated the aim of my project and took a great deal of care in formulating extremely helpful responses that have made this book much stronger than its earlier draft incarnations. My treasured colleagues and friends Chizuko Naitō and James Reichert have provided years of advice, inspiration, and warmth without which this project never could have been completed, and if there are tender moments in this book, they are surely the result of the ways they have touched this project and my life. I also enjoyed the invaluable support and caring mentorship of Norma Field, Chuanren Ke, and Daniel Ross (who first encouraged me to study fiction). They encouraged me to fuse my academic labor to life-sustaining practices outside the classroom and have been steadfast and generous with their counsel and kindness.

In writing this book, I was assisted and inspired by more people than I can recount, and I apologize to anyone I have neglected to acknowledge. For their encouragement and insights, I am particularly grateful to José Alamillo, Brian Bergstrom, Jonathan Besançon, Steven Carter, Wilson Chen, Wei-min Brian Chiu, Rey Chow, John de Boer, Edward Fowler, Hu Ying, Kota Inoue, Saúl Jiménez-Sandoval, Yōichi Komori, Kim Kono, Mariam Lam, Nancy Naples, Jocelyn Pacleb, Scott Schnell, Christopher Scott, Setsu Shigematsu, Nathan Shockey and Stephen Snyder. I am especially beholden to Thomas LaMarre for his wonderful friendship and for letting me accumulate countless personal, intellectual, and professional debts in a very short time. Thanks in large measure to Tom, I am enjoying a vibrant intellectual community in Montreal alongside brilliant and generous colleagues. In particular, Yuriko Furuhata, Sumi Hasegawa, Livia Monnet, Marc Steinberg, and Miwako Uesaka provide daily professional and personal solidarity.

The late Sharon Yamamoto provided crucial encouragement at the earliest stages of this project. Like many others working in fields related to East Asian studies, I miss her very much. Sharon suggested I take my book proposal to Duke University Press, where I was fortunate to be able to work with Ken Wissoker, as well as Susan Deeks, Mandy Earley, Mark Mastromarino, Reynolds Smith, and Sharon Torian. I have benefited enormously from this talented, patient, meticulous, and experienced team of editors. I also owe thanks to others who have kindly shared knowledge, practical support, and resources: Melaine Campbell, Ken Dean, the indefatigable Ronda Fenton, Grace Fong, Steve Jordan, Rebecca Kessler, Angela Lapenna, Dongwang Liu, Philip Lutgendorf, Indi McCarthy, Margaret Mills, Livia Nardini, Suan Ong, Anthony Paré, Csaba Polony, Sonia Ryang, Chiaki Sakai (a librarian whose skills and talents are the stuff of legend), Peggy Timm, Stephen Vlastos, Robin Yates, and Macy Zheng.

The research that went into this book was made possible by a generous three-year postdoctoral fellowship at what was then called the Stanford Institute for International Studies (now the Freeman Spogli Institute), a Japan Foundation Dissertation Fellowship, dissertation fellowships from the University of California Regents, the University of California President, and Graduate Studies at UCI, as well as grants from the University of Iowa's Center for Asian and Pacific Studies and Old Gold Summer Fellowship Program.

On intellectual, political, literary, and personal fronts, I am forever beholden to the dream team that sustains and motivates me every day, even when the intervals between when we talk or see each other are long. I consider myself honored and lucky to have comrades and friends such as Kamal Benali, Rushay

Booysen, Aziz Choudry, Theodore Harris, Wei-min Brian Chiu, Alfredo Heredia, Tomoyuki Hoshino, Kota Inoue, Susan Junis, Ramsey Kanaan, Youngran Kō, Christine LaMarre, Owen Li, Abby Lippman, Chizuko Naitō (whom I hold very close to my heart always), Keisuke Narita, Jocelyn Pacleb, Dylan Rodriguez, Setsu Shigematsu, Eric Shragge, Pamela Tallman, and Carla Williams.

I also thank my students at UCI, Stanford University, and the University of Iowa for sorting through very difficult subject matter in our classes together. While my gratitude truly extends to all of them, I acknowledge especially those whose insights and understandings contributed most directly and concretely to this project: Warren Allen, Traci Bruns, Cecilia Copeland, Angela Covalt, Elis Franzen, Nate George (without whom I could not have written much of part 2 of this book), William Hendrickson, Shiho Hirasawa, Suzanne Ii, Vernon Jackson, Sahar Mandegary Javed, Hyunok Jo, T. Ivan Kling, Peter Lee, Joshua A. Mitchell, Futoshi Nakagawa, Amanda Seals, Daigo Shima, Maiko Shiota, Seashia Vang, Lor Xiong, Shiori Yamazaki, and Armando Yañez. Jacob Boss (a.k.a. Galacticus) deserves special acknowledgement for his brilliant questions and for generously helping me put together the bibliography for this book. I am beginning a new journey now with some equally remarkable students in Montreal who have already taught me a great deal, and I look forward to learning how they will shape my future work.

The volunteer instructors, artists, and others who contributed to the University of Iowa's Youth Empowerment Academy (YEA!) invested time and energy in a short-lived program I discuss briefly in the conclusion of this book. Thank you to Vanessa Shelton, one of the most effective and resourceful educators I have ever met, as well as to Sean Baylor, Nancy Humbles, Tamara Ho, Miriam Landsman, David Martinez, John Nedved, Brad Richardson, Y'Shanda Rivera, Daniel Chornet Roses, Nicholas Taylor, Carla Wilson, Vershawn Young, and all of the University of Iowa student volunteers who shared their time and energy with the YEA! kids. All of our biggest thanks go to the YEA! kids, the real teachers and theorists.

The two people whose stalwart encouragement has given me the emotional strength to finish this book are Timothy Gauger, my love, and Kathleen Crume, my beloved mother. Tim embodies the best of the old dictum to "serve the people." His priorities, passions, and boundless energy fill me with hope for our collective future. For nearly four decades, my mother has used her mind-boggling super powers to make education meaningful and life-sustaining. As a classroom teacher and administrator, she has forever touched the lives of many youth in profoundly positive ways. I am very fortunate that Tim and Mom, who give so much to so many, share so much of their love with me every day in so many ways. I also owe thanks to Ralph Crume, Yukiko and Sachinari Naitō, Amanda, Benjamin, Janice, and Reuel Gauger, and Cindy Hinton for their kinship, warmth, kindness, and affection. Special praise and gratitude are reserved for the "little brothers" to whom I am indebted for countless drawings, jokes, "liberated" books, visits, songs, stories, letters, emails, games, culinary masterpieces, poems, noogies, pranks, and hugs: Anthony Corpuz, Eugene Fowler, Keenan Hinton, Alex LaMarre, Brennan Martinez, and Comrade Kyler J. Hinton, the real revolutionary who takes me to school. I hope this book honors the many young people, those I have known and those (like Anthony Soltero and Jonathan Jackson) I never met, who compelled me to pursue this project. Above all, I am grateful to my own little brother, James Patrick Hurley Jr. (August 7, 1971–July 1, 1995), to whom this book is dedicated and for whom it was written.

All translations in this book are my own unless otherwise indicated. In the pages that follow, Japanese names are written with the surname first except in the case of Japanese Americans and in quotations taken directly from sources in which this convention is not followed.

"Spics" BY ALFREDO HEREDIA

"Spics!" they yelled, and they meant us,
although they should've said "beaners,"
because we were Mexicans—a minor technicality.
In fact, Raúl, I later learned, was half Puerto-
Rican, which may have made him a Merican. But
it didn't matter then.

We were pissed off at being called out, and
Franky, who wasn't really a beaner, but a
Pilipino, a "flip" who grew up with Mexicans,
and was now a spic, was the first to throw them
the finger, and up it shot as Raúl grabbed
his crotch, the three of us shouting, "right here!"

They turned their car around, cut us off
before we reached the corner. And without
giving it much thought, as though it was
always meant to be, part of the universal scheme,
the great cosmic design, I kicked the front door back
when the driver put his leg out. He howled and
Raúl pulled him out and made him howl some more.

Franky planted his coke bottle firmly in someone's
face, and before we could do more damage, blue and
red lights flashed, a siren screamed, and the police,
who are always there when you don't need them,
had us hugging the ground, cheek to street.

In the courtroom, the judge, like a stoic patriarch,
raised his glasses, naked eyes, arctic blue, bearing
down on our late adolescent faces. "Young men," he
said, "I am going to be lenient." That was how
the army got us.

Written in the late 1980s, this unpublished poem by Alfredo Heredia dramatizes what might be considered a kind of "turf" war, although not in the usual sense. The dispute is not over a neighborhood, but over who can be violent, how, why, when, and where. The "turf" is violence itself. All of the parties involved are male, and the judge who appears in the final stanza represents the winners, the (white supremacist) state. The speaker and his friends are sentenced to redeem themselves for disallowed expressions of violence as soldiers for that state, which defines the turf and assigns the youth their "appropriate" roles within it. The poem clearly questions what it means to be, and who can be, "American" and the ways in which violence seems overdetermined for youth of color, "as though it was always meant to be."

As richly layered and provocative as "Spics" is, perhaps one of the most interesting aspects of it relates to why it has never been published. Heredia, in his words, "disavows" this poem. In the most declarative terms, he explained to me that he is now loath to participate in even representational violence: "I wouldn't write that poem or one like it now. When I was fourteen, I saw a boy my age get killed and later wrote about it in a piece of prose. I described it as a flashback. I don't think I could even write about that now, and that really happened. I don't want to romanticize violence. Writing that poem was a kind of showing off, a way of responding to the sense that this is what's expected of people like myself."[1] It was only by reassuring him that I would note his renunciation of this poem that he consented to its appearance here.

"Spics" is a fitting introduction to this book not only for the questions about representational violence the poet's disavowal raises, but also for thematic reasons. *Revolutionary Suicide and Other Desperate Measures* is a study of the stories we tell about youth and violence. Heredia's poem illustrates the power of stories to give meaning to behavior and events. For example, in the official version of the late adolescents' story, street violence is criminalized, and military service is a "deal" and, perhaps, even an opportunity. Heredia's disavowal of "Spics" is one type of response to the uneasiness that accompanies any exploration of the questions this book raises—questions such as: What does it mean for a society to cultivate an appetite for representational violence (often for profit) in its young at the same time that many of its youth experience real violence? Heredia's answers to such questions have led him to adopt a stance of total non-cooperation and non-participation, of refusing even to write himself into an act of violence.

To understand Heredia's position, one must consider the ways in which a late adolescent "boy of color" in the U.S. might see or experience himself as the agent of possible violence and, more critically, how the larger society might see that boy. For example, race and ethnicity are frequently invoked as if they explain flare-ups of so-called gang violence in juvenile halls in the U.S., and the drama of race-based affiliation within prisons and criminalized communities informs a considerable amount of filmic and other popular culture. The enduring familiarity with films such as *Scarface* and *Blood In, Blood Out* even among youth who were not yet born when the movies were released in 1983 and 1993, respectively, is notable. In our discussion regarding this phenomenon, Heredia expressed concern that *Blood In, Blood Out* and, to a lesser extent, Edward James Olmos's *American Me* (1992) allow ample room for youth of color, in his words, "to romanticize violence." Heredia recalled watching fifth-graders reenact violent scenes and dialogue from *American Me* and commented that "the medium is stronger than the message," which in the case of *American Me* can be interpreted as a broad critique of racist violence, both institutional and interpersonal.

Such movies can appeal to and fuel a romanticization of Latino gangs, as is undoubtedly the case for many white viewers. Heredia now feels he was, even if only in part, responding to that white audience's expectations when he wrote "Spics." After the poem was recognized at a Los Angeles poetry festival, Heredia recalls receiving a phone call from a white female filmmaker who was planning a documentary on poetry in the U.S. She told Heredia she was interested in his poem about "gangs in the army" and hoped he would consider reading it for her film. Heredia declined, uncomfortable with the way in which his poem was being received and the role he was being solicited to fulfill. The speaker of "Spics" and his friends are, of course, nowhere identified as gang members, but because they are Latino and Asian and because they fight, they were already coded as such for the filmmaker. She was looking for "gangs in the army" and not the army *as* the gang (or part of a larger gang).

The association between youth of color and violent "gangs" is so pervasive that the routine use of wrist twisting (or wrist locks) and psychotropic medication (both of which can make the excessive use of force and abuse harder to detect) as means to "control" young prisoners are not as familiar at the level of general public discourse as the notion that "gang tensions" on the outside spill over into juvenile halls. Thus, when many people hear that a young person has been found injured or even dead inside a juvenile hall, they may be more likely to imagine a ritualistic shanking committed by a rival gang member of a different race or ethnicity than a fatal overdose of medication or staff-inflicted injury.[2] The dramatic shanking fantasy even resonates with some youth who have actually served time in juvenile prisons and suffered the effects of untherapeutic medication or painfully executed "control" measures, which we might see as one example of how successfully we are conditioned to look to identity instead of institutions for the sources of violence—even in cases in which our own identity is suspect. By redirecting our attention to institutions, such as the nuclear family or juvenile "correctional" systems, and the often inadequate or misleading narratives available for understanding and expressing real experience, I seek to counter some of the prevailing myths that obscure the violent conditions many youth face and offer alternative models for reading and interpreting young people's rage.

I began this project in 1995 with a focus on how childhood experiences of violence are depicted in fiction written in contemporary Japan, but it became increasingly apparent that neither the genre nor the location could adequately contain answers to the most recurrent and urgent questions. The youth whose stories were being told and sold were already accustomed to crossing the line between fact and fiction. They had to in order to survive. Storytelling, as the second and third chapters of this book make clear, is often a critical survival skill for young people living with violence. Likewise, official and other adult responses and "solutions"—not to mention commercially lucrative forms of representational youth violence—do not "respect" geographic borders. Such conditions produce striking similarities in the experiences of and social responses to young people in Japan and the U.S. who are victims of violence despite the differences in how, for example, race and class are configured and understood in the two countries.

The comparisons I make between contemporary Japan and the U.S. in this book suggest that something fundamental links (or is shared by) these two countries. Depending on one's sensibilities, that core similarity might be described as neoliberalism, late capitalism, democracy, or authoritarianism, for example, and, of course, none of these labels is exclusively applicable to the nation-states of Japan and the United States. As a starting point for thinking about what Japan and the U.S. share, I will begin with the admittedly problematic notion of the "First World" to invoke an understanding of socioeconomic and geopolitical conditions informed by the Third World solidarity movements of the mid-twentieth century. These movements attempted to create channels (sometimes official, as was the case at the Bandung Conference of 1955, but more often not) through which oppressed people could make common cause with one another, resist domination, and assert the right to collective survival.[3]

As such, these movements were often oppositional and insurgent in character and simultaneously nationalist and internationalist. The notion of a First World from which a Third World seeks liberation suggests both a specific political history and a broad, fluid understanding of geopolitical differential power. Because the U.S. and Japan are not the only nations thought of as part of the First World, and each has populations within its respective borders who identify as part of the Third World, the label "First World" itself (like "capitalist" or "authoritarian") begs questions and comparison with other contexts. Furthermore, the notion of a First World has been defined in relation to (and by) those who have identified as part of the Third World, regardless of geographical location. This last point has particular resonance in the present study and warrants some elaboration.

I refer to Third World solidarity movements not to suggest that the U.S. and Japan are representative of a totalizing and geopolitically empirical or stable "First World" (after all, many of my examples come from movements within the U.S. and Japan that have identified as "Third World") but, rather, to shed light on how access to political theorization affects social and political movements. Throughout this book, I hope to show how the absence of opportunities for youth to develop political analyses to explain their anger or rage is a genuine problem. Third World and other solidarity movements have faced similar problems, which I draw on to shed new light on youth violence in Japan and the United States. Furthermore, several of the writers whose works I discuss connect youth violence in Japan and the U.S. to sociopolitical violence in the Third World. The Third World as a critical construct continues to be vigorously theorized and reworked in many ways at a number of levels. For example, the idea of Third World solidarity retains powerful resonance for some as a means to articulate identities (sometimes as a euphemism for people of color, but not always, as examples in Ireland and Quebec illustrate), agendas, and visions. Whether in the rhetoric of Hugo Chavez or Mahmoud Ahmadinejad railing against U.S. imperialism, the emergence of an "alter-globalist" political party in Quebec (Québec Solidaire) or in the street-level discourse of antiauthoritarian and anarchist people of color organizing in North America, the idea of Third World solidarity remains important today.

To better understand the enduring meanings of Third World solidarity, it is helpful to consider how even in its earliest history, the numbered designation of "worlds" did not denote fixed geographical locations. Instead, it served as shorthand for specific and contingent constructions produced through social movements and political struggles to address fundamental disparities. As Vijay

Prashad succinctly explains in the opening of *The Darker Nations*, "The Third World was not a place. It was a project."[4] The historical political project to which he refers began in the 1950s and was predicated on yearnings for national liberation, self-determination, and freedom from ongoing oppression. If, as Prashad argues, "The world was bettered by the attempt" to articulate a Third World agenda," we might consider that the world was worsened by articulations of a First World agenda that lays waste to the moral and political rights of the oppressed, including those who live and/or identify as members of the Third World within the borders of First World nation-states.[5] In the 1960s and 1970s, this was certainly the belief of groups such as the Black Panther Party and the San'ya Liberation League, for whom the U.S. and Japan were exploiters and oppressors of the Third World writ large, both abroad and at home.[6]

Despite differences in the ways in which discrimination (based on race or class, for example) is expressed in Japan and the U.S., people whose concerns have coincided with those of Third World solidarity movements have understood the net effects of their experiences of oppression as relatable. Thus, the struggles of migrant workers in the U.S. were immediately recognizable to the Japanese *burakumin* writer Nakagami Kenji when he visited a migrant workers' camp in rural Iowa in the early 1980s. In his essay "America, America," Nakagami writes, "I asked José, a Mexican, about the lives of immigrant workers and the immigration process. Their lives and migration patterns were very similar to those of mountain workers in places like Kishu [Nakagami's home region in Japan]." He further recounts, "My consciousness of the beauty of Iowa, named after an Indian word for beautiful land, was raised when I saw the makeshift shack where the migrant workers stayed. I don't want to criticize Iowa. I enjoyed the tender kindness of Iowans and yet felt I had just glimpsed another version of the hardworking Midwest deep in the heart of the heartland."[7]

Likewise, when Roberta Alexander and Elbert "Big Man" Howard traveled to Japan in 1969 as representatives of the Black Panther Party, they felt a much stronger connection to day laborers in the San'ya district of Tokyo and *zainichi* Koreans than to the (middle-class) student revolutionaries who had sponsored their visit. As Howard said at a press conference in Tokyo, "We, members of the Black Panther Party, recognize the exploitation, segregation, and social degradation of the workers of [San'ya] and the citizens of Korean background to be one and the same as to what we are subjected to in America."[8] "At the same time," as William Tucker explains, "the organizers of the San'ya Liberation League expressed solidarity and strong connections to the Panthers." Tucker, whose research on this subject is unparalleled, notes that of all of the places in Japan Alexander and Howard visited, "San'ya received the most attention" in the Black Panther Party newspaper. Tucker attributes this to a feeling of identification, a sense of "the movement of workers in San'ya as parallel to the [Black Panther Party] and urban Black movements in the U.S."[9]

The Third World thus was never geographically fixed in the Third World project, and the status of a nation-state was not conflated or commensurate with the status of everyone who might reside in it. The Third World might then be understood as a position—that of the "exploited, segregated, and socially degraded" to borrow Howard's words. While Japan and the U.S. might be widely regarded as First World nations, Alexander and Howard lived in the U.S. and saw both themselves and the "workers of [San'ya] and the citizens of Korean background" who lived in Japan as "exploited, segregated, and socially degraded." Third World solidarity movements emerged in this manner as a pattern of identification and affiliation based on relatable experiences of oppression. Students of color in the San Francisco Bay Area could see themselves as connected to anticolonial movements abroad and organized the Third World Liberation Front in 1969 because the Third World "project" included them. They, too, had cause to resist capitalism, white supremacy, and imperialism, and they, too, were "exploited, segregated, and socially degraded." The project was named according to historical and ongoing oppression and differential power relations associated with imperialism (i.e. "the Third World" oppressed by "the First World"), but the project's outcome would be the abolition of those expressions of oppression and differential power relations (and, according to some expressions of the project, all forms of oppression and differential power).

For more than half a century, those who have identified with a Third World project to liberate oppressed people have seen parallels in one another's situations that have fueled mutual recognition and solidarity. I wish to invoke their expression of mutual recognition and solidarity (and not any specific label such as "First" or "Third") at the outset, because, as the following chapters will make clear, the opportunities for and obstacles to mutual recognition and solidarity available to youth who experience violence in the U.S. and Japan are often strikingly similar and highly influential. The stories of youth addressed in this book emerge out of different contexts that are nonetheless clearly relatable and would likely lead many imprisoned youth in Japan and the U.S., for example, to see something immediately recognizable in their counterparts' lives, experiences, and feelings (were they able to meet one another). I understand the similarities in their situations as inextricably linked to economic, political, and social dynamics one finds in both Japan and the U.S. However, this is not to suggest that the relationship between Japan and the U.S. is unmarked by differential power.

It is impossible to write about contemporary Japan without considering the U.S. and the effects of its government, military, and media. There are roughly ninety U.S. military installations in Japan, approximately 75 percent of which are located in Okinawa, which shoulders this disproportionate burden for reasons inextricably linked to ongoing structures of domestic discrimination and the history of colonial oppression in Japan, even as U.S. military operational headquarters in Japan have shifted to the Yokota Air Base west of Tokyo, on the main island of Honshū. Currently, roughly 47,000 U.S. military personnel and more than 5,000 civilian Department of Defense employees are stationed in Japan at any given time.[10] Successive Japanese administrations' fervent support of this sizable U.S. military presence and recent political haggling over the proposed move of a single base (Marine Corps Air Station Futenma) do not, according to James Fujii, change the fact that Japan remains, more than sixty years after the end of the Pacific War, under U.S. military occupation.[11] For those living near U.S. bases, the complexities of what it means for the second-largest holder of U.S. national debt to be militarily occupied by that debtor nation do not mitigate the material concerns related to sexual assault, noise pollution, and incidents such as the crash of a U.S. military helicopter (which may have been transporting depleted uranium munitions) into a building on the campus of Okinawa International University near the Futenma base in 2004. Indeed, some Okinawans may find more room for mutual recognition with Chamorros in Guam than with people in Japan who live far away from U.S. military bases and personnel.[12]

This situation has inspired critiques of U.S. imperialism on the political left and right in Japan. For example, a shared opposition to U.S. political, military, economic, and cultural influence brought together an unlikely pair in 1998: Amamiya Karin, who at that time was an ultra-right-wing and nationalist punk rock singer in her twenties, and Shiomi Takaya, a middle-aged revolutionary leftist who had served time in prison for his involvement in planning the Yodo hijacking of 1970. As fundamentally different as their attitudes toward, for example, the Japanese emperor system may have been, they were united in their belief that the deleterious influence of the U.S. should be resisted. Amamiya and Shiomi shared their ideas on a trip to North Korea that is documented in Tsuchiya Yutaka's film *Atarashii kamisama* (The New God).[13]

Concern over U.S. influence also has loomed large in the political thought of a more "moderate" figure, the Nobel laureate Ōe Kenzaburō. In the late 1980s, during the so-called bubble economy years in Japan, Ōe rejected the characterization of Japan as a First World nation due to the relationship of enforced dependence on the U.S. In his essay "Japan's Dual Identity: A Writer's Dilemma," Ōe contends that, despite its status as an "economic giant," Japan is not an independent nation but, rather, a Third World nation dependent on the U.S. (for imports, food, "security," etc.) even while it acts like a First World nation and exploits other Third World societies.[14] For Ōe, Japan's dependence on the U.S. does not absolve the country of its aggression toward Korea, the Philippines, and China, the examples he cites. He explains, "Japan and the Japanese betray democratic aspirants in Third World countries" and "are often aggressors toward nations of the Third World, of which we ourselves are in fact a member."[15]

Any attempt to posit an illusion of sameness or "reciprocity" of influence would surely deflect attention away from the material effects of the dependence to which Ōe aptly refers, but this is not to say that Japan does not exert influence within the borders of the U.S. For many in the U.S., Japan or things Japanese play a significant role in everyday life—from what some call the "soft power" of cultural production and exports to the diffuse experiential realities of multi-generational Japanese America. Notable for the purposes of this book, which focuses on youth, is the widespread popularity of Japanese anime and videogames among youth in the U.S. For some youth, anime informs their fantasy lives, structures their peer interactions, and motivates them to study the Japanese language. In 1991, when I first taught a university Japanese class, the majority of my students expressed interest in business-related pursuits. The study of Japanese, to them, constituted a step toward career and economic advancement. More recently, I have found that, regardless of the university or its particular demographics, anime and videogames are often the interests my students cite as their gateway reasons for studying Japanese.[16]

Concurrent with my academic engagement with the relationship between Japan and the U.S. were my experiences working directly with youth in Japan and the U.S. over the course of two decades—for example, as a volunteer Court Appointed Special Advocate (CASA) with abused youth in the Orange County, California, dependency system and as founder and director of the University of Iowa Youth Empowerment Academy (YEA!).[17] One of my former "CASA kids," now a young adult, has experienced and embodied many of the connections that generated this book. He was twelve when I first met him, and our first conversation was almost entirely about anime. At the end of that conversation, he showed me a folder filled with drawings, poems, and magazine clippings. Aside from a few pictures that displayed understandable rage, the material in the notebook, particularly the poems, which spoke to feelings of loneliness and alienation, revealed a vulnerable and very open youth who was yearning to attach. The trauma and abuse he suffered (both in the home and in institutions such as hospitals, juvenile halls, and group homes), the racism with which he has had to contend, his creativity, his contradictory yet sincere love of films such as *Blood In, Blood Out* and *Scarface*, and his often surprising sense of humor in even the toughest situations have had a profound impact on this book (and my life). Although neither he nor the other youth, including my brother, who inspired this project are named or "studied," their presence is felt throughout. Admittedly, I was motivated to explore oppositional readings of high-profile "juvenile crimes" in part 2 because these young people I love have been so violated, so abandoned, and so reviled. Nonetheless, as I will explain in the chapters that follow, the misleading nature of conventional attitudes regarding youth and violence necessitates this shift toward that which is rarely seen, acknowledged, or addressed—the brutalized and vulnerable body of the youth we are coached to fear.

This book is divided into two parts, the first of which focuses on the moment of violation in early life and how it is rendered into memory and words. The second part focuses on adults' fears of angry youth, as well as the means of expression available to enraged youth in contemporary Japan and the United States. I hope to show that it is precisely our adult imaginations and the extent to which we idealize, vilify, or render unrecognizable childhood and adolescence that engender the violence we purport to loathe. Put in the simplest terms, if there are teenage "monsters" next door, they are very much monsters of our own creation. This is not to say that there is something uniquely pathological about the "adultness" of Japanese and U.S. adult societies but, rather, that the very processes of socialization to which we are all subjected often compel us to drive our children crazy. With the repeated caveat that the same may be said of other places (for similar or different reasons), one of the defining features of contemporary Japanese and the U.S. societies in the analyses that follow is their crazy-making propensity, which I see as pronounced in a common adjective used to avoid discussions of why some young people turn to violence.

Youth violence today is often described as "inexplicable" in both Japan and the United States. This book challenges the complacent and formulaic invocation of the "inexplicable" as a means of forestalling understanding and intervention and, instead, brings various traumatic origins of youth violence (whether directed at the self or at others) to the foreground. Each child's actions have meaning, and there are always explanations, but we are often coached not to see or to distort them (at all levels—from the individual or interpersonal to broadcast media). Our systematic and relentless betrayals of youth often begin with the denial of their experience, yet we continue to adopt an "adult" optic that puzzles over the way youth betray us. We sell their bodies while simultaneously treating them as markets and then excoriate and blame them for acting out precisely what we demand of them. Using fiction, journalism, film, writings by youth, and case studies as my texts, I chart a culture of child abuse that extends from the most private of spaces, the home, into the classroom, the marketplace, and the streets.

If in general we understand a culture to be the customs, patterns of relation, and belief systems through which a people perceive themselves to be affiliated and according to which they engage with others, then child abuse in Japan or the U.S., rather than a "cultural" problem, is in fact a culture itself. That is to say, child rearing, education, and socialization practices, and our very ways of seeing children in relation to ourselves as adults, may reflect and overlap with other expressions of cultural identity, but the abuse of children is no more or no less comprehensive as an identifiable culture than "Japanese" or "American"— even though we are more accustomed to seeing it as a function of culture (usually someone else's culture) or as pathological. As is the case with cultures in general, what we take to be "natural" or, at least, "neutral" must be continually learned and reinforced. (Cultures, after all, are "inherited" only insofar as they are taught and learned.) In Japan and the U.S., we invest considerable effort and massive resources (through advertising and the juvenile "corrections" system, for example) in cultivating in youth appetites for that which we routinely deny or punish them. These contradictory "lessons" we pass along to the next generation are often quite literally crazy making.

Youth in Japan and the U.S. learn to desire consumer goods, such as designer sneakers or handbags, and come to gauge their self-worth in relation to their acquisitions. When youth cannot afford to purchase what they are taught to want, they sometimes resort to extreme measures. We are familiar with this phenomenon through news reports of young people committing armed robbery or even murder to procure a desired good, or of Japanese girls engaged in *enjo kōsai* (compensated dating) with older men. Young people who can afford plenty are virtually guaranteed fame in this context in which the "right" to consume is held sacrosanct and the public display of consumption encouraged. The Hilton sisters are known in Japan and elsewhere precisely because they flaunt their excess and their consumption. Paris Hilton was arguably the least likely to suffer the worst effects of imprisonment, yet more media attention was devoted to her brief jail sentence in the summer of 2007 than to that of perhaps any other young person in a U.S. prison, including Omar Khadr.[18] The fact that so many of the goods youth in Japan and the U.S. learn to desire are produced by youth elsewhere working in abysmal conditions underscores the far-reaching effects of the disregard and responsibility for global childhood suffering characteristic of the prevailing neoliberal economic policies pursued by the governments of Japan and the United States.

The first chapter of this book, "Survivor Discourse, the Limits of Objectivity, and Orpha," establishes my theoretical approach to childhood suffering—how it is understood, manufactured, represented, and simultaneously hidden from view in contemporary Japan and the United States. I also identify the ways in which childhood trauma differs significantly from adult-onset trauma or oppression. Briefly, children, unlike populations of adults who may be subjected to violence, intimidation, and so on, are for a period of time necessarily dependent on adults for survival, a developmental reality that points to the limits of the applicability of adult liberation theories to the problems of institutional, state, and familial child abuse.

Chapter 2, "Shizuko, the Silent Girl," concerns a controversial autobiographical novel (released in 1993) about childhood sexual abuse by a well-known Japanese *manga* author, Uchida Shungiku. I explore the ways in which this novel functions as oppositional storytelling and, at the same time, feeds into existing markets for sexualized images of children, particularly girls. I introduce this topic by discussing the title itself: *Fazaa Fakkaa* (Father Fucker). Central to my analysis is the question of how the rhetoric of consent invoked by the title relates to experiences of torture and dissociation as they are depicted in the novel and in real life. I also look at the ways in which creative storytelling is connected to the young protagonist Shizuko's survival and how this echoes what the author elsewhere describes as her own "figuring out" process that culminated in the novel.

Bastard out of Carolina, an autobiographical novel by Dorothy Allison, was also published in 1993 and, like *Father Fucker*, tells the story of a girl who was sexually abused by her stepfather and who belongs to a community perceived as more likely to produce abusive homes. In the case of *Father Fucker*, the girl grows up in a "broken home," and her mother works in the sex entertainment industry (as a hostess and dancer). In *Bastard out of Carolina*, the girl grows up in a poor white family in South Carolina. This novel is the subject of the third chapter. Like Shizuko, Bone, the protagonist of *Bastard out of Carolina*, relies on creative storytelling and childhood play to manage the daily terror with which she lives, but her experience as a young storyteller is radically different from Shizuko's due to the presence of some caring and involved adults. In this chapter, I also discuss how the identification of a "bad self" (congruent with the tendency toward self-blame) shapes the melodramatic stories Bone tells as a girl and how the adult narrator remembers and reinterprets these childhood stories.

The second half of the book deals with youth as imagined and real agents of violence and explores how the incapacitation of many of today's youngest generations serves certain state and corporate interests. Even the most casual observer of juvenile halls in Japan and the U.S. is immediately struck by the disproportionate presence of youth perceived as ethnically, culturally, or racially "different" from the dominant population. Rather than understanding this as simply a side effect of racism or prejudice, I analyze the epidemic incarceration of oppressed youth as a constitutive element of "Japanese" and "American" societies. Clearly, the widespread use of psychiatric medication and violence in juvenile "correctional" institutions assists in the incapacitation of youth who might otherwise pose a threat, not in the misleading sense echoed throughout much of the mass media (which, after all, routinely fuels exaggerated fears of the teenage menace), but as an oppressed population large enough to constitute an opposition of consequence. In other words, "Get 'em while they're young," and they will not be able to organize and resist later.

Chapter 4, "Engendering First World Fears," explores images of children as either threats or threatened in the 1990s and early twenty-first century, as well as how fear and rage have been maintained in recent years as the dominant national feeling states in the U.S. and Japan. Each of the cases and stories I analyze in this chapter reveal something about how adult society in both countries is understood and defined in relation to youth and how those very understandings are reinforced and amended to exact social and political compliance. I also highlight the escalating criminalization and abuse (institutionally and otherwise) of youth as a phenomenon that serves both state and corporate interests. I end the chapter by exploring how one contemporary Japanese writer addresses these questions in a work of fiction. Hoshino Tomoyuki's novella *Uragiri Nikki*

(The Treason Diaries) draws together two of the most feared figures in Japan and the U.S. from recent years—the "teenage super-predator" and the "terrorist—and in effect places them in the same army.

In Chapter 5, " 'Killer Kids' and 'Cutters,' " I introduce the words of actual youth and analyze how they represent their own experiences and problems such as "juvenile crime" in ways that diverge sharply from official and mass-mediated discourse. I discuss a range of interpretations of the defining "incident" that catapulted the problem of the "teenage super-predator" onto the center stage of public discourse in Japan, eclipsing government scandals and many other news stories: the killing of Hase Jun in May 1997. A boy who used the alias "Sakakibara" in letters claiming responsibility for the murder had already attacked two other children, killing one of them (Yamashita Ayaka), when he decapitated Hase Jun and left his head in front of a school gate. I look at the new vocabularies youth in Japan and the U.S. have developed or claimed to identify and communicate their understandings of events such as this one and the Columbine High School shootings. The problem, as it is narrated by youth, points to very different causes than the predictable theses presented on the nightly news (or in state legislatures). In this chapter, I focus on the mangled and thwarted attempts to communicate desperate youth make when denied more direct means of communication.

The last chapter moves beyond the stories of children per se to address violence in the lives of young adults living in Japan and the U.S., particularly those who struggle for an analysis that suits their rage. My discussion focuses on the writing of Hoshino Tomoyuki, who attempts to provide disaffected readers with possibilities for a political analysis through which rage might be understood and perhaps even channeled. Chief among his concerns is the Japanese emperor system, and my discussion of Hoshino's fiction engages histories of anti-imperialist discourse in Japan and the United States. I look especially to his novel *Ronrii Haatsu Kiraa* (Lonely Hearts Killer; 2004) to explore the question: What happens when young people are denied opportunities to develop a political analysis to explain their rage? Or conversely, how does the presence of such an analysis affect both the meaning and outcome of acts of violence? Hoshino's work opens up avenues to compare and connect children's rage to histories of militant and revolutionary resistance ranging from anarchism in the early twentieth century (and today) to the Third World solidarity movements mentioned earlier.

While much of this study concerns fiction's role in communicating and defining childhood trauma, fiction is also equally capable of engendering trauma. The wildly popular 1970s horror sci-fi manga *Hyōryū Kyōshitsu* (Floating School), by Umezu Kazuo, begins with conflict between a boy and his mother.[19] The boy has a treasured marble, which the mother throws away while cleaning his desk. Upset when he discovers what his mother has done, the boy confronts her while she is chopping vegetables in the kitchen. The mother turns around, brandishing the knife, and the boy asks if she intends to stab him. They argue, and the boy announces, "You're not my mom anymore. I'm never coming home again." The mother replies, "Fine, see if I care." The boy leaves in a huff, walks to school, and then a sudden and inexplicable explosion catapults his school building into a post-apocalyptic future world, a frightening desert landscape populated by mutants and monsters.[20] All that is left behind in the present where the school once was is a giant crater. The message here is clear: If you defy your prescribed role, if you "talk back" to your parents, if you are "bad," something terrible will happen and you will suffer, a message that is hammered home throughout the series as the boy is reminded constantly of how much he misses and needs his mother. This is much more than a dramatization of separation anxiety. It is an admonition to obey your parents—and, by extension, the rules of society—because if you do not, life as you know it will end.

When we compel our youth to "obey," telling them not to defy their prescribed roles (whatever those roles may be and regardless of circumstance) or else risk losing that which (or "everything") they hold dear, we should not be surprised when some young people opt out, resist, or defect altogether. In the case of *Floating School* and other literature that reinforces rigid models of appropriate behavior, there is no room to accommodate youth for whom "good citizenship" or "filial piety" might mean something very painful or risky, such as the demand to endure physical abuse. For the child who literally must resist and fight back to survive, Umezu's series sends a potentially dangerous message.

Some youth violently reject the admonition to observe the rules of the very social contracts that structure their oppression as a means of survival, and what thus appears to be "criminal" or "disobedient" may be a young person's only available means for expressing a will to live. If that is the case, then a work of fiction such as Hoshino Tomoyuki's *Uragiri Nikki* (The Treason Diaries), which brings together "teen killers" and "Third World guerrillas" from the headlines of 1997 and 1998, may have something in common with the manga I just described in that both respond to anxieties and fears of violent youth, fears that the world as we know it will end if kids start to resist. While the manga portrays this as apocalyptic, Hoshino leaves open other possibilities. What follows is a sustained, albeit far from exhaustive, attempt to make sense of the cultural and experiential landscapes out of which such narratives emerge.

Finally, I am indebted to the late Huey P. Newton, co-founder of the Black Panther Party and the author of *Revolutionary Suicide*, not only for the title of this book, but for providing the inspiration behind much of its analytical framework. Newton's analyses (including his application of the First World–Third World distinction) are far from dated when brought into congress with other effects of global capitalism (such as "unevenness"). As a young man, Newton developed a political analysis to explain his rage and, with the help of many others, sought to transform unjust conditions through direct and meaningful action, some of which I describe in the second part of this book. Throughout, I hope to honor Newton's internationalist perspective and, at the same time, the ways in which certain internationalisms, oppositional nationalisms, and anti-nationalisms coalesce in the words and work of today's youngest radicals and revolutionaries whose vision and commitment give me hope for the future. Vijay Prashad calls this the "internationalist nationalism" of the Third World project, whose proponents have "looked outward to other anticolonial nations as their fellows."[21]

As I discuss in chapter 6, Huey P. Newton believed that by aggressively and unrelentingly pushing for more of the world's resources, for more power and more control, the First World was over-reaching toward eventual self-annihilation. In the meantime, all that pushing takes its toll on each new generation of children. Our youth are raised amid distortions that we treat as natural; thus, many young people can only blame themselves or lash out in misdirected rage when they sense that *something* is not right. Youth are often told that they (and not a society, community, or government) are each personally responsible for "choosing the right path," behaving appropriately, and overcoming suffering through hard work. We dismiss, deny, or ignore the real horrors and struggles with which many youth live, making it difficult for them to trust their own experiences and perceptions, and making it more likely that they will convey the distortions to yet another new generation. Therefore, adults in Japan and the U.S. today are less prepared to interpret the desperate measures to which some children resort as "blowback" than as simply "inexplicable."

PART 1

"Livid with History"

"In Remembrance" BY JANICE MIRIKITANI

We gather at your coffin,
Uncle Minoru.
Mother, with her hands like gardenias,
touches your sleeves.
We whisper of how well you look
peaceful in your utter silence.
How much we remember.
Why so much now, at death?
Your kindness, Uncle,
as you crafted paper monkeys,
multicolored birds
to climb and jerk on a stick
to amuse children who gathered
at your innocent dark eyes,
always slightly moist.
We would jump on your back, riding you
like a silent horse,
as you lumbered on your hands and knees
from room to room.
        How much we remember . . .
We rode your shoulders,
knotted with hurt,
dressed in faded denim, smelling like

laundry soap and fish.
You never complained of it
only through those dark moist eyes,
and your smile that drew
living animals to you, even wild birds.
Obachan said they could smell
the wounds hiding in your throat,
the wound in your heart
pierced by unjust punishment, racism, and rejection
sharp as blades.
     When did you vow silence, Minoru?
After the camps,
after you buried your daughter?
You slumped into a light
of your own and let life ride you.
Your daughter thrown broken
on the road by a drunk driver
who mumbled she flew from nowhere like a dumb chicken,
stretched out $200, not one apology,
and said we were safer in the camps.
     Was there nothing left to say, Minoru,
as you slapped away his hot white hand?
     How much we remember . . .
When they took you to Amache Gate
locked us up like herded horses,
your dark innocent eyes, moist
with disbelief at charges of espionage,
your shoulders staggered from the lies.
Fear like a cold finger
pressed at your heart.
The sky scummed over with clouds
and punishment without crime
stabbed between the blades of your back.
     Was there nothing left to say?
Minoru, the children who rode you
have tongues like birds.
We chatter. We remember

the mounds of hurt at your shoulders.
Could we but massage them to soothe
the pain, but death
makes our regrets scattered as apologies.
We did not expect them
to rip the coat of pride from your bones
nor the melody from your throat.
    Yes, there is much to say.
We will not leave your memory
as a silent rancid rose.
Our tongues become livid with history and
demands for reparations.
Crimes are revealed like the bloody lashes
of a fallen whip:
    the falsehoods, deletions, the conspiracy
    to legalize mass imprisonment.
No, we will not forget
    Amache Gate, Rohwer, Poston, Heart Mountain,
    Minidoka, Jerome, Gila River, Manzanar, Topaz,
    Tule Lake.
Our tongues are sharp like blades.
We overturn furrows of secrecy.
    Yes, we will harvest justice.
And Uncle, perhaps
your spirit will return
alive in a horse or bird,
riding free in the wind
life surging through
the sinews of your strong shoulders.
    And yes,
the struggle continues on
with our stampede of voices.[1]

Janice Mirikitani's poem "In Remembrance," written for her uncle who died in 1984, refers to the long-term effects of the internment camp experience and the pain and anger that require both a voice and an audience. Vowing to "overturn furrows of secrecy" and remember the "falsehoods, deletions, the conspiracy to legalize mass imprisonment" with tongues "livid with history," Mirikitani pays tribute to her uncle, the "silent horse," who was subjected to "relocation" along with 120,000 other Japanese Americans in 1942 and later lost his daughter. However, Mirikitani does not portray her quiet uncle as having been only a victim, as her descriptions of his strength and refusal to participate in the drunk white man's attempt to buy his compliance reveal. Telling traumatic histories, such as the internment of Japanese Americans during the Second World War, poses a unique dilemma, because, on the one hand, the details of suffering must be spoken, yet on the other hand, many traumatized and oppressed people who have demonstrated tremendous courage to survive are wary of the ways in which stories of their suffering can perpetuate the lack of agency characteristic of victimization.

In her discussion of the ways in which several generations of Japanese Americans have dealt with the subject of the internment, Donna Nagata describes this dilemma: "There is also a fine line between focusing on the suffering created by the internment and focusing on the strength and resilience with which Japanese Americans have been able to respond to this trauma. Overemphasis on suffering runs the risk of portraying the Japanese Americans as 'damaged' victims, while overemphasis on their coping strengths runs the risk of minimizing the negative aspects of the internment."[2] This dilemma is reflected in many survivors' movements' simultaneous wish to portray those who have endured trauma as strong and capable and to acknowledge the reality of victimization. Documentary films featuring interviews with internment camp survivors and their children, such as Emiko Omori's Rabbit in the Moon, can give us a glimpse into individual experiences of this dilemma as survivors recount memories and describe why, when, and how they began to speak about their experiences, as well as why those conversations continue to be painful.[3] Remembering and finding words for memories of the internment camps can resurrect old pain at the same time that it can involve new demands and dangers, many of which defy simple description. Mirikitani's poem points to a way out of the dilemma Nagata so succinctly describes, a way to acknowledge strength and suffering without glamorizing the suffering as is so common in melodrama—or, as the writer and essayist Dorothy Allison has said, to demonstrate that "suffering does not ennoble. It destroys."[4]

Because it is exceedingly difficult for stories of great suffering to be spoken in the aftermath of that suffering, it is not surprising that poetry and fiction provide unique vehicles through which stories of traumatic experience can, and often do, emerge. Nevertheless, writing trauma in the form of "fiction" involves clearing enormous hurdles, not the least of which is language itself. To write about trauma, one must first find words to convey what no one wants to hear or say, to speak the unspeakable. Survivors who find the words to write about their own traumatic experiences face further struggles in keeping or sharing their words, as Dorothy Allison, the author of *Bastard out of Carolina* and a survivor of childhood abuse, explains: "I didn't start writing, or at least I didn't start keeping the writing, until 1974 when I published a poem. Everything I wrote before then—ten years of journals, ten years of poems and short stories—I burned because I was afraid somebody would read them. And always in the back of my mind there were my mother's whispers: They'll send you to detention, you'll wind up in a county home. You don't want to do that."[5]

Further complicating efforts to represent traumatic experiences are the dynamics of individual responses to trauma that also may make it exceedingly difficult for survivors to speak out and be heard. In his essay "Truth and Testimony: The Process and the Struggle," Dori Laub argues that the crucial process of testimony is a "ceaseless struggle."[6] Not only must survivors struggle against external admonitions to repress; they contend with what Laub describes as a confusing and contradictory "imperative to tell," which is equally fraught with challenges.

> The survivors did not only need to survive so that they could tell their stories; they also needed to tell their stories in order to survive. There is, in each survivor, an imperative need to *tell* and thus come to *know* one's story, unimpeded by ghosts from the past against which one has had to protect oneself. One has to know one's buried truths in order to be able to live one's life.
>
> This imperative to tell and to be heard can become itself an all-consuming life task. Yet no amount of telling seems ever to do justice to this inner compulsion. There are never enough words or the right words, there is never enough time or the right time, and never enough listening or the right listening to articulate the story that cannot be fully captured in *thought*, *memory*, and *speech*. The pressure thus continues unremittingly, and if words are not trustworthy or adequate, the life that is chosen can become the vehicle by which the struggle to tell continues.[7]

As Laub indicates, some survivors for whom words are never enough may elect to help others who have lived through similar trauma or choose other paths that might offer the hope of somehow "correcting" the injustices of the past and providing for others that for which they themselves may have longed. Capturing Laub's notion of the "inner compulsion" to tell, Mirikitani's poem conveys how the pain suffered by her uncle and her community has made her tongue "livid" with a history that must be told.

Impeded by the challenges that Laub describes, challenges that point to how the virtual impossibility of telling is not always or only the result of a tendency or desire to forget, many traumatized people are successfully discouraged from speaking about their experiences. The literary scholar Gurleen Grewal connects self-censorship to the maintenance of trauma's power to destroy when she notes that the "traumatized do not heal under suppression (amnesia), although forgetting is a characteristic response to trauma."[8] Concurrent with these internal conflicts and obstacles are the external pressures to "move on" with one's life, to "forget about the past," or, as is also common, to deny the trauma altogether. When, despite these overwhelming barriers, the silence is broken and survivors are able to trace back through time to remember and recount historical trauma, both individuals and communities can be transformed, or, as bell hooks describes it, "The telling of our history . . . enables political self-recovery."[9]

Finding the Words and the Space to Tell

People who have lived through traumatic events often identify themselves as "survivors"—and not "victims"—as one means of asserting personal agency and distancing themselves from earlier experiences of powerlessness. The word "survivor" acts as a semantic repository for individual and collective yearnings for dignity and recognition and, as such, as a way to pay tribute to what was not crushed ("spirit," "courage," "inner strength," for example). Thus, communities of "survivors" can experience a sense of affiliation or solidarity through their shared suffering and a perception of shared strength. As strong as the belief may be that survival has the power to overcome what victimization takes away, when we use the word in certain contexts and speak of "merely" or "barely" surviving, we refer to a very different experience, something closer to the edge of death than dignity. What makes one survival an extraordinary and valiant process and another akin to perpetual agony lies not only in the material effects of a traumatic event or illness itself, but also in how that survival is understood and how it is communicated. Telling stories is therefore crucial for the individual "survivor" and her community.[10] But perhaps no aspect of survival is more difficult.

Leo Etinger has explored how the differential power relations behind human-generated horror render communities of traumatized people "the losing party in [a] silent and unequal dialogue." Etinger's analysis reveals how the very structure of oppression impedes acknowledgment of trauma by either the traumatized or the traumatizer. He writes, "War and victims are something the community wants to forget; a veil of oblivion is drawn over everything painful and unpleasant. We find two sides face to face; on the one side the victims who perhaps wish to forget but cannot, and on the other all those with strong, often unconscious motives who very intensely both wish to forget and succeed in doing so."[11] When those "motives" to forget involve great personal or political interest—when the power and privilege of the traumatizer(s) are threatened by disclosure—the efforts to silence those who have been victimized can be highly organized, officially sanctioned, and violent.

Thus, because of the tremendous obstacles facing anyone who attempts to speak the unspeakable, expressions of traumatic suffering, what has been called "survivor discourse," is rendered almost impossible—almost, because it exists despite the overwhelming mechanisms in place to not only suppress it but to prevent its very formation. Living through life-threatening trauma does not in and of itself prepare one to speak or write as a "survivor." One must first identify the trauma, which all too often has been sequestered far away from language, and find an audience willing to listen before thoughts, memories, and feelings can emerge as survivor discourse. In their article "Survivor Discourse: Transgression or Recuperation," Linda Alcoff and Laura Gray have defined survivor discourse as the "relatively new" proliferation of disclosures of trauma (such as those by survivors of childhood sexual abuse), but survivor discourse writ large is as diverse and as old as the range of historical human trauma.

Certainly those who have experienced war and gone on to speak and write about the horrors of individual and shared trauma in battle have produced what could also be described as survivor discourse.[12] Nonetheless, written and spoken attempts by survivors to communicate traumatic experience have been, as Alcoff and Gray explain, "excluded speech, constrained by rules more often implicit than explicit but nonetheless powerful. At various times and in different locations survivor speech has been absolutely prohibited, categorized as mad or untrue, or rendered inconceivable."[13] Implicit, varied, and frequently difficult to detect, forces of suppression are unleashed to ensure that traumatic stories, if they surface at all, can only surface in bits and pieces (or in "over-determined" and scripted forms). Such censorship is often proportional to the nature, dimension, and duration of the traumatic event itself.

If the trauma is suffered by many, the silencing of their stories requires greater vigilance and ferocity. For example, at the level of general public discourse in the U.S., slavery and its ongoing multigenerational effects remain subjects met with such intensely defensive white discomfort and denial ("Don't blame me for what my ancestors did") that material details (such as the ways in which Africans were chained next to the rotting corpses and waste of one another throughout the Middle Passage) are less common in contemporary discussions of race relations than is the pseudo-logic deployed to protest some phantom "reverse racism" and deflect attention away from the many ways in which whites in the U.S. still benefit from slavery's legacy. That thinly veiled white supremacists could enlist as their most visible spokesperson an African American, Ward Connerly, in their efforts to repeal affirmative action in California only underscores the success of the dominant white culture's historical amnesia.[14] That is to say, Connerly's very presence in the political campaign to ban affirmative action demonstrated how contemporary popular discussions of race relations and social justice frequently rely on members of oppressed groups to lend credibility to the forgetting or minimizing of horrible histories and their ongoing effects.[15] In the minds of many whites, Connerly came to embody a perceived end of racism and white domination, and he provided those who already benefit from white supremacy with further justification for seeing racism as a problem of the past.

When racism has been the subject of mainstream/corporate news programming or special documentaries in the U.S. in recent years (even before Barack Obama assumed the presidency), it has all too often and increasingly been portrayed as a problem of retrospection, consigned to a distant past disconnected from the present. The language of California's Proposition 209, described as a "civil rights" initiative, characterized affirmative action as an unfair source of inequality—as if we had passed through and beyond the racist phase of U.S. history—when, in fact, the proposition used the language of liberation to reinforce the dominant white power structure by casting whites, and white men in particular, as a besieged group unfairly disadvantaged by "quotas" and "preferences" and thereby eclipsing even the most quantifiable privilege whiteness affords.[16] The "special preferences" canard is particularly misleading when invoked to portray whites as "victims" in that white people, women in particular, have benefited from affirmative action more than any other group.[17]

Speaking or acting out against the suppression of horrible truths can be as dangerous as participating in ongoing suppression can be lucrative. Unlike Connerly, whose success is inextricably linked to his rejection of white-supremacist reality, the journalist and former Black Panther Mumia Abu-Jamal's outspoken critiques of white supremacy have left him vulnerable to the wrath of those he challenges. He has lived on death row for the past thirty years after being sentenced to death in what Amnesty International and others have described as a profoundly unfair murder trial.[18] The weakness of the original case against Abu-Jamal has required those who continue to deny him a fair retrial to launch highly organized attacks on his character, and their efforts to demonize him have escalated as Abu-Jamal's analyses of U.S. imperialism, the prison regime, the racist disenfranchisement of voters, and other issues have become more widely available (even in spite of the refusal of network media and National Public Radio to broadcast his radio commentaries).[19]

In 1997, the former Black Panther Geronimo Pratt was released from a California prison after it was revealed that key trial testimony came from a paid police informant and evidence proving he could not have committed the murder for which he had been imprisoned for twenty-five years was suppressed at trial. The Federal Bureau of Investigation and State of California knew (due to telephone wiretapping of the Black Panther offices) that Pratt was in the San Francisco Bay Area at the time when he supposedly killed a teacher in Santa Monica. Pratt's case is yet another example of how those who speak out and encourage us to believe (and organize in response to) horrible truths and realities, such as the violence of white supremacy, are often punished and silenced for doing so.[20] In the case of the Black Panthers, the surveillance, slander, infiltration, and "psy-ops" characteristic of COINTELPRO tactics were severe and coordinated enough to remain effective for decades.[21]

Given the historical and continued pervasiveness and success of the myriad forces of suppression, the burden to communicate experiences of unspeakable trauma has rested with those who have survived or are still experiencing the trauma, those who encounter the greatest obstacles—internally and externally —when it comes to telling their stories. In her work on confronting white supremacy in the U.S., bell hooks writes, "Even those of us righteously committed to black liberation struggle, who feel we have decolonized our minds, often find it hard to 'speak' our experience. The more painful the issues we confront the greater our inarticulateness. James Baldwin understood this. In *The Fire Next Time*, he reminded readers that 'there has been almost no language' to describe the 'horrors' of black life."[22] Because, according to hooks, the "pain of awareness" is "too great," stories of African American suffering are rarely spoken, particularly to white people. Even when white police officers in New York City fired forty-one shots at Amadou Diallo, an unarmed black man, killing him (1999); when our evening news anchor recounts how James Byrd Jr., a black man in Texas, was literally dragged to his death while chained to the truck of a proud white supremacist (1998); or when we recall the seemingly endless list of names such as Martin Lee Anderson (killed in a juvenile "boot camp" in 2006 at age fourteen), Sean Bell (killed by police in 2006 at twenty-three), and Oscar Grant (killed by police in 2009 at twenty-two), many in the U.S. are unprepared to relinquish the familiar myth of the strident and angry young black male criminal long enough to conceive that whiteness is terrifying and terrorizing in very real ways. The difficulty in telling, combined with the near-refusal to listen to, real stories with real details of white-supremacist violence softens and airbrushes out the rough and brutal edges of most of what we do hear.

When representations of violence are routinely seen and heard, it is rarely because they tap into collective wishes for social justice or a greater understanding of the effects of violence in our lives. As is the case with other categories of representation, the thought provoking or the socially significant is not necessarily popular or lucrative. Clearly, a considerable amount of representational violence (much of which exploits dominant cultural myths about how race, ethnicity, and gender relate to violent behavior) does sell. As Henry Giroux explains, however, blanket condemnations of all forms of representational violence miss the important distinctions between "the stylized violence of the spectacle and violence that can illuminate important messages about the basis of humanity and inhumanity." Giroux goes on to identify three forms of visual representational violence, which he calls "ritualistic" (predictable horror and action genres), "symbolic" (which attempts to connect feelings and meanings to violence), and "hyper-real" (exploitative and aestheticized "ultraviolence").[23]

Giroux's three terms, which overlap and blend into one another, are not fixed or self-contained categories that can be used to define every example—nor should they be. However, the tendency to lump all representational violence into the same category (and thereby avoid the most pressing moral and political questions) is still very evident in a wide range of public discourse coming from groups and individuals whose opinions about violence and the media (as all neutral or all deleterious), for example, may differ. Giroux offers useful tools for looking at what kinds of representations of violence circulate with regularity in contemporary life and what kinds are ignored or excluded. The novelist Barbara Kingsolver, prompted by a letter she received from a reader, provides the following response to thinking about differing meanings of representational violence: "The simple, intense exposure of a vicious act, in film or in literature, is entirely different from a story that includes both the violence and its painful consequences. I can't even call these two things by the same name. . . . I find I'm prepared to commit an act of violence in the written word if, and only if, it meets two criteria: first, the act must be embedded in the story of its consequences. Second, the fictional violence must be connected with the authentic world."[24] In part 1 of this book, I explore examples of the kind of fiction Kingsolver advocates here, and in part 2, I allow room for another possibility: representational violence designed to prepare and inspire audiences to defend or liberate themselves.[25]

Stories that bring us into contact with pain stemming from violence in the "authentic world" are particularly few when it comes to widespread and multigenerational violence carried out by dominant and powerful individuals, communities, cultures, and institutions. Perhaps nowhere is this more evident than in the U.S., where even genocide and slavery can be romanticized, minimized, and fetishized. For example, members of the Skull and Bones secret society at Yale University reportedly stole the remains of the Apache freedom fighter Geronimo and still make "use" of them.[26] Until recently, Eddie Rickenbacker's, a bar in San Francisco, maintained and defended a display of what it claimed were the teeth of Monasetah, one of America's "comfort women" taken by Custer and his army. The bar's owners even noted that Custer is said to have "knocked out her teeth."[27] A simple trip to virtually any antique store will produce evidence of "old-timey" nostalgia for slavery in the form of salt-and-pepper shakers or figurines. That some white Americans can "have fun with" the remains or racist caricatures of the oppressed and colonized demonstrates how white supremacist U.S. society needs (or, at least, permits) the crimes on which it was built and continues to be maintained to be "forgiven," erased, or commodified for "enjoyment." Much the same can be said of some of the ways in which childhood suffering is marketed to adult consumers, as I will explain in chapter 1.

CHAPTER 1

Survivor Discourse, the Limits of Objectivity, and Orpha

Over the past four decades, stories about childhood trauma have steadily become a mass media mainstay in everything from television talk shows to bestseller lists in both Japan and the U.S. Not surprisingly, the most conventionally successful examples can be characterized as inspirational or tabloid. In the U.S., for example, the popularity of David Pelzer's autobiographies (*A Child Called "It," The Lost Boy*, etc.), which recount his own childhood experiences of abuse and the dependency system, and several television miniseries about the murder of JonBenét Ramsey fit comfortably into established genres of the uplifting and the scandalous, respectively.[1] In Japan, volumes of letters describing memories of abuse and maltreatment were collected in a popular book series and website entitled *Nihon ichi minikui oya e no tegami* (Letters to Japan's Most Despicable Parents), and television specials about celebrities who have beaten the odds and overcome illness, accidents, domestic violence, or other hardships provide a steady stream of inspirational viewing to complement the proliferation of *iyasu-kei* (soothing, healing-style, or therapeutic) literature.[2]

Sometimes the inspirational and the tabloid merge with the melodramatic or the camp, as one finds in Miike Takashi's *Katakuri-ke no kōfuku* (The Happiness of the Katakuris; 2001), a musical-comedy horror film about a family whose country inn is the site of multiple gruesome deaths.[3] While playing in the yard, seven-year-old Yurie, the youngest member of the Katakuri family, comes across a pile of decomposing corpses (who proceed to rise as zombies for a song-and-dance number), and her family's response to her discovery is to "sing away" the trauma. Specifically, their song instructs the young girl to "look forward" and "be positive." This comic enactment of the admonition to repress is presented as both tender and inspirational, the premise being that she will, of course, "get over it."

The inspirational and the tabloid are also evident in news media accounts of high-profile incidents, particularly in the tendency to focus on certain violent crimes as isolated, extraordinary, aberrant, or shocking. This tendency would have us believe at times that there is an increase in school killings, for example, and at other times that these isolated incidents are rare spectacles for us to view or ponder from afar. Whether we are presented with an inspirational story of a courageous person who saved others or a tragic story of an innocent victim, the incident itself is often portrayed as shocking and "inexplicable." Sensational characterizations of an attacker as "crazy," "sick," "deranged," "hateful," or "demented" offer diagnostic (if vague) conclusions that forestall understanding. For example, if we accept the opinion expressed by some reporters and analysts after the shootings at Virginia Tech in 2007 that Seung-Hui Cho was "demented," we are not compelled to look further. In most corporate mass media reporting, Cho's experiences of racism and class oppression, which were certainly discussed at great length and with empathy in some circles, did not warrant meaningful exploration because he was simply (if tragically) "demented," and the temerity to suggest there may in fact be more to explicate and understand was preemptively framed as inappropriate and disrespectful to the victims.

When news stories about high-profile crimes circulate internationally, the tendency to forestall understanding is often pronounced even in the most responsible reporting. In his article of May 27, 2007, Bruce Wallace, staff writer for *The Los Angeles Times*, described the "grisly crimes alarming Japan," such as the case of a twenty-year-old in Tokyo who had murdered and cut up his sister in January 2007.[4] This incident was covered extensively in Japan at the time, and Wallace accurately conveys the sense of "alarm" fueled by the Japanese media's coverage of ensuing murder stories. Wallace also carefully avoids assigning a peculiar cultural (Japanese) or historic (contemporary) cause to the series of crimes he relates by referring to cases of dismemberment from other countries and earlier historical periods. While refreshing in its refusal to rest easy with cultural peculiarity as an explanation, Wallace's article nonetheless ends with the message that "some people" are simply so filled with "hate" that their actions cannot be explained. Specifically, Wallace quotes Jimmy Sakoda, a retired homicide detective from Los Angeles who had "close ties to Japanese police during his career," as saying, "When someone dismembers a body, that's total hatred . . . hate beyond reason."

This book is, in part, a response to what is often misidentified as a recent increase in "inexplicable" child abuse and youth violence in both the U.S. and Japan but could be more accurately characterized as an increase in reported—to both police and news agencies—incidents. However, my primary concern is the simultaneous attention to stories of youth and violence and assessment of these stories as beyond reason or understanding. Child abuse and youth violence have often been discussed together to lament a perceived breakdown in social and family structures, but the more profound connections, which are not unique to recent generations of young people, continue to be suppressed. That some in both Japan and the U.S. assert a specific cultural or national identity by insisting that theirs is a community that values family, one in which "the family" is of primary importance, only further suppresses the more troubling relationship between child abuse (writ large) and youth violence.

The emergence of survivors' networks, self-help literature, and nonprofit organizations dedicated to preventing abuse during the latter decades of the twentieth century (a time when the deployment of images of sexualized children and teenage "super-predators" in Japan and the U.S. also escalated) and the growing awareness of the reality and effects of abuse among mental health professionals and survivors' networks have opened up possibilities for a growing number of survivors of abuse to "come out." This growing awareness and space for survivor discourse and movements have developed alongside the emergence of the False Memory Syndrome Foundation in the U.S., a nonprofit organization that supports parents whose children have accused them of abuse, and a host of debunkers. Breaking through the Manichean framework of such highly charged cultural spaces remains difficult, especially for youth. This is in large measure exacerbated by the inadequacy of the terms according to which discussions of abuse occur.

The Politics of Power and Children

Many of the concepts so useful in understanding trauma in adult and multi-generational communities are insufficient when applied to the case of children. So completely is the parent–child—and adult–child—relationship structured in terms of dependency that we cannot identify it as a relationship of differential power per se; differential power relations can only serve as a euphemism given the lopsidedness of the adult–child relationship. As adults, we discuss children and their futures; we make decisions on their behalf. School boards, politicians, religious organizations, and parents vie for the moral high ground, claiming theirs is the truly pro-child agenda far above competing versions of what is "best for the children." Some of the most fiercely debated issues in contemporary politics in the U.S. (such as juvenile criminal justice and the death penalty, same-sex marriage, gun control, welfare, health care, and immigration) are frequently discussed and debated in terms of how they affect children, and educators, politicians, and pundits strive to prove that theirs is the agenda espousing the most child-centric model of "family values." The very material needs of children, who are, indeed, uniquely dependent, leave them especially vulnerable, as a group and as individuals, to their adult caretakers—from those who make policies to parents.

Decision making in the adult caretaker–child relationship is unilateral, particularly in the case of the very young who cannot yet articulate an opinion, feed or clothe themselves, or safely navigate their surroundings without assistance. Parents clearly have the greatest and most immediate access to their children, especially in states such as the U.S. and Japan where the nuclear family's privacy and parental rights may be seen as hallmarks of a free-market neoliberal democracy's ability to provide a better society. Parents whose children are taken into state custody or whose parental rights are terminated in these countries are, as a result, frequently portrayed as deviant, abnormal, or atavistic. The United Nations Universal Declaration of Human Rights of 1948 includes two articles (16 and 26) asserting the importance of family and parental rights, and the subsequent reaffirmations of parental authority are too numerous to mention here.[5] The erroneousness of the myth that First World countries lead the vanguard in the official protection of children's rights is particularly evident in the case of the U.S., which (along only with Somalia) refused to ratify the United Nations Convention on the Rights of the Child of 1989.[6]

Henry Jenkins writes, "If politics is ultimately about the distribution of power, then the power imbalance between children and adults remains, at heart, a profoundly political matter."[7] At the same time, the differential power models that are so useful in understanding injustice among nations and corporations, among adults, fall short of explaining the position of the child in relation to the grownup. As liberation theorists such as Frantz Fanon have so successfully demonstrated, the colonized adult "Native," for example, can never appropriately be seen as infantilized and dependent (even when the colonizer's "Prospero complex" would have it otherwise), for to do so is to "explain away" colonialism and deny the "Native" individual subjectivity. Fanon, in critiquing Dominique-Octave Mannoni's *Prospero and Caliban: The Psychology of Colonization*, wrote that to espouse Mannoni's claim that the "germ" for a colonized person's "inferiority complex" is "latent in him from childhood" is to pretend that any "so-called dependency complex" antedates colonial racism.[8] Ideas such as Mannoni's (which infantilize and pathologize those whose lives and communities have been disrupted at every level by imperialist expansionism) have served as justification for countless attacks on indigenous rights and cultures and have fueled the destruction of societies and communities considered somehow fortunate to be helped out of their own histories and traditions and into enforced dependency. But a child, unlike the colonized, occupied, or otherwise oppressed adult, is for a period of time *necessarily* dependent on adults for survival, a developmental reality that points to the limits of adult liberation theories' applicability to the problem of child abuse.

Having all been children, we can conceive of childhood dependency in particular and personal ways. We have all "been there." Yet when it comes to discussing the ways in which adults harm children, many adults feel uncomfortable and turn away from such stories. Since children rarely have the language to speak their experiences, our collective denial is made all the easier. We may oscillate between romanticizing children at play in a world free of adult stress and responsibility and lamenting how "horrible" youth are today. But we rarely engage in sustained and serious efforts to listen to children who struggle to communicate how they experience their realities to us. Anyone who interacts with severely abused youth knows it can be very difficult for children to comprehend and describe what has happened to them. Even those taken away from daily torture may, for example, speak lovingly of a parent who burned, beat, and raped them—or blame themselves, saying that they "made" a parent angry or somehow caused the abuse. It is not until years have passed that some adult survivors are able to find words to begin to recount what they endured and extricate themselves from the belief that they were "bad" and deserving of maltreatment.

Orphic Survival, Creative Writing, and the Model of the Good Reader

Central to the analyses that follow is the claim—counterintuitive perhaps, yet still demonstrable—that the very process by which an abused child manages repression can be transformed into a vehicle for speaking or writing about the abuse. That is to say, waiting among the fragmented and atomized shards of the abused child's personality might be a way to integrate the traumatic experience into a more fully aware adult survivor identity.[9] This seed or fragment and its possibilities, identified by Elizabeth Severn (a patient of Sándor Ferenczi) who called it "Orpha," can be understood as the "organizing life instincts" that propel the victim toward self-preservation.[10] Like the art of its likely namesake Orpheus, Orpha's "music" can be both mysterious and beneficial. To better understand the significance of Severn's and Ferenczi's notion of Orpha, it is helpful to revisit the legend of Orpheus and the meanings attached to Orphic literatures and beliefs in classical Greek and Roman traditions. Orpheus's descent to the Underworld to find his dead wife, Eurydice, is a familiar story that has inspired countless variations and allusions. Using his musical gifts to charm the spirits and win access to the Underworld, Orpheus searched for Eurydice, who had died from a snakebite. Her liberation required that he refrain from looking back at her and at hell, but Orpheus, afraid that Eurydice might not be behind him, looked back in contravention of the rule, and she disappeared. The message here, to understand Orpha, is that Orpheus's music could work magic, but his desire to look back led to pain and amplified or prolonged grief. As conceived by Ferenczi (and Severn), Orpha similarly refers to a traumatized person's simultaneous belief in (or experience of) the efficacy of a skill (such as musical performance) and fear of looking back.

Although he charms the gods and spirits of the Underworld with his music and they allow him to take Eurydice back from death, Orpheus is unable to resist looking behind to ensure that she is truly following him even after he is warned that doing so will mean that he will lose her forever. There are many other stories of Orpheus's musical powers, such as the lyre performances that won the Argonauts safe passage through dangerous situations or stormy seas, and the religions, cults, or societies (described, for example, by Plato and Aristophanes) known as "Orphic" were in part defined by their belief in the efficacy of the "charms and incantations of Orpheus."[11] Common to the different myths and legends is the portrait of Orpheus's ability to use music to pass through tremendous dangers. Orpheus's ability to overcome adversity relies on what might best be described as creative distraction or trance. He fails only when he looks back and breaks the trance, an element of his story that surely made sense to Severn, who had repressed memories of sexual abuse until undergoing psychoanalysis with Ferenczi.

Severn saw her literal survival prior to analysis as rooted in a fragmented self she called Orpha. Like the magical Orpheus, whom one noted classicist explains "refuses to be submerged," Severn's Orphic fragment fought against psychological entombment in her childhood past.[12] It warrants at least casual mention here that Orphic religions left behind literature and artifacts resembling toys dedicated to the "divine child," and the figure of the child seems to have been central to Orphic worship.[13] Although Ferenczi makes no mention of such historical practices, the appropriateness of Severn's choice of the term "Orpha" to describe the remaining fragment of a tortured child's personality is striking.

Like Orpheus who was instructed not to look back, the abused child is taught to look forward and away from traumatic experience. As Ferenczi noted in writings that departed from the teachings of his mentor, Sigmund Freud, every message that the abused child hears is designed to deny the traumatic abuse or prevent the child, whose communication skills are developing, from accessing a language that can speak to the trauma.

> In most cases of infantile trauma, the parents have no interest in impressing the events on the mind of the child, on the contrary, the usual cure is repression: "it's nothing at all"; "nothing happened"; "don't think about it"; "katonadolog" ["soldiers can take it," in Hungarian]; but nothing is ever said about these ugly matters (for instance of a sexual nature). Such things are simply hidden in a deadly silence; the child's faint references are ignored or even rejected as incongruous, with the unanimous concurrence of those around him, and with such consistency that the child has to give up and cannot maintain his own judgment.[14]

Ferenczi's observations on the reality of abuse and mechanisms of repression have given his early contributions long-lasting significance and relevance.

In his clinical diary, Ferenczi earnestly reflected on his own limitations and errors so as not to adopt what he saw as his teacher's arrogance, writing that Freud "is the only one who does not have to be analyzed."[15] Ferenczi further characterized Freud as rigid in his adherence to his theories.

> One learned from him [Freud] and from his kind of technique various things that made one's life and work more comfortable: the calm, unemotional reserve; the unruffled assurance that one knew better; and the theories, the seeking and finding of the causes of failure in the patient instead of partly in ourselves. The dishonesty of reserving the technique for one's own person; the advice not to let patients learn anything about the technique; and finally the pessimistic view, shared only with a trusted few, that neurotics are a rabble, good only to support us financially and to allow us to learn from their cases: psychoanalysis as a therapy may be worthless.
>
> This was the point where I refused to follow him. Against his will I began to deal openly with questions of technique. I refused to abuse the patients'

trust in this way, and neither did I share his idea that therapy was worthless. I believed rather that therapy was good, but perhaps we were still deficient, and I began to look for our errors.[16]

Ferenczi concluded that the "antitraumatic in Freud is a protective device against insight into his own weaknesses."[17]

Ferenczi went so far as to share his disappointment and critique with his teacher, writing in a letter dated January 17, 1930, "I do not share for instance, your view that the therapeutic process is negligible or unimportant, and that simply because it appears less interesting to us we should ignore it. I, too, have often felt 'fed up' in this respect, but overcame this tendency, and I am glad to inform you that precisely in this area a whole series of questions have now come into a new, a sharper focus, perhaps even the problem of repression."[18] Ferenczi contends that analysis fails when the analyst ignores material at odds with prevailing theories. "I admitted that caught in my own theoretical postulates, I had, in a superficial and careless manner, presumed modes of feeling of an adult, sexually mature person," he explains as a preface to his critique of Freud's tendency to impose theories of adult sexual subjectivity onto even very young children.[19] Freud also leaned in a similar direction in *The Aetiology of Hysteria*, but later wrote that stories of abuse were "only fantasies which my patients had made up."[20]

Severn brought Ferenczi in direct contact with Orpha, the fragment of her personality that he describes as "a singular being, for whom the preservation of life is of 'coûte que coûte' significance." Ferenczi described this fragment as a "guardian angel" of sorts that "anesthetizes" the suffering body by providing solace.[21] In her essay on Ferenczi's work with the traumatized, Nancy Smith takes up Severn's notion of Orpha to elaborate on the long-lasting effects of trauma on the self and argues, "[Orpha] allows for a marshaling and preserving of vital life organizing functions after trauma, within the strongest remaining fragmented portion of the traumatized individual's personality."[22] Smith goes on to explain that the reliance on the "Orphic process" is proportional to the onset and severity of the trauma, and those who once desperately held onto a "fragmented portion" of their personality to survive will continue to do so.[23] Nevertheless, when this Orphic fragment is a person's sole means of survival, other opportunities for growth, reflection, or experience may be precluded. Thus, for the "person surviving via heroic Orphic functioning," Smith explains, there "can be no grieving." It is only by moving away from a reliance on Orpha for survival and toward what she calls "intersubjective connection" that the once traumatized person can slowly begin to speak about that which Orpha sought to overcome.[24]

The Moral Imperative to Tell and to Listen to Stories of Abuse

As well as serving as a unique vehicle through which trauma can be rendered into words, the use of fiction for survival is very much in keeping with a definition of Orphic survival as creative, artistic, or even magical. Writing fiction can offer "trance-inducing" means toward overcoming the prohibition to glance back. The importance of storytelling for survival is the subject of two autobiographical novels written by adult women who survived prolonged childhood sexual abuse. The novels, *Fazaa Fakkaa* (Father Fucker) by the *manga* artist, film star, and salsa singer Uchida Shungiku and *Bastard out of Carolina* by the novelist, speaker, and founding member of the Lesbian Sex Mafia Dorothy Allison, were both published in 1993. The following two chapters in part 1 examine how these novels break away from the dominant pattern according to which the sexual abuse of children (particularly girls) had been narrated in prior fiction (typified by what in Japan is known as the "Lolicon" or "Lolita complex" genre). Unlike stories told from the vantage point of the perpetrator, these novels focus on the subjectivities of the abused girls themselves and how creative storytelling—Orphic expression, as it were—enables the young protagonists to survive repeated and violent sexual assault.[25]

Father Fucker and Bastard out of Carolina call into question the ways in which fiction (or literature) is usually differentiated from real life and personal experience. Advertised as "autobiographical novels" (*jidenteki shōsetsu*) in their respective markets, these works undo many of our assumptions about the meanings of truth and fiction. Put in the simplest of terms, these novels are ultimately about the lived truth that can perhaps only be communicated in fiction. Uchida and Allison craft protagonist selves who live, who survive, precisely because of the stories they create for themselves. The very material and real power of storytelling to save lives is written into fiction by women who themselves survived by writing, a parallel "story" lending another level of import to the stories of the two fictional girls, Shizuko and Bone. While there is a variety of historical literary traditions (such as the Japanese *shishōsetsu*, the German *Bildungsroman*, or various versions of the embellished poetic memoir) that have blurred the lines between life and literature, these novels, particularly *Bastard out of Carolina*, make very clear to readers how "fictional" storytelling can communicate truths that might otherwise be suppressed or buried in nonfiction, "objective" speech, or everyday conversation. And at the core of these stories of experiences of abuse is the acknowledgment of the special role of storytelling in the lives and cognitive development of children.

Both novels also begin by invoking the intersection of oppression in the adult world and the bodies of abused "lower-class" children, which arguably allows room for some of their respective audiences to distance themselves from the protagonists and their communities—and, consequently, from the ongoing realities of child abuse. The relative success of each novel (both of which inspired filmic adaptations) cannot be divorced from this potential space for dis-identification. It is often easier for us to acknowledge that marginalized and stigmatized children are abused. The protean and everyday ways in which class, for example, is expressed, are evident in jokes about sexual abuse in the U.S. that end in hackneyed punch lines about "in-breeding" in low-income or "redneck" communities. Even the abused protagonist of *Bastard out of Carolina* wrestles against such stereotypes in trying to understand what is happening to her when she tells us, "I knew what the act was supposed to be, I'd read about it, heard the joke. 'What's a South Carolina virgin?' 'At's a ten-year-old can run fast.' "[26]

Conventional attitudes regarding class and regional differences in the U.S. hold that it is more scandalous, more shocking, and more interesting to imagine that the affluent daughter of well-to-do white Boulderites, JonBenét Ramsey, was sexually assaulted and killed than it is to imagine a poor white girl from the South having been impregnated by a male relative. The face of a heavily made-up child of privilege plastered across magazine and tabloid covers occupies a space in our imaginations and in our culture that makes these events seem rare, belying the everyday reality of fatal child abuse.[27] The shock characteristic of media coverage of fatal child abuse (in both the U.S. and Japan) reveals how tenaciously we cling to myths of unconditional parental love—unless the families involved can be seen as deviant, backward, or otherwise "unfit." Cultural identity is so often expressed in terms of family relationships and family values that it takes little investigative expertise to find a group of adults who will readily agree that the lives of children in other communities are very sad, difficult, or pitiful. For example, those in the U.S. who protested in hopes that Elián González would remain with distant relatives in Miami rather than be returned to his father in Cuba often relied on the demonization of Cuba as a state in which all children are de facto abused (by a presumably "negligent" and "unfit" government) in their arguments.

The differential sentencing of parents whose actions (or lack of actions) lead to the death of their children further reveals how class affiliations and perceptions of status (as linked to moral integrity, guilt, and so on) underwrite much of the contemporary U.S. legal system. For example, on August 8, 2003, the ten-month-old son of Mark Warschauer, a professor at the University of California, Irvine, was found dead of hyperthermia, strapped into his car seat on a hot day. Warschauer had left his son, Michael, in the car for more than three hours while he worked in his office. Not long after this incident, a university police spokesperson, Steve Monsanto, said, "With cases of that type, I'm not familiar with any case where charges haven't been filed." When explaining what would happen next, Monsanto said the campus police had referred the case to the Orange County District Attorney and that "you would be hard-pressed to find a situation where the D.A. wouldn't [press charges]."[28]

Indeed, John Darrell Morgan of Fontana (east of Irvine in Southern California's "Inland Empire") was sentenced to a one-year prison sentence for having left his daughter Angelina, who was three years old, in his Chevrolet Astrovan one year earlier. Angelina also died of hyperthermia. Unlike Warschauer, who was working in his office while his son was forgotten in the car, Morgan left his daughter strapped in the car because he passed out unconscious (a reaction to prescription painkillers he had been taking for one day) while unloading groceries in his driveway.[29] Warschauer, by contrast, was never charged with any crime even though Steve Monsanto had been confident that the D.A. would press charges against him. Orange County Deputy District Attorney Matthew Murphy told the press, "Despite the feeling in our office about the tragic death of the child, the law in this area is very clear."[30]

"Kaitlyn's Law" (named for Kaitlyn Russell, a baby left alone in a car, where she died), which was enacted in California in 2001, stipulates that "a parent, legal guardian, or other person responsible for a child who is six years of age or younger may not leave that child inside a motor vehicle without being subject to the supervision of a person who is twelve years of age or older."[31] The penalties for violating Kaitlyn's Law, which functions as a type of "enhancement clause," include fines and do not preclude additional charges for violations of Section 192 of the California Penal Code, which addresses various types of voluntary and involuntary manslaughter.[32] In understanding why Morgan was sent to prison and Warschauer faced no charges even though Morgan had been incapacitated at the time of his daughter's death and Warschauer claimed to have forgotten his son, it is helpful to consider that the professor may have been afforded greater sympathy by other professionals, such as the D.A., who could be predisposed to seeing Warschauer as their peer. In other words, leaving a child to die in a hot car may be a crime so long as we do not identify with the parent in question. Murphy told *Los Angeles Times* reporters that his decision not to file charges took into account Warschauer's "unquestionable love for his child, supported by dozens of witnesses and an Internet site devoted to the memory of his son."[33] Antipathy toward affluent professionals can and often does influence juries' deliberations and public opinion in some high-profile trials, but the decision to press charges and pursue a prosecution is made by other professionals.[34]

When faced with fatal child abuse in one's home community or peer group, many go to great lengths to depict the offending parent(s) as outsiders—if not to attempt to justify or deny the abuse altogether. It is easier in contemporary Japan, for example, for many to accept that the children of a working-class truck driver in Kobe would be left unfed to die than to believe an elite Tokyo University graduate would beat his fourteen-year-old son to death with a metal bat. Attitudes that belied a fierce classism predictably shaped public responses to these events, both of which attracted media attention in the late 1990s. The truck driver and his wife were vilified as "monsters" and unfit parents while the elite Tokyo professional was described in sympathetic terms. The "metal bat incident" of 1996 is useful as a point of reference for how public responses to elite or privileged parents who kill children differ from reactions to murders involving marginalized or poor parents, as well as how they differ from attitudes and fears about children who kill. Journalists reporting on the "metal bat incident" described the father's accounts of the murdered boy's violent behavior at home and portrayed the father's actions as the frustrated attempt by a loving man to protect his other family members from possible harm.[35] Public willingness to identify with the father in this case fueled both apologist journalism and the lenient sentencing (up to three years).

The "metal bat incident" became the story not of a murdered boy but of a well-intentioned father driven to desperate measures by his son's violent temper. The murdered boy's presence in most public discussions of the case mattered only insofar as it excused or explained the father's actions; he was, in effect, lost in the collective yearning to disallow the possibility of deadly abuse perpetrated by a father conforming to the fiercely lauded and idealized model of middle-class success. We are more comfortable with the image of a terrible teen than that of a middle-class father murdering his son. As will be addressed at length in part 2, violent parenting is frequently overshadowed, if not erased, by the more comforting and predictable image of the teenage (usually male) menace. In the U.S., for example, images of teenage "super-predators" and "gang members" have fueled a wide array of anti-youth legislation, such as California's Proposition 21 of 2000, which have made it possible for more young people to be tried as adults, placed in adult prisons, and subjected to death-penalty sentences. In May 2007, the Japanese Diet introduced an array of draconian juvenile crime laws, including one that lowered the age at which a child can be imprisoned to "about twelve." Some Japanese lawmakers had been trying to eliminate the minimum age altogether.[36]

The intense focus on seemingly isolated events, such as the "metal bat incident," would have us believe that they were completely aberrant and uncommon when, in fact, abuse in privileged circles is often effectively hidden from view. A reader/viewer who maintains distance when confronted with stories of abuse outside her community may not be surprised that "they" would do such things to their own children. Many abuse stories are, after all, reported in ways likely to reinforce such a reader's sense of superiority by confirming "their" depravity. These reductive binaries, when applied to class divisions, are quickly undone by Sandra Butler, who observes, for example, that "among the more affluent, incestuous assault is simply a better-kept secret."[37] Access to attorneys and distance from the scrutiny of social-service agencies that monitor the poor in the U.S. assists some families in the covering up of child abuse. As Ferenczi noted, the ways in which cover-ups are expressed may differ according to cultural or class contexts, but "such incidents are much more frequent than one would imagine. Only a very small proportion of the incestuous seduction of children and abuse by persons in charge of them is ever found out, and even then it is mostly hushed up."[38]

If child abuse is seen as atavistic, there is no room for the many stories of abuse that emerge from what are perceived as "evolved" communities and families. Just as anthropologists who have studied the maltreatment of children in "primitive" societies have reinforced idealized notions of childhood in their home cultures, child-abuse prevention and intervention programs targeting marginalized and poor communities are bound to the myth that abuse is a symptom of "backwardness," of poverty, of race and ethnicity, or of "underdevelopment." Health professionals, social workers, and teachers in the position to intervene are far less likely to report child abuse among their peers than abuse occurring outside their class or community, a result of the kind of social pressures that may have contributed to Freud's recanting of his early observation that sexual abuse occurred with regularity in his society. The ease with which certain groups are positioned as disdainfully "Other" or in need of "assistance" arguably contributed to the success of Uchida's and Allison's novels, which tell the stories of children their respective dominant cultures expect to be abused.

Checking Out and Checking In

Father Fucker and Bastard out of Carolina are the stories of two young girls who are violently and repeatedly sexually abused by their stepfathers, but the stories are not told to us by the young girls, Shizuko and Bone; rather, they are narrated by the girls as grownups, the adult survivors. (For some readers who erroneously contend that a "real" father would never do such a thing, the horror may be mitigated by the depiction of stepfathers and not biological fathers as the abusers.) While it is surely beyond the abilities of anyone to remember childhood years in full detail, memory for the narrators of Father Fucker and Bastard out of Carolina is fraught with significant gaps, competing versions of events, and fears and anxieties that remain compelling long after the danger has passed. One function—or perhaps what would be best designated the subtext—of both narratives is to communicate the extreme difficulty survivors encounter when trying to organize their memories and articulate their experiences, because the aftereffects of prolonged, repeated trauma combined with the ways in which severely abused children develop patterns of psychologically dissociating or "checking out" of their physical realities during the abuse make it very difficult for the adult survivor to piece together traumatic episodes and recount them in a chronologically coherent narrative.

The Japanese psychiatrist Nishizawa Satoru echoes a widely held belief among those who work with traumatized youth when he argues that children who are unable to escape an abusive situation learn to escape the only way they can, through dissociation.[39] An example of this would be imagining oneself somewhere else, going numb, being unable to see or feel anything, or staring intently at the ceiling while being raped. Ferenczi's patients in 1932 described similar states, as he explains: "This 'being gone' is not necessarily a state of 'not-being,' but rather one of 'not-being-here.' As for 'where,' one hears things like: they are far away in the universe; they are flying at a colossal speed among the stars; they feel so thin they pass without hindrance through the densest substances; where they are there is no time; past, present and future are simultaneous for them; in a word they feel they have overcome time and space."[40] Checking out in this way complicates later attempts to remember the abuse for obvious reasons. Both novels I discuss in the next two chapters focus on the actual years during which the protagonists were abused, and the way in which this content is related dramatizes the problem of how experiences of severe trauma at an early age affect fundamental ways of understanding one's own experience and subsequent difficulties in communicating those experiences to others.

The difficulty involved in recounting severe trauma is represented in *Father Fucker* and *Bastard out of Carolina* through descriptions of the struggles Shizuko and Bone face when attempting to trust their own perceptions and experiences at the same time that those experiences are being directly and forcefully denied. The repetition of fierce denial and the distortion of their reality by members of their families contribute to and help maintain false narratives or pervasive family fictions, which regularly deny the daily terror each girl suffers and main-tain the myth that they are the cause of any trouble in their "good" families— the families everyone acts as if were real. Both girl protagonists, to differing degrees, are designated scapegoats for discord in their families. Shizuko is not "obedient" (*sunao*), and Bone is too "stubborn." To better understand how these distortions are expressed and how they affect the narrators' ability to interpret their own life experience, we must confront the tension between the versions of events imposed on Shizuko and Bone and their own memories of how they were abused, a tension so inextricably woven into the way the stories are told that these novels demand a great deal from a reader. By resisting the tendency to minimize, naturalize, normalize, or marginalize the horror (or identify with the perpetrator), and thereby precluding the possibility of a "fun read," we can engage in the difficult practice of reading as bearing witness— whether as a show of solidarity, with eyes "livid with history," or with what Ferenczi called *Gegenliebe*, or "counter-love."

In the following two chapters, I adopt a model of reading inspired by the notion of counter-love and the role of child advocates. For many years, I served as a CASA for abused children, and this experience informs my approach to *Father Fucker* and *Bastard out of Carolina*. The role of a CASA by definition is a biased and unidirectional one. The *ideal* advocate's sole concern is the child's safety and well-being, and she tries to understand, as much as possible, what it feels like to be that child. She is "appointed" by the court but is not part of it. She does not represent or work on behalf of state institutions or the family of origin. She allies herself with the child and uses her position to further the child's interests, such as developing toward eventual autonomy in a safe en-vironment. Similarly, the ideal reader, as I envision her in the following two chapters, is an ally-advocate who reads closely enough to discern details and clues that can support the fictional child's liberation. This type of close reading as advocacy is necessary work in setting up part 2, for any meaningful discussion of how youth express rage should include an understanding of from where that rage might emerge.

CHAPTER 2

Shizuko, the Silent Girl: Uchida Shungiku's *Fazaa Fakkaa*

Uchida Shungiku's decision to call her autobiographical novel *Fazaa Fakkaa* (Father Fucker) warrants some discussion. The use of two widely known English words, one of which is vulgar, for the title helped to generate attention and impact the sales of a novel that might otherwise have been relegated to the conventional category of *joryu bungaku* (women's fiction), particularly given its "domestic" setting.[1] Before one opens the book to begin reading, the eponymous protagonist is described as a "fucker"—not a survivor, victim, or girl. The agency seemingly assigned to the protagonist through this characterization begs to be considered in relation to the politics and marketing of sexualized innocence. Much of the previous fiction addressing the sexualization and sexual abuse of girls in Japan, such as Nosaka Akiyuki's *The Pornographers*, was recounted from the vantage point of the adult abuser or would-be abuser, and similarly skewed and distorted representations continue to abound in some popular pornography (called "Lolita eros" and associated with an audience's corresponding "Lolicon" or Lolita complex) and adult comic books in contemporary Japan. One can also find material narrated by the abused or exploited (who, of course, are not always seen as such) that appeal to a Lolicon readership.

In a talk presented at the University of Iowa in 2006 and translated by Nathan Shockey, the literary and cultural critic Naitō Chizuko described what she calls a "Loliconization" phenomenon in contemporary Japan: "I use the term 'Loliconization' to mean the commodification of children, girls, and young women as sexual symbols in society. The term derives from 'Lolita complex,' which was originally used as a general term to represent pedophiliac sexual desire. However, in contemporary Japan, its abbreviation, 'Lolicon,' has become widespread thanks to its connection with *otaku* culture, and today it no longer represents any one peculiar sexual preference. In other words, the term 'Lolicon' has been standardized to represent a broader societal desire."[2] Naitō describes this "broader societal desire" as replacing the "symbol of 'woman,' which is exchanged as property among men" with "the proxy symbol of the 'young girl.' " In other words, she writes, "Precisely because of the youth of the 'young girl,' she lacks a strong will, and since she is innocent and still has a 'blank' interiority, the male gender is able to freely project its ideals and delusions onto this symbol of the 'young girl.' Put simply, such a symbol possesses a very favorable set of circumstances for the expression of masculinized desire."[3] A similar Loliconization (with its attendant sexualization of girls), while perhaps not as conspicuous as it is in urban Japan, is also evident in many North American communities. Images of sexual activity involving actual children may be hidden from view yet remain an enormous, if illegal, moneymaking industry of global dimensions. In her talk, Naitō also discusses how the contemporary Japanese novelist Shōno Yoriko takes on the transnational market in Loliconized culture in her novel *Dainihhon Ontako meiwaku-shi* (which Nathan Shockey translates as *The Troublesome History of Dainihhon Ontako*). According to Naitō, "[The fictional country of] Dainihhon takes 'Loliconism' as a matter of national policy, exports *lolicon* goods overseas, and aims for complete globalization of *lolicon* and *otaku* culture." Underscoring Shōno's critique of differential power across nation-states' borders, Naitō adds, "The nation of Dainihhon treats 'Mars' like a colony, creating a 'Martian girls red-light district' that commodifies and abuses girls."[4]

International sex tourism continues to place girls and boys around the world —most notably, in places where dollars, euros, and yen trump local sustainability and autonomy—in daily danger for profit and the "entertainment" of North American, Japanese, and other First World sex tourists. In countries that rely on foreign currency obtained through tourism, there may be little or no local intervention in the sexual exploitation of children, a reality that cannot be divorced from the neocolonial or client relationships between local governments and aggressively expansive (often U.S. or Japan-based) multinational corporations.[5] Travel writers and promoters make little effort to conceal what they are selling in advertisements that often feature young women and children wearing little clothing and making overt offers of sexual "entertainment" or more thinly veiled promises of exciting nightlife.[6]

Images of children as "seductive" are ubiquitous. For example, Judith Herman identifies a myth of the "Seductive Daughter" that she traces back to the biblical story of Lot, whose daughters are described as having "seduced" him, a myth that persists today in what she calls a "modern American version":[7]

> The modern American version of the Seductive Daughter is familiar to everyone. She has been immortalized in the popular literature as Lolita. Vladimir Nabokov's immensely successful novel has been understood on many levels, but on perhaps the simplest level, Lolita is a brilliant apology for an incestuous father. . . . The Seductive Daughter lives on, an active inhabitant of the fantasy life of the millions of ordinary citizens who constitute the readership of *Chic, Hustler, Playboy, Penthouse,* and the like. What is more surprising to learn is that the Seductive Daughter also appears regularly in the professional clinical literature.[8]

In Japan, children who are sexually abused by family members are misassigned agency as soon as the abuse is rendered into language. The word for "incest" (a term that is problematic in its associations even in English, as is evident in the use of prepositions such as "with" in many dictionary definitions) in Japanese is kinshinsōkan, a word meaning "sexual relations with close relatives" and that contains the character (sō or ai) for "mutuality" or "reciprocity." That a well-known cartoonist would publish a novel based on her experiences of childhood sexual abuse and call it *Father Fucker,* invoking the linguistic and cultural myths that assign agency to sexually abused girls, could not have been a marketing accident, and the myth of consent will remain a problem in the discussion that follows.

Uchida's deft marketing sense contributed to what became in the 1990s a diverse and lucrative business bearing her name. Uchida "goods," such as comic books, essay collections, and music compact discs, along with periodic television appearances and film roles (including the mother in *Visitor Q* [2001], a film by Miike Takashi that treats sexual abuse as spectacle), have made her somewhat of a household name in Japan. While many U.S. readers may not have heard of Dorothy Allison, Uchida Shungiku has been a celebrity, albeit one whose popularity has waxed and waned. Given the notoriety of its author and the escalation of the marketing of Uchida goods following *Father Fucker*'s publication, many readers may be more prepared to see the words "Father Fucker" as shocking or provocative than to recognize the irony in such a title.

In a book of essays, Uchida Shungiku describes the origin of this title, shedding some light on how she (and, by extension her protagonist, Shizuko) came to be called "Father Fucker":

"If your stepfather hadn't done you, you never would have become such a great *manga* artist, huh?" About four years ago, my boyfriend at the time said this to me. "Father Fucker!" is what that same boyfriend cruelly accused me of being one year later. I wondered what I was if even my boyfriend would go so far to call me that, and I could not stop crying. But about six months later, I ended up thinking that if I'd cried that much, I'd better figure this out, and with that I began to feel better.[9]

For Uchida, "figuring out" and "feeling better" meant writing, but once she had brought her completed first novel to the publishers, she saw how the emphasis on maximizing profit would determine the way her story would be marketed. She recalls, "Every single day [at the publishing house] I was asked the same question over and over again to the point where it was all I heard: Is it true? And then when they'd tell me they had to sell copies, so why not go ahead and put 'autobiography' on the jacket cover, I realized how it works and replied, 'By all means, since you are publishing it for me, I don't want to risk all the hassle of the book not selling. Go ahead.' But I hadn't expected that everyone would be so interested in whether or not it was true."[10] In this moment, not only her work but Uchida's life became a commodity subjected to the dictates of the marketplace.[11]

In interviews and essays in the 1990s, Uchida indicated that the novel does draw on aspects of her own childhood, but even her books of essays at the time (which include drawings of nude or seminude women or nude photos of herself) were heavily advertised and shaped by what publishers and Uchida's eponymous corporation determined would sell well. That is to say, sexual abuse was once again distorted to conform to the crude, larger signifier "sex." The content of her work, however, complicates this pattern. The following is an example of the elliptical descriptions of her childhood Uchida provides in her nonfiction writing: "My stepfather came into the home where I lived with my mom and my younger sister and created a paradise for him and only him, which I kicked down and left for rubble when I ran away. But . . . I am not 'poor little sexually abused Uchida-san.' "[12] In light of the dynamics of trauma described in the previous chapter, it is not surprising that much is left unsaid in her discussions of her own trauma and that those gaps take shape only in fiction. Again, literature offers avenues and possibilities of expression unavailable in other registers, such as everyday conversation or even the psychoanalytic session.

Father Fucker epitomizes the complexities of "survivor discourse" in that not only are barriers to telling represented in the story, but the book itself was received with considerable hostility and outrage, and Uchida was rebuked for telling her story publicly as a novel. Exploitation by the publishing house did not protect Uchida from the harsh criticism that her novel was untruthful and distasteful. Rather, the novel's promotion exacerbated certain criticisms (according to the "any publicity is good publicity" model of profit generation). Telling stories of childhood abuse—sexual abuse in particular—can be so threatening to those who wish to ignore and deny it that even a practice as immaterial as demonstrating "good manners" or filial piety can be picked up as justification for dismissing the reality of abuse. Uchida expresses frustration with this kind of criticism, "After publishing *Father Fucker*, I was criticized for 'disclosing my real parents' faults,' but I couldn't help wondering what that was about. People even believe that in romantic or married relationships, anything a man does to a woman should be kept secret. What is up with that? I don't know."[13] A diverse and powerful array of forces of suppression are evident in the very context in which *Father Fucker* was unleashed: the exploitative shaping of survivor discourse for profit; the dismissive voices of conservative debunkers; the self-righteous voices of the guardians of polite conversation; and the very real pain and lingering repression of the writer herself, who courageously (if not necessarily always consciously) was (and continues to be) living out a complex, contradictory, and confusing process of "figuring out" her experiences and feelings in public.

The space Uchida's novel has opened up for public and personal conversations about abuse cannot be underestimated. For some survivors, the novel offers a shared language, and I have met with women in Japan who described finding the words to describe their own experiences by reading *Father Fucker*. The novel offers many readers who are also survivors of sexual abuse a way into thinking about how their own experiences have affected them. Although psychoanalysis has been of interest to literary critics, and literature has interested psychoanalysts, for some time, the clinical possibilities for fiction's role in analysis and trauma recovery have only recently begun to be explored. Dana Bryon Staub explains in "The Use of Fiction in an Analysis" that a novel can be used by a therapist and client to enter into a discussion of the protagonist's traumatic experiences, allowing the reader/patient to find ways to talk more freely about her own experiences.[14] When I have used the novel and its film adaptation in classes at the University of California, Irvine; Stanford University; and the University of Iowa, I have been continually amazed by how my students want to continue discussing it with me even long after a class has ended and how many of them choose to write about the novel for term papers. The novel, in very tangible ways, has provided a space via Shizuko and her story through which my students and I can enter into conversations about abuse and related suffering.

In discussing Uchida's novel with students, I have found that the level of classroom discussion can be deepened and intensified by producing what Shoshana Felman has succinctly described as a "crisis":

> [Teaching] takes place precisely only through a crisis: if teaching does not hit upon some sort of crisis, if it does not encounter either the vulnerability or the explosiveness of an (explicit or implicit) critical and unpredictable dimension, it has perhaps not truly taught: it has perhaps passed on some facts, passed on some information about some documents, with which the students or the audience—the recipients—can for instance do what people during the occurrence of the Holocaust precisely did with information that kept coming forth but that no one could *recognize*, and that no one could therefore truly *learn, read, or put to use*. . . . My job as a teacher, paradoxical as it may sound, was in fact that of creating in the class the highest state of crisis that it could withstand, without "driving the students crazy," without compromising the students' bounds.[15]

Felman's description of the process and response to stories of traumatic suffering she brought into the classroom in many ways speaks to my own experience teaching *Father Fucker*. Unlike those critics who rebuked Uchida's "impolite" and "unseemly" story of Shizuko's horrific childhood, my students routinely are able to respond to the "crisis" the story introduces in our midst and, through discussions and papers, find ways to "talk back" to the title and put their readings to both personal and academic use.

Along with the title's characterization of the protagonist, derisive name-calling serves as her reason for reflecting on her childhood and deciding to "figure it out" by telling her story. *Father Fucker* begins with her description of her journey back to childhood:

> People often tell me I have a face like a prostitute. When I tell them that I have had all sorts of job experiences that involved hostessing, they often ask, "Did you also do, um, you know," implying selling my body. They ask in a lighthearted tone as if it were only natural. I haven't let it show on my face, but I have hated that. Soon after I turned sixteen, I ran away from home and started out homeless, and I frequently thought that the one thing I wouldn't do is sell my body. Even when it looked like someone would ask me just to try

it, I would refuse. Still, without any ill will, people will ask me in complete earnest, "Did you do that?" I got asked this so many times that more than getting angry, I thought it was strange. After all, the people asking me this were not particularly cruel or callous. So for them to ask me like that meant I must really look like I have been a prostitute. But I truly hated having people say that to me. I had lived my life thinking that was the one thing I would never do. I don't care what other people think about me, but why do I have that kind of face?

Yesterday, I finally remembered. I was a prostitute. . . . My pimp was the person who raised me up until the age of sixteen, and furthermore she was my biological mother. My customer was her lover, the father who raised me.[16]

In addition to being labeled "Father Fucker" and marked as "looking like" a prostitute from the outset, the protagonist's very name, Shizuko, which literally means "quiet child," is connected both to the way she is denied a voice and her struggle to later claim it. One can hardly say "reclaim" in the case of one silenced before she can speak. Readers learn that while still a toddler of three or four, Shizuko was already conditioned to accept injustice and physical pain through repeated acts of violence and neglect, groomed, as it were, by her mother and biological father for the sexual abuse she later suffers.

The adult narrator's earliest memory of physical abuse, which occurred prior to her entrance into kindergarten, is having been hit in the head by her biological father with a dresser drawer "because" she asked him to bring home money at the instigation of a neighborhood adult who knew Shizuko's mother was supporting the family (12–13). In concert with this training to expect violent punishment, she is taught by her father to keep secrets, a lesson that deforms her developing ability to communicate what she knows and what she sees. When one of her father's girlfriends accompanies Shizuko, her sister, and her father to a beach outing, he tells Shizuko that she must not tell her mother (the implied punishment being further violence). The adult Shizuko includes these early lessons as part of a picture of her childhood prior to the years in which she was violently sexually abused by her stepfather, but it is up to the reader to think about how such early experiences limited or perhaps determined how Shizuko would interpret and organize her subsequent daily terror and pain.

The pressure to keep silent when afraid is further enforced by the physical surroundings in her first home, where, for example, the outdoor toilet is unlit—the bare bulb that went out having never been replaced (35–36). Just as her parents fail to attend to the burned-out light bulb, they consistently fail to attend to her physical well-being, conveying the message that she has no choice but to endure hardship and fear. While it was not uncommon for homes to have outdoor toilets in the early 1960s in Japan, when the thirty-seven-year-old narrator would have been a toddler, the unattended bulb (only the first of many bad memories involving bathrooms and bathtubs) speaks more to the culture in Shizuko's home than to the historical moment.[17] Later in the novel, her stepfather has a teenage Shizuko bathe in an outdoor tub that is not only exposed to the wind, rain, and bugs but, more important, to the eyes of their backyard neighbors. The fear of violent "punishment" makes it difficult for Shizuko to question—let alone find words for—the discomfort she experiences when, for example, she is expected to bathe where she can be seen (by her stepfather or neighbors). The adult narrator also notes the irony of not having been allowed to bathe in the bug-infested tub while menstruating because her stepfather considered menstruation "dirty" (137). The discomfort and fear associated with toilets and baths serve as a backdrop for much of the abuse, which escalates in both degree and frequency throughout the novel.

Just as she learns to accept uncomfortable toilet and bathing facilities without protesting, she is forced to accept that her own physical boundaries can be violated. There are two scenes in particular when these two factors converge, the first being when her stepfather beats her and throws her into a bathroom while yelling, "Stay in there forever! A piece of shit like you should live in the toilet!" (140).[18] The other scene occurs away from home when she is frightened after having passed bloody tissue in a hospital bathroom stall and convinced herself that her health and well-being are not worth the attention of a nurse and that she has been through worse, leading her to flush the "evidence" down the toilet. Her struggle to trust her own perceptions and to reject the guilt assigned to her (with its implication that she deserves to suffer) is further complicated when, at various points in her childhood, she is sexually assaulted by strangers. For the child already sexually abused in the home, being molested by a stranger can confirm what she perceives to be her difference. These experiences outside the home are further distorted at home into proof that she is "odd" and sexually promiscuous, crazy-making designations that continue to be asserted even as her stepfather routinely rapes her.

The novel includes scenes from Shizuko's very early years that depict a home environment in which sex and her mother's sexuality are confusing. Shizuko relates memories of her mother's sexual jokes and crotchless underwear, things that she is not able to interpret or even identify until long after the fact. In recounting her story in this way, piecemeal and by association, she is able, even without providing the reader with every detail, to communicate an environment and climate that later facilitate the constantly escalating sexual abuse. Whereas the young Shizuko is limited by the silence imposed on her, the older narrator grabs hold of related memories. She provides explanatory and descriptive memories that are linked by *how* they affected her as opposed to *when* they occurred, even when she remains unsure as to what was a dream, what was a story she was told, and what was her own experience. Bessel van der Kolk and Onno van der Hart have described traumatic memories as "the unassimilated scraps of overwhelming experiences, which need to be integrated with existing mental schemes, and be transformed into narrative language."[19] *Father Fucker*'s narration, its ordering and description of events, and its interrogation of the role (of "bad daughter") imposed on the protagonist dramatize this necessary process of integration and rendering into narrative that van der Kolk and van der Hart describe. Given the author's own account of what led her to write the novel, one cannot help but wonder about what this process meant for Uchida herself, what it allowed her to "figure out."

The representation of how Shizuko is blamed for her abuse and the discrepancy between her own experience and her parents' interpretation of her role in the family is frequently couched in terms of her difference. Her position as the "weird" one requires fierce reinforcement, and to this end, her mother frequently juxtaposes Shizuko's "badness" to her sister's "goodness." Her younger sister, Chie, who is not physically abused (although she does witness the violence), does not respond to Shizuko's suffering with sympathy. Shizuko's story, which casts Chie as a toady or an "Uncle Tom" figure who identifies with the aggressor, discourages musings into her younger sister's subjectivity beyond reductive notions of "rivalry" or "cruelty." This portrait is complicated if we shift our focus as reader-advocates to the younger sister and question how the events described might be seen from Chie's perspective. Such a shift mimics the way in which Shizuko herself undoes her parents' distortions by retelling her childhood to reveal the abuse masked by her parents' fictional versions of a family—or, in other words, their family fictions.

If we consider, for example, that Chie is present for the derisive name-calling (when their stepfather calls their mother "fat" or says Shizuko "needs psychiatric help") and constantly escalating violence, we might imagine how a child in such a situation could want to avoid becoming the next target. As rich as such a de-centered reading of how Chie is perhaps lost in the text could be, the problem of how she survives in the home and how Shizuko experiences her sister's different role in the family fiction would nonetheless still raise the ultimately unanswerable question that faces all survivors of trauma: "Why me?" This question invokes what Claude Lanzmann has described as a fundamental obscenity. To ask why is to endow horror with logic. Lanzmann, in responding to discussions of the Holocaust, asserts, "It is enough to formulate the question in simplistic terms—Why have the Jews been killed?—for the question to reveal right away its obscenity. There is an absolute obscenity in the very project of understanding."[20] Taking heed from Lanzmann's observation, in looking at Father Fucker, I will offer a reading that draws more from questioning "how" the abuse is represented than "why" Shizuko is beaten and raped while her sister is not.

Shizuko recalls how her mother's discriminatory practices, such as clothing purchases (red dresses for herself and Chie and a blue one for Shizuko), marked her as different. The unrelenting positioning of Shizuko as different, as subject to different standards and different treatment, is underscored by Chie's response to her sister's abuse. For example, in one scene Chie and their mother return home to find Shizuko on the floor surrounded by broken glass after having been raped by her stepfather. The narrator tells us, "My sister was just silent and looking at me" (255). Rather than vilifying Chie as having been complicit or even interpreting her as having been terrified that she could be the next target (she is only thirteen or fourteen years old in this scene), these moments are important in helping us understand Shizuko's reliance on Orpha, Ferenczi's concept of the fragmented self that enables survival discussed in the first chapter. After their mother and Chie return home to find Shizuko on the floor and we are left with Chie's silence, as is the case in so many other scenes, there is no immediate response that questions the abuse or acknowledges Shizuko's experience of it. It is as if Chie expects and accepts her sister's suffering. How, then, we might ask, is Shizuko able to reach the point at which she, as the adult narrator, can tell us what happened? Without anyone in her immediate surroundings to challenge the abuse, how did she come to understand that she did not, in fact, "deserve" it?

One clue as to the nature of Shizuko's Orphic process (and perhaps Uchida's, as well, given the author's own careers as a manga artist and singer) is the description of her early creative attempts to express herself and construct fantasy worlds. Through drawing manga, Shizuko creates a world of her own, a fantastic world in progress as it is dramatized in the 1995 film adaptation of the novel.[21] In the film, when Shizuko dissociates and enters her imaginary world, she appears within the world she is drawing. In her dream world, a manga hero-like imaginary friend appears to her, encouraging her and showing similarities to the film's more idealized version of the biological father, and her manga world comes to life. The imaginary friend asks her, "So, you are going to be a manga artist?" She tells him that she is going to Tokyo, and he comments that he likes her drawings, a stark contrast to the stepfather who ridicules her drawings as "a waste of time" in both the film and the novel. Orphic storytelling and fantasy figure prominently in the therapist Dana Bryon Staub's discussion of Alice, a patient in whom the "strongest part of her personality was the part engaged in fiction/storytelling."[22] Like Alice's, Shizuko's survival is depicted through her ability to imagine a different reality, one over which she can exercise control.

Shizuko creates imaginary ways out of her painful reality, but it is not until she is much older that she begins to develop a way to understand the reality of the abuse. By narrating her story, she demonstrates skill developed through her Orphic process and applies that skill to her personal history, paralleling perhaps Uchida's own application of her talents as a writer to her childhood experiences. Shizuko signals that this application took time. The narrator's understanding of her abuse is described as a very recent development. She explains at the outset, "Up until yesterday, I had completely forgotten that I had been a prostitute" (5). After Shizuko explains that her experience as a "prostitute" was, in fact, prolonged and repeated child abuse perpetrated by her stepfather, the "customer," and her mother, the "madam" or "pimp," our conventional understanding of both pimping and family relationships is disrupted. We are also confronted with the question, "Why yesterday?"—why this experience, or this understanding of it, had been "forgotten" until now. Shizuko does not provide an answer to this second question. To decipher the codes and uncover the forces that made her forget (and later remember), we must pay attention to how abuse was denied as it happened, for as we witness the twisting and deforming of her remembered youth, we find avenues toward explaining the forgetting.

Bombarded by criticism that she is "weird" and "disobedient" and that her troubles are her own fault, the young Shizuko struggles to think against or out of the distortions imposed on her, but her attempts to disentangle herself from those distortions are constantly sabotaged. It is not until she turns sixteen that Shizuko can run away from the dangerous stories and her dangerous home. At sixteen, she describes her home life to a boyfriend, whose sympathetic reaction assigns blame to her family, providing her with the first corrective reading of the abuse. Soon after, she is raped and beaten by her stepfather, despite her repeated protestations. She describes finding the courage to leave after this brutal attack as epiphanic, born of a sudden realization that propels her to break away: "That's right. I don't really have to be here" (257). As pivotal as the boyfriend was, however, we must also see her decision to run away as the culmination of years of struggling—carried out very much alone.

Recovered Memory and Oppositional Storytelling

The adult Shizuko has escaped from her abusive family, but her process of emotional or psychic separation is ongoing and in progress even as she tells her story. Naitō Chizuko discusses the significance of fiction "in progress" in her insightful essay on the difference between literature that imposes closure and literature that invites the reader to hold onto an imaginary and potential space, continuing the explorations incited by reading an author's words.[23] Naitō describes how the curious concept of an "ending" (ketsumatsu) to a story is perhaps most obviously demonstrated by looking at so-called unfinished stories, such as Meian, which Natsume Soseki was writing when he died. "Unfinished" works often inspire speculation, and Meian was even given an imaginary "completion" in 1990 in a sequel (Zoku Meian) by the contemporary writer Mizumura Minae. Naitō reminds us that every act of reading can invite us to take up a story line or a character's life and that we all can, and often do, linger in the space created through writing and reading.

Naitō's broadened notion of reader-response theory posits a shared space that a reader can revisit and revise, as well as use to sustain an ongoing relationship with a text. We may feel attached to characters, or we may imagine our own resolutions to troubling situations or amend "endings," but regardless of our particular relationships to a work of fiction, by imagining and wanting to stay with a story or a character, the story for us is necessarily "unfinished."[24] In this sense, Naitō reminds us that literature and stories can be our shared language, a phenomenon encountered whenever we refer to characters in stories (fiction or film, for example) to communicate an experience, attitude, or quality. Whether we speak of someone's "Oedipal complex" or, as I did earlier in this chapter, described someone as an "Uncle Tom," we draw on these shared languages and stories. In the case of *Father Fucker*, the very structure of Shizuko's narration involves us, for only by deciphering which words and which descriptions are remnants of the distorted self imposed on her by her parents can we, too, understand what was distorted—and at what price. As is the case with other fiction depicting child abuse and its fallout (such as Kōno Taeko's short story "Snow"), *Father Fucker* can be read as psychological detective fiction.

For example, Shizuko clearly signals to the reader that there is a significant disparity between her mother's interpretation of events and her own perceptions even before she begins recounting early memories. She even relates how this disparity led her to disavow relations with her mother and sister as follows: "Even if I try to line up *my memories* with the *stories* I heard from my mom, they don't match up very well. Eleven years after I ran away from home, I decided to cut all ties to my mother and sister once and for all at the end of an argument we had" (7; emphasis added). Beyond warning us that she and her mother do not share the same views as to "what happened," she positions her "memories" (*kioku*) in opposition to her mother's "stories" (*hanashi*). Although throughout the text, many of her mother's stories are qualified with grammatical signals that indicate that Shizuko's memories differ from what she remembers her mother as having said, these clues are frequently subtle, such as the use of quotations, paraphrasing, or words that attribute information to other sources. Peppered everywhere, yet never the focus of a given passage, these clues can easily be missed if we do not heed the narrator's warning.

Pre-memory, what happened before Shizuko was born or before she can remember, poses fewer challenges to readers, because Shizuko cannot corroborate or contradict for us the distortions of what she herself did not experience. Her knowledge of how her biological parents met and their early years together, for example, is entirely dependent on her mother's accounts, but even this she does not take for granted, writing, instead, "*I heard* they met at a dance hall" (9; emphasis added). Even in the most uncontested stories, her words and those of her mother are clearly differentiated. She employs grammatical qualifications (such as "I hear" or "according to") over and over to remind us that these details do not come from her direct knowledge or experience of events. Shizuko distinguishes what she knows and remembers from what she has been told *because she had to in order to survive.* (We might imagine this extending through the intervening years between the novel's end and the moment of narration.) Her disavowal of her mother's stories creates the space in which Shizuko's story can be told, and the reasons for this become increasingly apparent as we learn more of Shizuko's story and her mother's distortions of events.

Her mother's version of events, which assigns blame to Shizuko, and the impact of this scapegoating is also established in these early passages. For example, the reader learns that Shizuko's mother told her (at an undisclosed early age) about how difficult childbirth was and how her physical stress and varicose veins were compounded by having to return to work immediately after giving birth. Having heard this story ("Hearing this story, I"), Shizuko felt overwhelmed with guilt and, according to her mother (once again, this qualification is employed), promised to become a doctor when she grew up so she could relieve her mother's pain, for which Shizuko was led to assume responsibility (11). Shizuko does not provide the reader with a chronological reference that would indicate when this conversation took place, but by including this memory near the beginning of the novel, she gives the reader a snapshot to illustrate how burdened she was by feelings of responsibility for her mother even at a very young age. The distortion that a child could be responsible for a mother's pain in childbirth imposes intent where clearly none is possible. The false agency in ensuing distortions often involves the mother's substitution of Shizuko for her biological father.

The marked difference between the way the narrator describes her mother's treatment of her and her sister, as well as the mother's insistence that Shizuko's behavior causes the abuse, is connected early on to the mother's feelings about her first husband (Shizuko's biological father), to whom she frequently compares Shizuko. She had hoped that giving birth to Shizuko would transform her husband from a philanderer into a devoted husband, but instead he urged her to have an abortion and continued his relationships with other women. One could imagine that, being unable to express her resentment and anger directly at the absent father/partner, the mother instead aimed it at Shizuko, whom the mother describes in the harshest terms. This does not apply to Chie. Significantly, when her younger sister demonstrates the good penmanship that their father had, their mother does not compare Chie to their biological father; "On no occasion did my mom ever comment on the ways Chie was like our real dad. All she always ever said, like she was chanting the *nenbutsu*, was that I was like our real dad" (66). Such comparisons ("chanted" by her mother like a nenbutsu, or *namu amida butsu* [prayer to Amida Buddha]) are, for Shizuko, examples of how she was an outsider even in her own family, positioned beyond or away from home with her absent father.

Some scenes are drawn only from her mother's "stories" (which often highlight and assign value to temperamental or attitudinal differences between Shizuko and Chie) and not stories for which Shizuko has a competing memory. In these cases, Shizuko uses other narrative methods to call into question the veracity of her mother's version of events. For example, her mother told Shizuko that when she was a little girl, an adult woman, perhaps her father's sister, came to stay with them, and that woman and Shizuko argued a great deal, but Chie got along with the older woman without trouble. In retrospect, the adult survivor Shizuko expresses her skepticism regarding the accuracy of this portrayal by noting how the story portrays Chie in glowing terms by means of contrast. She explains, "Compared to [how she said I interacted with that woman], my mom said Chie was a good-natured kid who could get along with anyone" (28). In her mother's family fiction, Chie got along well with others and lived up to others' expectations of what a "good daughter" should be, but Shizuko caused trouble. With this division already firmly in place by the time Shizuko's stepfather moved in, the script, as it were, for what would transpire was already partially written.

Shizuko's role as the "bad" daughter and family outsider is quickly picked up by the stepfather, who, as we see in a scene in which he leads Shizuko and Chie over a condemned bridge, draws on the mother's schema to distort and twist events in ways that continue to blame Shizuko for that over which she has no control (98–100). Shizuko knows they should not cross this bridge and she hesitates while her stepfather and Chie go ahead, leaving her behind. She recalls being worried for Chie, "as her big sister," but Chie was "unbelievably . . . enjoying the thrill" (98). Shizuko was left to decide whether to stay behind and incur his wrath or traverse the bridge, both options carrying the risk of physical danger. After the stepfather and Chie reach the other side, Shizuko is spotted on the bridge, and a crowd tries to coax her safely across. When she reaches the other side, she searches the crowd in vain for her stepfather and Chie like "Rocky looking for Adrian." When she does find them, she is met with hostility and reprimand. Her stepfather calls her an "idiot." She is "in trouble" (for getting caught) when, in fact, she was coerced into a dangerous situation by the very man who is now rebuking her.

Her parents tell Shizuko that to be a "good daughter" and avoid further "punishment" she must be more compliant and "obedient." When her stepfather touches her breasts in front of her mother, Shizuko protests, but her resistance is met by her stepfather's complaint that she is not "obedient" or "agreeable" (sunao), and her mother follows this up by admonishing her in a similar way: "Shizu-chan, please be more obedient (Please try to get along)" (89). This pattern escalates to the point where her mother eventually sends Shizuko off to be raped, warning her not to disobey or "go against" her stepfather. The message here is not to obey so that the abuse will stop; it is to obey and endure so that the abuse can continue. The confusing message that Shizuko needs to accept abuse obediently to be a "good daughter" is never challenged. Being "obedient" means repressing any instinct to protect or assert herself. Shizuko struggles to understand just what the word "obedient" means in these moments, which signals to the reader that even as a child, she was able to recognize that something was wrong with her family's vocabularies and stories.

In the film based on the novel, we watch the mother wash rice noisily and intently, rhythmically rinsing the rice against the metal bowl as if to drown out the sounds of her daughter being raped. In the novel, the mother not only actively avoids acknowledging the abuse, she acts as "pimp" to avoid becoming the abused herself. For example, she asks Shizuko to find out what her stepfather does on Sundays and holidays that keeps him away from their home all night. Her mother relies on Shizuko to voice the question about his other family that she is afraid to ask. When Shizuko asks the question, she bears the brunt of his anger in her mother's stead. Her mother's use of Shizuko to say what she herself will not say (and endure what she herself will not endure) is inextricably linked to another aspect of her family fiction, one that involves a considerable amount of what Shizuko describes as "melodrama."

In her representation of her first marriage, the mother portrays herself as having been battered and neglected by a philandering and seldom-employed husband who spent their money on gambling and other women. Shizuko describes her mother's relationship with her stepfather less sympathetically. For example, when her stepfather beats her mother and then threatens to leave her while walking away, Shizuko describes her mother pleading with him, "Please come back!" Shizuko describes her mother as looking like a "character in a melodrama" (62). While not vilifying battered women as participants in their abuse, a myth that continues to impede the prevention of domestic violence, we cannot read such a passage and overlook the difference between inequality of power in adult–adult relations and the dependency characteristic of adult–child relations. Sandra Butler points to how child abuse can be occluded in some mothers' responses to marital oppression:

> The voices of incest victims' mothers echo the estrangement many women
> feel from their dreams and expectations and the sharing and closeness they

had anticipated in their marriages, as well as their competitive and awkward feelings about their children. The result is a message many mothers—not just those of incest victims—send to their children as they try to meet the demands placed on them as wives and mothers: "Your father first and you second. It would be too dangerous to fight back, because if I lose him I lose everything. For my own survival I must leave you to your own devices. I cannot defend you, and if necessary I will sacrifice you to your father."[25]

A mother perhaps immobilized by fear and confusion may not formulate such an obvious message in thoughts or words, but Butler's description speaks to the way in which a mother such as Shizuko's can fail to respond when her children are in danger. Rather than revealing the weaknesses of individual mothers, however, this points to larger problems, as Laura S. Brown explains: "Similarly, if we continue to blame nonparticipating mothers for their husbands' incestuous attacks on their daughters by engaging in long discourses on how these women must have set up their daughters, or were triangulated with them, or had abdicated their mother role (or you fill in the blank), we are excused from asking what kind of culture continues to reproduce fathers who rape their own children."[26] Certainly, the tendency to respond to publicized cases of children sexually abused by fathers with outrage directed at the mother for "failing to protect the children" runs the risk of deflecting attention away from the abuse itself.

Not surprisingly, this tendency is endemic to many cultural and religious ideologies, in both Japan and the U.S., for example, which continue to encourage wives to place their "husbands first," and this points to the widespread success of patriarchal family configurations that make it even more difficult for a child to survive abuse in the home. In the U.S., one need only watch "family programming" on the syndicated Trinity Broadcasting Network (or read the columns of James Dobson of the evangelical and right-wing Christian non-profit organization Focus on the Family) to hear religious leaders encouraging women to defer to their husbands to create righteous Christian homes. Similar messages abound in Japan, where they can be informed by the emperor system or Confucian family ideologies, Christianity, or any number of other belief systems that can lend themselves to an acceptance of women's roles as ancillary to those of men. The emperor system in particular, as I will address in part 2, relies not only on a rigid social hierarchy but also on related notions of ownership (of, for example, national or ethnic "purity") and patriarchy (with the god-emperor as father of the nation and individual fathers as "mini-emperors" in the home), both of which are certainly evident in the depiction of Shizuko's stepfather, who, we are told, was born in Manchuria (a site of Japanese imperial expansion and aggression), proudly carries a scar from having been struck by a Russian soldier's bullet as a child, and loves military songs (which would surely have included some that celebrated the emperor and imperial project). The status of mini-emperor he cultivates in the home extends from enforced terms of address, as I will explain, to his claim to total moral authority.

Idealized notions of motherhood that serve the interests of patriarchy run far deeper and wider than any single religious or cultural ideology, regardless of how pervasive or powerful that ideology may be. In their introduction to a collection of essays on the myriad ways in which children are increasingly casualties in "small wars" waged against them, Nancy Scheper-Hughes and Carolyn Sargent summarize Jill Korbin's critique of "an uncritical overattachment to the idealization of maternity and mother-love, an attachment that can prevent family, friends, and even well-seasoned professionals from perceiving the intent of some women who are determined to kill their children."[27] The problem here is clear: On the one hand, we have belief systems that deem a mother's unconditional love as natural and universal; yet on the other hand, those same belief systems make it very difficult for many mothers to express how their daily lives are less than ideal because they feel bound by our collective attachment to idealized motherhood. This is certainly the case in Japan, where child abuse intervention counselors often describe their female clients' complaints that motherhood is not like what they anticipated, not like it is represented in magazines and on television. And, as is the case in the U.S., the response to a news story about a mother who kills her children frequently involves shock and outrage at this "unnatural" behavior, treating fatal child abuse as if it were uncommon when, in fact, it is quite ordinary.[28]

On March 26, 1998, for example, a "young mother" (*yanmama*) in Japan left her two toddlers in the car with the engine running (for air conditioning) while she played Pachinko for nine hours. She checked on them twice, leaving them juice and candy, and the two children died. Analyses of this incident in the Japanese popular media portrayed the mother as lacking "normal maternal instincts," reinforcing notions of a biologically determined ability to parent. Similar examples from North American news sources will be familiar to many readers. As Jill Korbin explains, "Only some of these cases capture public attention," making it seem as if they are rare when they are not.[29]

Without denying the difficulty involved in escaping a violent spouse or the trauma suffered by a battered woman whose children are also abused (and who may, in fact, also abuse her children), it is still possible to argue that Shizuko's perception of her mother's participation in a "melodramatic" moment reveals what can be read, at the very least, as missed opportunities for "good enough" parenting.[30] Without hammering the message into readers' heads by telling us, "She could have saved me, but she didn't," Shizuko's narration demonstrates it. For example, when the mother calls her lover, the stepfather, back after he has beaten her (as if his presence were the sole means of attaining the distorted dream of a "family" for which she yearns), we see the meaning of her pleas from Shizuko's perspective. Her mother's "melodramatic" desperation seems fake in Shizuko's retelling—not in the sense that it did not happen; it was artificial (like playacting) compared with the materiality of Shizuko's own pain. Her mother's "melodramatic" story does not correspond to Shizuko's experience. The mother's version masks the abuse with melodramatic pathos and stock characters: the suffering wife; the violent womanizer; and the two daughters—one good, one bad.

Shizuko's assigned role as the bad daughter ("sick in the head," according to her stepfather) serves also to maintain her mother's relationship with her stepfather. The narrator describes feeling as if she was being manipulated and abused by her parents for their amusement. For example, after Shizuko writes a letter addressed to them in honorific language ("To Mother Dearest and Father Dearest" [Okaasama, Otōsama e]), her stepfather is angry that he was not shown the proper deference by having his name written first. Her mother sends her to talk with him, and when she asks what he wants, he replies, "I don't know! What a pest!" Shizuko describes feeling like an "ingredient" or "material" (zairyō) necessary for such exchanges: "My stepdad and mom smirked like they were enjoying themselves by sending me back and forth like that. And this kind of thing happened over and over again. Even as a child, I could sense there was something creepy going on with them. It wasn't long before I realized I was being used as an ingredient to create that dynamic" (54–55). Although the stepfather insists that Shizuko address him with the honorific for father, "Father Dearest" (otōsama), her mother tells Shizuko that she herself chose to use this form of address. Shizuko recalls that her mother told her that in kindergarten Shizuko announced that from that point on, she would refer to her parents as otōsama and okaasama (57). However, Shizuko remembers several conversations in which her stepfather did, in fact, insist on this method of address, and she describes not having liked using it. To see past the distorted "double talk" (which was also used to enforce and maintain the story that Shizuko was "bad") requires that the reader trust in Shizuko's perceptions, just as Shizuko herself struggles to come to trust her own perceptions as an adult narrator. Put simply, the reader-advocate's role is to side with Shizuko.

In addition to casting Shizuko as the "bad daughter," her mother (and, later, stepfather) find fault with those on the "outside" who challenge the myth of the "good" family, such as the woman who told Shizuko to ask her biological father to bring home money when she was a toddler and the teachers who later tried to foster Shizuko's developing talents and dreams. When she decides she wants to write manga, Shizuko tells her elementary school teacher, who gives her a drawing pad (67). Happy with the gift and excited about her new dream, Shizuko eagerly returns home to tell her mother, but she is not met with the kind of encouragement she wants and anticipates. Her mother angrily objects to Shizuko's wish to draw manga and insists that she return the drawing pad. When the stepfather arrives home and learns of Shizuko's manga-writing aspirations, he is even angrier. Having already determined that Shizuko will become a doctor, they perceive manga writing as frivolous and "stupid." The direction their conversation takes, however, reflects the interest they have in disparaging differing opinions or practices to maintain the fiction that their family is "good." Instead of looking at the meaning of how fostering a child's interests might encourage her to excel in many areas, they see the teacher as having acted inappropriately by meddling and giving Shizuko a drawing pad. Her stepfather exclaims, "What idiots. All these damned teachers are complete idiots!" (71). Shizuko goes on to tell us that "no matter who the teacher was, he'd put them down, calling them cheapskates," and that both her mother and stepfather even spoke ill of her teachers' "personal lives" (71). Their litanies of other people's problems are described as increasingly frantic and desperate in proportion to the escalation of the abuse at home.

Torture, Dissociation, and the Rhetoric of Consent

By the time she was fifteen, Shizuko tells us, her daily life had become unbearable, her stepfather's cruelty having escalated to routine beatings and rape. The degree to which his "spin" on the abuse determined Shizuko's understanding of events is evident even in the adult narrator's description of her teenage years. As she recounts increasingly violent abuse, Shizuko falls back on stories from her childhood that held her responsible for the abuse she suffered. She seems to shift in and out of the role of adult survivor, making it possible for us to think of the narration as representing a survival or "recovery" in progress and not yet complete. Shizuko's reliability as a narrator is complicated by her incomplete separation from the language and logic of her abusive upbringing, and it is up to the reader to connect the way in which the abuse is narrated to the events described. Shizuko's narration is "spotty" both in terms of chronology and perspective, dramatizing the phenomenon widely accepted by contemporary psychologists and researchers that "memories of prolonged or variably repeated childhood abuse . . . appear to be retained in spots, rather than as clear complete wholes."[31]

As indicated earlier, while being abused, it is common for a child to dissociate and "check out," a phenomenon echoed in Lenore Terr's description of a wide variety of "defenses and coping operations," such as "massive denial, repression, dissociation, self-anesthesia, self-hypnosis, identification with the aggressor, and aggression turned against the self."[32] Bessel van der Kolk and Onno van der Hart elaborate on how dissociation has been a focal point throughout the history of psychiatric research, explaining, for example that more than a century ago "the very foundation of modern psychiatry was laid with the study of consciousness and the disruptive impact of traumatic experiences."[33] They describe in detail how early psychotherapists understood that certain events "would leave indelible and distressing memories—memories to which the sufferer was constantly returning, and by which he was tormented day and night."[34] Despite the obvious dimensions and frequency of this phenomenon, however, they write, "For the past seventy years, psychoanalysis, the study of repressed wishes and instincts, and descriptive psychiatry virtually ignored the fact that actual memories may form the nucleus of psychopathology and continue to exert their influence on current experience by means of the process of disassociation."[35] But with the advent of newer neurological testing procedures, in addition to rapidly expanding data drawn from clinical practice, van der Kolk and van der Hart note that we now have a better understanding of the origins of dissociation: "Under extreme conditions, existing meaning schemes may be entirely unable to accommodate frightening experiences, which causes the memory of these experiences to be stored differently and not be available for retrieval under ordinary conditions: it becomes dissociated from conscious awareness and voluntary control."[36] The long-term effects of such dissociation, they conclude, are not so mysterious, because those "who have learned to cope with stress by dissociation often continue to do so in response to the smallest strain. Subconscious memories thus come to control ongoing behavior."[37]

"Massive denial" in children subjected to prolonged and repeated abuse extends to the children's social relationships outside the home, and they "valiantly try to look normal at school, in the neighborhood, and on the play-ground," according to Terr.[38] Consequently, the very means by which a child might survive chronic abuse contributes to how difficult it can be, even for those who are very attuned to the dynamics of child abuse, to identify severely abused children and intervene. In Shizuko's case, we see that, even when the horrors of her daily life do spill over into the "outside" world, no one knows how to respond to the unexpected and terrifying violence of her stepfather, and no one intervenes on her behalf.

Selective Attention

Toward the end of her eighth-grade year (when she is fifteen), Shizuko begins to have sex with her boyfriend and classmate, Hiroki, and soon after fears she is pregnant. Her mother also becomes suspicious, noticing signs of pregnancy such as morning sickness, and she warns Shizuko that if her stepfather finds out, he will kill her (175). Shizuko recalls maintaining the daily hope that her period will finally come. It becomes increasingly difficult to deny her preg-nancy, and her mother eventually reveals Shizuko's condition to her stepfather, whose first reaction is to call Shizuko a "whore." Shizuko tells us that she "did not know the meaning of the word" at that time (184). He then beats Shizuko "more times than [she] could count" and eventually demands to know with whom she has had sex (186). He takes Shizuko and her mother in a taxi to Hiroki's house and "characteristically" worried about what "people" (the taxi driver) might think, remains silent and composed for the duration of the ride. Upon arriving at Hiroki's house, he blows up again, unable to contain his rage, screaming at Hiroki's father, "You want me to do it to your wife? Huh? What do you think?" Shizuko remembers thinking that was a very curious question, perhaps because it conflated the categories of "wife" and "stepdaughter." Her stepfather proceeds to attack Hiroki, and after Hiroki runs off, he begins to beat Shizuko again. Before leaving for home with the mother, the stepfather turns to Shizuko and says, "Don't bother coming home. I'll let this family have you!" (187–88).[39]

Shizuko's initial reaction on being left at Hiroki's is one of relief, of being "lucky." She soon witnesses an entirely different way to express anger, when Hiroki's parents sit the two of them down and ask if they understand the gravity of their situation. Hiroki's mother asks Shizuko whether she would like to take a bath. For Shizuko, who had been effectively isolated and unable to make friends, this is a new experience: "Raised with the warning that I was not to make friends, I had never bathed at another person's home before" (190).[40] Restricted social interactions and limited experiences with people outside the family are characteristic of abusive homes as Judith Herman explains:

> Families in which child abuse occurs are socially isolated. It is less commonly recognized that social isolation does not just happen; it is often enforced by the abuser in the interest of preserving secrecy and control over other family members. Survivors frequently describe a pattern of jealous surveillance of all social contacts. Their abusers may forbid them to participate in ordinary peer activities or may insist on the right to intrude into these activities at will. The social lives of abused children are also profoundly limited by the need to keep up appearances and preserve secrecy. Thus, even those children who manage to develop the semblance of a social life experience it as inauthentic.[41]

The contrast between her parents and Hiroki's leaves Shizuko feeling envious. Hiroki's response to witnessing some of the culture of Shizuko's home, on the other hand, predictably leads to retreat. She remembers that after her bath, she saw Hiroki studying at his desk and guessed that he was still intending to go to school the next day. Sensing an immediate shift in their relationship, Shizuko feels distant from the boy to whom she had grown so attached, and tellingly, their awkward discussion about a homework assignment proves to be their last conversation.

Returning to a more urgent and immediate narrative voice (the differences between the narrative present and past become porous when she describes events from a point closer to her younger self by using dialogue), Shizuko reconstructs her return home and how she was bombarded by questions from her stepfather—such as "Where did you do it? Did you do it here?"—and asked by her mother to "apologize to your father." Her stepfather also accuses her of "doing it" with her homeroom teacher, a teacher Shizuko liked a great deal, and then he "examines" and "punishes" her:

> "Lie down."
> My dad stretched me out and rubbed and poked at my belly.[42]
> "When I kicked you around before, I was hoping it would make you miscarry, but no such luck . . . the damned position is wrong, it's a breech."
> . . . My stepfather was gradually getting excited by this bogus medical examination, and he took off my underpants and started poking around my genitals.

"Don't you ever do that again for the rest of your life. Never again for the rest of your life."

I was silent.

"To make sure you can't, I'm going to sew you shut. And I'm going to do it to you right now. You can still have a baby by Caesarian section, so don't worry."

As if I wouldn't worry.

So, my stepfather actually started making preparations to sew up my vagina. . . .

"You're only kidding, right? Are you serious? Are you really going to do it?" My mother sobbed and pleaded with him over and over again, but my stepfather quietly continued on with his preparations. I just blankly watched on. As usual, I shut down and did not feel anything. After a while, he commanded me to "wash yourself in the bath," and he stood up. (196–98)

Shizuko recalls frequently "shutting down," being "silent," and "staring at the ceiling" in her recollection of this terrifying episode. The previous night she had been beaten by her stepfather in front of Hiroki and his parents, and no one had intervened to stop the abuse. The abuse expanded outside the confines of their home, making it increasingly difficult for Shizuko to imagine that her survival could involve physical escape from pain. Like many victims of repeated torture and abuse, Shizuko describes her ability to survive the abuse in the moment as stemming from her desperate attempts to see herself as powerful. She imagines herself to be "strong" and unaffected by fear, and she promises herself that no matter what he does to her, she will not be broken. Much like an Orphic reliance on imaginative storytelling, fantasies of exaggerated strength (or even rescue) can be as central to survival in the moment as they can be disruptive to long-term survival after the danger has passed.

Certainly, no one in her immediate surroundings gives Shizuko any cause to think that she does not deserve to be abused or could be saved. As the "surgery" scenario unfolds, Shizuko's portrait of her mother's limitations indicates why imagination provided a necessary function for her:

Although my mom seemed frightened that my stepfather would really sew my vagina shut like he said, she never once said "Stop." To me, it seemed like that's what she wanted too. From the beginning I had never thought she would save me, and I solemnly washed myself in the bathtub. I opened my legs wide and leaned back down on the "operating table" my stepfather had made by spreading out some newspaper.

My mom no longer questioned him. And, of course, she didn't stop him. . . .

I was silently staring at the ceiling. The surgery never got underway.

My stepfather said, "Your pulse is too high. I can't perform surgery like this."

I took this to mean, "I have scared you," which made me angry. Because no matter what my stepfather tried to do to me, I believed I could be strong and not get scared, plead with him, or kiss his ass.

"Nope, it's useless with your pulse so fast. You will sleep here. Because I have something to discuss with you in a bit."

My stepfather didn't take me to the kids' room, but to his and my mom's room, and he put me on their bed. Because it wasn't my usual bed, I couldn't relax, but I thought he'd brought me in here because my sister was in the kids' room. (198–200)

Shizuko does eventually fall asleep until she is awakened by movement and the smell of pomade and is raped by her stepfather. The next morning, she asks her mother, "Why did Dad do it with me?" (201). Her mother tells Shizuko that he thought he might induce a miscarriage.

A particular word Shizuko uses in the question above and in many other passages related from the vantage point of the adult survivor to describe being raped requires some discussion. Her use of the conjunction *to* (meaning "and" or "with") to describe the sexual abuse in *Father Fucker* as "sex *with* my stepfather"—as opposed to a grammatical pattern that would more accurately reflect the unidirectionality of rape—is a distortion that stems from the myth that she was somehow a participant in her stepfather's violence (245). We can look at this "with" as both a discursive expression of the stepfather's power and a signal reminding the reader of the discrepancy between the consent implied by the "with" (her stepfather's version of the story) and Shizuko's own experience as the abused. Unlike other competing interpretations of events in the text, such as how her mother's "stories" differ from her "memories," Shizuko does not attribute this particular phrasing ("sex *with* my stepfather") to another source, providing some insight into the way in which the impact of repeated rape by her stepfather differs from her earlier experiences of abuse and discrimination. By looking at what is communicated by this word choice and how its functions in a particular point in the narrative, we can see how, even as an adult survivor, Shizuko has yet to extricate herself completely from the distortions so brutally imposed on her. While she does, at times, use grammatical constructions that indicate an awareness of the unidirectionality of rape, the "to" appears more often.

Shizuko's frequent use of "with" to describe sexual abuse reflects how the family cover-up skews the lopsided nature of parent–child relations, as if Shizuko could consent to "sex with her stepfather"—a fiction most clearly illustrated when her stepfather is upset that her vagina is "not wet" and accuses her of "thinking about something else" instead of sex "with" him (252). This discursive absolution of the perpetrator's responsibility is similar to what occurs with the use of sō (reciprocity or mutuality) in kinshinsōkan (incest) in that, by introducing the language of consent, attention is deflected away from the sexually abused child's inability to consent. By using the "with" to describe rape as "sex with her stepfather," the adult Shizuko reveals the extent to which she has internalized her parents' distorted portrait of her as an active participant in her abuse. Our job as readers is to notice such remnants of the abuse and its traumatic effects, to undo the "with" and its distractions, and to see past the "stories" and words to the truth of the abuse.

Shizuko's early attempt to undo the "with" is strongly discouraged by her mother, who is portrayed as policing Shizuko's resistance. In one critical scene, Shizuko is called to the bedroom by her stepfather in what had become a pre-rape ritual, but before going, Shizuko picks up a knife. As narrator, she lets the reader know that she fully intended to stab her stepfather and bring an end to her abuse. She is stopped by her mother, who makes her put down the knife. Although her mother claims to be acting in Shizuko's best interest, the immediate circumstances reveal the limits (and irony) of such "parental" concern, for in knowing that her daughter has been summoned to be raped, the mother says, "Since you are still a child, you probably can't understand this, but I am thinking about your own good in saying this to you. That is the one thing you can't do. If you do, it will be the end." Her mother's "concern" for Shizuko not to kill her stepfather is expressed at the same time that the mother watches her daughter walk away to be raped by him. Taking the knife will be the "end" of something the mother does not want to end. The confusing message that her mother is "thinking about [Shizuko's] own good" at the same time that her mother is acting as Shizuko's "pimp" triggers a return to a dissociative state, which Shizuko describes as her "usual" feeling as if she were looking at herself from a far-off and disconnected space. (In part 2, I explore stories in which youth do not put down the knife.)

Shizuko recalls breaking out of the daily terror induced by the traumatizing abuse long enough to contemplate murder as a means of escape. Her mother's "concern" pulls her back in, enforcing the martial law within the home that requires Shizuko to be ritually raped so the family can survive. Her mother's willingness to overlook, distort, or deny Shizuko's suffering is made even more blatant in the ensuing scene when she remarks—after catching Shizuko smoking in the bathroom—that she had thought Shizuko had been coming home smelling like cigarette smoke after having "been with a man." Her mother's insistence on portraying Shizuko as sexually promiscuous when she is being raped regularly at home reinforces the image of Shizuko as "bad" (promiscuous or "loose") and in need of discipline, a term that all too often is a euphemism for abuse (not just in this case).

An Army behind Each Word

The memories Shizuko can recall and piece together for the reader must stand for other memories left unsaid, because, as I discussed earlier, profoundly traumatic memories are fraught with proportionally profound gaps. Seared into her memory is the rape that led to her decision to run away, and it is also the most detailed memory of being raped the adult narrator relates. In the scene in which the stepfather admonishes Shizuko for "not being wet," the physical pain of rape is so severe that even her highly developed ability to "check out" cannot numb it. The severity of the pain propels her to break out of her usual state of "feeling nothing":

> "Please, it hurts. It hurts," I said.
> "You can take it."
> My stepfather continued his actions.
> "I'm serious; it hurts, it hurts, it hurts," I kept saying.
> But my stepfather still kept at it, and then he suddenly yelled, "Shut up!"
> And he smacked me down with all his might. He kept beating me like that, and I never said a word. (253)

She goes on to describe her head hitting a glass door and being beaten with a guitar and a dresser drawer, the same "prop" her biological father had used to beat her when she was a toddler. Her mother and sister come home, and her mother, seeing Shizuko lying on the floor, asks her, "What did *you* do?" (255; emphasis added).

This experience leads Shizuko to what she recalls as her "sudden" decision to run away from home. Her growing capacity to challenge the "bad" daughter story is accelerated by the escalation of the abuse, and she stays up all night planning her escape. Shizuko's discovery of her agency and how very different it is from the false agency imposed on her by her parents disrupts the pseudo-logic of the "with" and the rhetoric of consent that pretends she is a participant in or otherwise responsible for her own abuse. Her ability to run away from home and escape is severely hindered by a number of forces, not the least of which is her stepfather's surveillance. Allowing the possibility that she can leave and act on that new idea demonstrates extraordinary courage in the face of extraordinary adversity. It should be noted that in the sequel to Father Fucker, the hope we may feel after she runs away is crushed when her family finds her.[43] The sequel makes clear how running away from home did not guarantee the certainty that the knife might have.

The "with" and its myth of consent can also serve as a starting point for thinking through one of the differences between the biological father's abusive behavior and the stepfather's—not, to reiterate an earlier point, to understand the "why" so much as the "how." The stepfather enters the home in a sexualized consumer context. As a customer at Shizuko's mother's nightclub, his entrance into the family is made possible by his wallet and not by models of affiliating, caretaking, or parenting. The latter responsibilities are clearly secondary or irrelevant to what he perceives as the privilege his money and status command. The money and household appliances he provides are ongoing "payment" for the attention and obedience, particularly sexual, to which he feels entitled. When Shizuko's mother's story (which casts Shizuko as the "bad daughter") comes into contact with the stepfather's consumer fiction (which casts her as a "whore"), the two are woven together in each other's service and at Shizuko's expense.

In one of her early studies, Judith Herman found that the sexually abusive fathers and stepfathers in her research asserted their authority in the family by force, and they supervised and restricted the lives of their partners and children, "often virtually confining them to the house."[44] We find similar descriptions of the stepfathers' behavior in Father Fucker and Bastard out of Carolina. However, the mothers of Shizuko and of Bone in Bastard out of Carolina have significantly different responses to the abuse of their daughters. Shizuko's mother knows her daughter is being abused, but she blames Shizuko. Bone's mother, a much more sympathetic parent at least for the narrator of Bastard out of Carolina, is horrified and ashamed as she learns more and more of the truth, yet she is ultimately unable or unwilling to put her daughter's well-being ahead of her feelings for her husband. If we borrow the language of social theories of sexual abuse in the family, Shizuko's mother is closer to the model of a "colluder," and Bone's mother, to a "helpless dependent." Models such as "colluder" and "helpless dependent," however, are useful only insofar as they offer descriptive categories for behavior that, even in these two novels, does not "stay put." Rather, it defies any easy or consistent label. As will become even more apparent in the case of *Bastard out of Carolina*, fiction allows for the contradictions and complexities that a diagnosis often does not.

CHAPTER 3

"Mama, He Treats Your Daughter Mean":

Dorothy Allison's *Bastard out of Carolina*

The man raped me. It's the truth. It's a fact. I was five, and he was
eight months married to my mother. That's how I always began to
talk about it—when I finally did begin to talk about it.

—Dorothy Allison, *Two or Three Things I Know For Sure*, 41

I know the use of fiction in a world of hard truth, the way fiction
can be a harder piece of truth. The story of what happened, or what
did not happen but should have—that story can become a curtain
drawn shut, a piece of insulation, a disguise, a razor, a tool that
changes every time it is used and sometimes becomes something
other than we intended.

—Dorothy Allison, *Two or Three Things I Know For Sure*, 3

Whose Suffering Matters

It goes without saying that our private lives and stories are surrounded and shaped by larger stories, even those we may not identify or mention as related to what we experience or remember.
Much of Dorothy Allison's autobiographical novel *Bastard out of Carolina* takes
place in Greenville, South Carolina, in the 1950s, during the decade after Bob
Jones University established its campus there. The year 1955, a crucial one in
the novel (a time when the narrator tells us Greenville "was the most beautiful
place in the world"), was also the year of the bus boycott in Montgomery,

Alabama, which is 300 miles from Greenville. Neither Bob Jones University, notorious for its prohibition of interracial dating (in effect until March 2008), nor the boycott appears in the novel. That in and of itself is perhaps only of passing interest. Nonetheless, when race is addressed explicitly in the novel, it remains peripheral or thoroughly mediated through the white narrator protagonist's subjectivity. The larger story of white supremacy in the U.S. in the 1950s, in other words, is rendered into backdrop details ancillary to the personal saga of one white girl who suffered terrible child abuse.

This relegation of race to the margins is possible because the girl is white, because white supremacy and even its feminist expressions not only permit her access to the role of victim but require that her assumption of that role be at least somewhat disconnected from its relationship to the brutalization of people of color for it to be valued.[1] Significantly, the author introduces her novel with a quote from James Baldwin, and the narrative proper occasionally draws readers toward the realities of white supremacy, but it stops short of implicating the girl or her family (particularly her uncles) in any privilege or power asserted through their whiteness. Rather, race is most often invoked to identify the white girl *with* people of color, to portray her as more like blacks, for example, than other whites. In this chapter, I look at how the novel chronicles that abused girl's shifting relationship to her own legitimate rage, as well as her power, both real and imagined. I want to begin by situating that process in its enraged and embattled historical moment and bring the elliptical and transient glimpses of race to the foreground, because if this is, as I contend, a story about a girl's redemption through Orphic storytelling, it is very much the story of a white girl, albeit one who is marked a "bastard" and "trash."[2]

My analysis of race in *Bastard out of Carolina* begins with a recognition of the pseudo-logic at work in the "American justice system" writ large that often casts boys and men of color who commit crimes as threatening or dangerous and white girls and women who commit crimes as pathetic or led astray and thus more in need of psychiatric/therapeutic than correctional/punitive institutionalization, the latter being a characterization against which the novel's young protagonist rebels in her fantasy life and the former being a problem I explore more fully in part 2. Put simply, the white girl or woman is seen as in need of "protection" and the boy or man of color as someone from whom to "protect" white society (especially white women and girls). This gendered and racialized formula regarding the protection of white womanhood and the concomitant policing and brutalization of men of color has its antecedents in various plantation and colonial configurations of race and gender. My inflection of this pattern's subtle presence in *Bastard out of Carolina* underscores how white supremacy has continued to function as a dominant (if often unspoken) socialization mechanism in the U.S. and is present even in many stories of white female victims that might challenge other forms of discrimination and oppression.

Prohibitions and allowances delimited along lines of race, ethnicity, gender, and sexuality are articulated in the policies and history of Bob Jones University, located on the very grounds where this novel is set. In fact, perhaps nowhere in contemporary North America is institutionalized white supremacy more openly touted, and, as Yasuhiro Katagiri, professor of American history and government at Tokai University, explains, Bob Jones University also represents a constituency to which certain conservative politicians have sought to appeal:

> On February 2, [2000], [George W.] Bush appeared before enthusiastic students and faculty members at Bob Jones University in Greenville, South Carolina. "We are conservatives," Bush began his remarks, "because we believe in freedom and its possibilities, family and duties, and faith and its mercies." For the Texas governor, Bob Jones, where former President Ronald Reagan, former Republican Presidential Nominee Bob Dole, and other prominent politicians had previously spoken, was an appropriate place to address his conservatism on the very opening day of his campaign for the South Carolina primary. But the history of the conservative and fundamentalist Christian institution was also colored by its racial bigotry, manifesting a sordid past which was redolent of the "Old South."
>
> As an avowed opponent to interracial marriages, the university had enforced a disciplinary rule prohibiting interracial dating among its students since the 1950s. This particular campus regulation, coupled with the school's practice of racial discrimination in its admission policy, forced Bob Jones to lose its federal tax-exempt status during the 1970s. After a thirteen-year battle with the Internal Revenue Service, the South Carolina institution was finally told by the United States Supreme Court that its disciplinary rule against interracial dating and marriages was discriminatory and that the racial discrimination practiced on its campus violated "a most fundamental national policy." Upon hearing the Supreme Court's eight-to-one ruling, Bob Jones, Jr., then president of the school, intransigently denounced those nine sitting justices as "eight evil old men and one vain and foolish woman" and further "refused to sacrifice" the university's "convictions for tax exemption."[3]

Explicit mention of race and ethnicity in *Bastard out of Carolina* also often comes in the form of comments about sex, about interracial "dating" and "miscegenation." For example, the protagonist recalls her maternal grandmother saying, "My granddaddy, your great-great-granddaddy, he was a Cherokee," and calling him a "black-eyed bastard" (26–27). What marks the young protagonist as the "strangest girl-child" in the family is her "blue-black hair," which the grandmother attributes to the girl's great-great-grandfather through stories in which, the narrator recalls, "everybody seemed legendary" (26).

The story of the "legendary" Cherokee great-great-grandfather is at once a source of uncomfortable difference and the kind of romance and exoticization that finds its ultimate expression in co-optation and genocide. One means of "conquering" is to assimilate, to consume the conquered, to make them "part" of you, and as Andrea Smith makes clear, "Colonial relationships themselves are gendered and sexualized."[4] She also explains how the notion of assimilation itself is disingenuous, writing, "[The] colonized group can never be completely assimilated—otherwise, they would be equal to the colonists, and there would be no reason to colonize them. . . . [While] Cherokee women were promised that assimilation would provide them with the benefits of the dominant society, in fact assimilation efforts made them more easily subjugated by colonial rule."[5] Similarly, the grandmother's story upholds the white supremacy it might seem to challenge. It constitutes a transgression of Bob Jones's values but is still an expression of the colonizer's assimilation fantasy—exoticized "strange" difference that can be mastered, absorbed, diluted, manufactured, and owned.

When one of Bone's cousins speaks of "colored" in the family tree, the dual effect is comparable; they are not "pure" white, but that is what makes them "interesting." However, Bone notes a significant difference when it comes to blackness, one that reveals a tendency to see American Indians as "legendary" and part of the historical past (and thus not the present) in contrast to the immediacy of "color" (blackness). The difference is clear at the level of feeling states. For example, she describes heightened affect ("tenderness") in response to phenotype: "People were crazy on the subject of color. I knew, and it was true that one or two of the cousins had kinky hair and took some teasing for it, enough that everyone was tender about it" (54). That "tenderness" is immediate but not explored. The "tender" topic of racialized relatives (in the present) and the romantic and taboo presence of the American Indian great-great-grandfather (in the distant past) are valenced through the subjectivities of Bone and her cousins who are "called out" for perceived difference.

Behind all of this is an idealization of white women as a means of asserting white masculinity, or, as Kevin Alexander Gray explains, " 'Defilement' or being 'spoiled' during the Jim Crow era most often meant banishment—or stripped of being 'white' for one's 'nigger-loving' ways. White men used 'protecting white womanhood,' the first plank in the Klan platform, as a pretext for controlling white women, but in some respects it trapped the men in a psychotic effort to prove their own sexual dominance."[6] Perhaps no assessment speaks more to the violence perpetrated by white men in *Bastard out of Carolina*. Efforts to control white women and girls are most obviously elaborated in the character of Glen, as I will discuss, but along with the occasional overt references to race and ethnicity is an unspoken question as to what role Bone's family, particularly her uncles, might play in the lives of local blacks. Bone leaves open room for this question when describing her relationship with her uncles: "Though half the county went in terror of them, my uncles were invariably gentle and affectionate with me and my cousins" (22). One is left to wonder, which half? Bone never tells us.

It is reasonable to imagine the terrorized half of the county would have been the black half. In the 1950s, the city of Greenville had two high schools (Sterling and Washington) for black students, many of whom lived in fear of their white neighbors, for good reason. The black population of Greenville in the 1950s was all too familiar with lynching and murders, such as the infamous case of the twenty-eight white men who tortured Willie Earle to death in 1947 and later admitted guilt in court only to be found "not guilty" by a jury of their (white) peers. (Greenville County, as some readers might recall, also refused to celebrate the Martin Luther King Jr. holiday until 2005.) The terrorism under which black people lived in Bone's hometown is never linked to the terrorism in her home, but it is my contention that her suffering is inextricably linked to the larger white-supremacist milieu out of which her story emerges (one that is not so much "Southern" as hemispheric). The extent of white supremacy's grip on Bone's world, as Gray reminds us, is evident in the political-institutional arm of its power, "In 1956, [Senator Strom Thurmond of South Carolina] authored the infamous Southern Manifesto—a document signed by 19 of the 22 southern senators that urged the south to defy—as they put it—the Supreme Court's 'clear abuse of judicial power' in outlawing segregation in public schools. In 1957, he executed the longest filibuster in history while trying to halt the first Civil Rights Act proposed in the Senate and backed by Eisenhower."[7] As much as Bone's uncles and the rest of her family benefit from the distance their whiteness affords them from the brunt of the oppression we might associate with Strom Thurmond, the Klan, or Bob Jones University, some of Bone's relatives share cause to distrust the legal system with the black people we can imagine they terrorized.

When Bone's abuse or other harm is discovered, her outraged family members do not call the police as a first response. Bone's Uncle Earle even says, "The law never done us no good" (5). His experientially based distrust of a legal system and law-enforcement apparatus based on the protection of private property shapes a predictable understanding of and relationship to "the law." Uncle Earle is not alone in recognizing that the more valuable the property, the greater the degree of protection that will be provided to it and its owners. Likewise, the fewer the resources or property involved, the less will be available to redress injustice or harm. For communities without what are considered to be valuable assets, the reluctance to turn to "the authorities" has been, and continues to be, a necessary survival strategy, because they know all too well for whom "the law" is written and enforced. As Bone's mother reflects, "We're not bad people. And we pay our way. We just can't always pay when people want" (82). And while Uncle Earle does call on a lawyer to obtain a settlement for one of many (alcohol-related) car accidents in which he is involved, the general lack of trust in "the system" is a recurring theme in the novel.

Some have taken such details as evidence that Bone's family "does not have access to the power which is usually the privilege of whiteness in this country," a position that suggests a uniformity of "white power" expressed and exerted only in specific places, in specific ways, and in specific dialects. Such claims minimize how terrifying whiteness itself can be for even the most romanticized (or, in one reviewer's words, "beautiful") person of color to emerge in Allison's writing.[8] They also run the risk of limiting one's ability to understand the terror with which Bone lives—white supremacy's destructive toll on white people. Bone lives in highly charged interstices, as a victim in her home, as "poor white trash" outside "the system," as a girl in a society defined by white men, as not "white enough," as a "bastard," and, although not described as such, as a beneficiary of the privilege her whiteness still guarantees her. The following reading of her story attempts to tackle what she experiences on her terms, as Dorothy Allison presents it, but takes as its starting point this "strangest girl-child's" position in the larger society.

Bone's position as a white girl is perhaps most striking in the following passage:

Shiny brown faces kept pressing against the glass and then withdrawing, stern blank faces that we could barely tell from one another.

"Niggers," Grey whispered proudly. "Scared of us."

I wrapped my fingers around the banister rail, working splinters loose from the dry wood, and leaned over to look for myself. I had never seen colored people up close, and I was curious about these. They did look scared.

"Their mama won't let them come out." Little Earle was chewing a splinter off the railing and picking another. "We heard her this morning, telling 'em she'd beat their asses if they even opened that door. She sure an't happy we moved in here." (83–84)

This mother's justifiable fears, which we might associate with, for example, the corpse of Willie Earle, are never given voice in *Bastard Out of Carolina*. The indistinguishable (to the white children) and anonymous faces of black youth matter only insofar as they are experienced by white people. This is the problem of the Americas in its reduced form. The suffering of white people, of white women in particular, is deemed more important than the suffering of people of color. We often see this problem played out in Hollywood films. The racism expressed by Winona Ryder's character in the film *Girl Interrupted* or the brutal murders of women and men of color by Uma Thurman's character in *Kill Bill* are permitted or excused because the white women's trauma and pain are presented as sufficient justification for what would otherwise be criminalized or offensive speech or behavior. Put simply, their suffering matters more, so much so that it renders any trauma and violence they inflict (particularly on people of color) inconsequential. As much as *Bastard out of Carolina* reveals about the dynamics of childhood trauma and as compelling a novel as it is, we must read it in this American context in which the suffering and endangered white girl or woman is an icon of white supremacy.

Learning to Decipher and Tell

Father Fucker and *Bastard out of Carolina* are in many ways stories about the inability to tell a story. Both protagonists, Shizuko and Bone, create for themselves fantasy worlds that contrast sharply with the daily abuse and constant state of fear that mark their childhood years. Instructed by adults to accept or ignore what is happening to them, these characters demonstrate a similar turn toward creative expression and imagination, toward Orpha's music as described in chapter 1. In addition to the ways in which Shizuko, for example, is told she must "obey," both girls contend with unspoken pressures to "roll with life's punches" or to "tough it out" (*shikkari shite* in Japanese). In Bone's case, suffering is endowed with religious (specifically Evangelical Southern Baptist Revival Circuit) significance, and she learns "everything that comes to us is a blessing or a test" (160). Even after the abuse is discovered and Bone is "rescued," she is told to forget about what happened, the logic being that to "dwell on the past" would only perpetuate her victimization and suffering.[9] In both novels, the abuse is minimized and erased by messages, implicit and explicit, from adults who want Shizuko and Bone to behave as if nothing happened.

Both Uchida and Allison have publicly written of and discussed their personal experiences of making sense of childhood abuse through writing.[10] Dorothy Allison describes how finding words and building new vocabularies to express her particular experiences, her memories, and her feelings have been paramount to her personal survival.

> Why? I am asked. Why do you bring that up? Must you talk about that? I asked myself the same questions until finally I began to understand. This was a wall in my life, I say, a wall I had to climb over every day. It was always there for me, deflecting my rage toward people who knew nothing about what had happened to me or why I should be angry at them.
>
> It took me years to get past that rage, to say the words with grief and insistence but to let go of the anger, to refuse to use the anger against people who knew nothing of the rape. I had to learn how to say "rape," say "child," say "unending," "awful," and "relentless," and say it the way I do—adamant, unafraid, unashamed, every time, all over again—to speak my words as a sacrament, a blessing, a prayer. Not a curse.[11]

The same could be said of the challenges facing Bone, who, although adept at telling stories of legendary villains and heroes to her playmates as a child, can only tell the story of her abuse as an adult narrator.

Bone's childhood imaginings parallel what Allison has described as her own discovery of the power of fictional worlds. Just as Bone experiences satisfaction not only in entertaining her playmates, but also in creating fantasy worlds in which girls can be strong and even "mean," Allison writes of how her stories of powerful women offered corrective alternatives to her own powerlessness as a child. Here again, we see how what cannot otherwise be conveyed (in prayer, for example) can be explored, developed, and transformed in a creative register, through storytelling:

> "Let me tell you a story," I'd begin, and start another one. When we were small, I could catch my sisters the way they caught butterflies, capture their

attention and almost make them believe that all I said was true. "Let me tell you about the women who ran away. All those legendary women who ran away." I'd tell about the witch queens who cooked their enemies in great open pots, the jewels that grow behind the tongues of water moccasins. After a while the deepest satisfaction was in the story itself, greater even than the terror in my sisters' faces, the laughter, and, God help us, the hope.[12]

Allison's transformation into a survivor-storyteller whose autobiographical novel is informed by her own experiences conforms to generally accepted views regarding human development, as well—notably, the ways in which we all "tell" our stories in different ways at different times. Communication is not static, and our methods of expression change with age. As children, our abilities shift and change a great deal from year to year, as has been established by developmental psychologists such as James Garbarino and Frances Stott, who write, "As children develop, their physical, emotional, and intellectual states and abilities change. The range of what is possible not only increases but changes in nature. . . . We see children proceeding through a series of qualitatively different stages. A three-year-old is different from a nine-year-old in many ways, some of which are relevant to the child's communication with adults."[13] The interplay between "normative" communication patterns in childhood development and the kinds of brutal silencing we have seen in *Father Fucker* further contribute to the virtual impossibility of an abused child, such as Bone, being able to describe details of the abuse. Reading novels such as *Father Fucker* and *Bastard out of Carolina* can serve as practice for us as adults to re-enter childhood experience and perception along with the adult narrators and to cultivate an attentiveness to what is not clearly or comfortably articulated. By becoming better readers in this respect, we undoubtedly become more attuned to the communication of children in our own lives.

We are growing ever more accustomed to notions such as "survivor guilt" and the special burden felt by those who survived the atomic bombings of Hiroshima and Nagasaki, for example, to speak up for not only themselves, but for those who did not survive, yet we rarely think of victims of childhood abuse as part of an oppressed group, many of whom do not survive. In addition to the children who are murdered by parents and caregivers, there are countless more who are unable to survive the lingering effects that leave them vulnerable to violence as adults or who kill themselves. The pain of each individual victim is not diminished by how "ordinary" child abuse is. In thinking of the thin line between who survives and who does not, I am often reminded of the story of

Miyakoshi Asae, who was at home with her sister when the atomic bomb was dropped on the city of Hiroshima. Miyakoshi was in the bathroom at the moment of impact, and she describes her memories of that day:

> Because of my partial deafness, I did not hear anything. Suddenly I found the house collapsed around me and myself trapped in the lavatory. Perhaps irrationally, I cried out for help over and over again, and finally a man broke the door in and pulled me out.
>
> Looking around for my sister, I saw her lying sprawled in the corridor, the right side of her body covered with terrible burns. She had probably been washing her hands, with her right hand stretched over the wash basin, when caught by the searing heat. I put my sister on my back and fled barefoot to Hijiyama Park. Her face was festering with burns, and her right eye was hanging out. I pushed the eye back into its socket and tried to use gauze mask to hold it in place, but her ear had melted away, and there was nothing to attach the mask to.[14]

Miyakoshi's sister died four days later. The bathroom door that served as the barrier between Miyakoshi and her sister has come, for me, to represent the arbitrary and very thin line dividing those who survive violent trauma from those who do not. Although this does not suggest an erasure of responsibility (Miyakoshi exclaims that she "detests the United States"), Miyakoshi's story highlights the lack of "rhyme or reason" to explain why one person is relatively spared in the bathroom and another outside is vulnerable to a bomb's worst force. For Bone and Shizuko, for Allison and Uchida, Orphic functioning—through storytelling and manga drawing—provides a protective barrier, a bathroom wall, behind which at least their creativity and imagination can remain intact, if only in fragments. But imagination alone does not make it possible for every abused child to survive. A community's response to abuse can play a decisive role for many children, and therein lies one way in which *Bastard out of Carolina* depicts a story of abuse and survival quite unlike Shizuko's.

Shizuko grew up without any extended family or community; she had no place to seek refuge from the daily abuse and no one, as we have seen, in her home gave her cause to believe that she did not deserve the beatings and rape. Any gestures of support or concern, such as those from a teacher or neighbor, were distant and could not break through the walls of isolation and secrecy that kept the abuse hidden and allowed it to continue. *Bastard out of Carolina* tells a very different story of abuse—despite the striking similarities between it and *Father Fucker*. Both were published in the same year and are narrated by adult survivors (each of whom has one younger sister) who describe having been sexually abused by a stepfather. These parallels are, indeed, uncanny. But unlike Shizuko, Bone, the protagonist of *Bastard out of Carolina*, has a large, extended family that, in spite of its many crises and shortcomings, intervenes when the abuse is discovered, making a critical difference in the way in which Bone is able to survive and give words to what happened to her as a child. Put in perhaps misleadingly simple terms, Bone grows up with a sense of community and affiliation that Shizuko lacks.

Although Shizuko describes early memories of her abusive biological father, Bone, the eponymous "bastard," has no memories of her father. She does not know where he lives or even his name because "Granny refused to speak it after she had run him out of town for messing with her daughter." Thus, Bone—Ruth Anne Boatwright—bears the last name of her mother's family (3). Her identification with her mother's family, and its many strong women and troublemaking "Boatwright boys" (whose "hands never hurt" Bone), is central to her survival and her status in her Greenville community. In contrast to the four other people who make up Shizuko's family (her mother, sister, father, and stepfather), more than a dozen family members play significant roles in Bone's life, and some of these family members intervene—although not equally effectively—when the abuse is discovered. Bone also has memories of happier and safer times before the onset of abuse, memories we do not find in *Father Fucker*, which tells the story of a girl whose earliest memories are of being abused.

Bone recalls enjoying the company of family members on front porches during the summer when she was five years old. To escape the scorching summer heat and humidity, they would drink iced tea and listen to the radio. The security that characterizes Bone's earliest memories provides a stark contrast to Shizuko's memories of being beaten and afraid as a toddler. During that summer of 1955, the year of the Montgomery bus boycott, the man who eventually abuses Bone is already spending time at the diner where her mother works, and soon after he enters Bone's life as her stepfather, but during that summer she is still safe, "perfectly happy at Granny's side" and "worshipping" her uncles (21–22). One of the ways Bone survives is inextricably linked to her memories of this summer, a connection she acknowledges in her description of the lasting power of these early experiences to provide ongoing comfort: "*When I think of that summer*—sleeping over at one of my aunts' houses as easily as at home, the smell of Mama's neck as she bent over to hug us in the dark, the sound of little Earle's giggle or Granny's spit thudding on the dry ground, and that country music playing low everywhere, as much a part of the evening as crickets and moonlight —*I always feel safe again.* No place has ever seemed so sweet and quiet, no place ever felt so much like home" (22; emphasis added). Whereas remembering for Shizuko offers the possibility of self-recovery through understanding but not a reprieve from pain, remembering the summer of 1955 offers Bone a feeling of safety. The two narrators describe experiences of abuse that are similar in many ways, as will be evident in the discussion that follows. However, their very different experiences as toddlers render them very differently prepared for organizing and representing their childhood years as adult narrators. When comparing these two novels, therefore, we must consider differences in the age of the onset of abuse and how, specifically, the representations of each character's first five years are reflected in narrative differences.

In her discussion of how child abuse differs from adult-onset trauma, Judith Herman distinguishes between trauma that disrupts a life and a life formed in a state of constant traumatic disruption. Bone and Shizuko are both abused as children, but only Shizuko is born into violent domestic abuse. While Herman's claims about the developmental effects of childhood trauma are evident in the experiences of both characters, her distinction between childhood and adult trauma can be applied to an analysis of how the protagonists' differing ages at the onset of abuse are related to subtle differences in the two narratives. Herman writes:

> Repeated trauma in adult life erodes the structure of the personality already formed, but repeated trauma in childhood forms and deforms the personality. The child trapped in an abusive environment is faced with formidable tasks of adaptation. She must find a way to preserve a sense of trust in people who are untrustworthy, safety in a situation that is unsafe, control in a situation that is terrifyingly unpredictable, power in a situation of helplessness. Unable to care for or protect herself, she must compensate for the failures of adult care and protection with the only means at her disposal, an immature system of psychological defenses.[15]

The timelines in question differ only by five or six years and thus should not serve as cause to minimize the abuse Bone describes or its relationship to the style of narration. But Bone's memory of a safe summer before the abuse points to a critical contrast in the two narrators' relationships to memory and community, as well as how their descriptions of the abuse and family members reflect fundamentally different experiences as toddlers.

Shizuko's memories provide the structural framework for *Father Fucker,* and the chronology and context of those memories are not always clear. Shizuko struggles to tell her story to make sense of it, and the struggle to tell shapes the narrative we engage as readers. Bone's storytelling allows her to take control of what she could not as a girl, and the memories that she relates are part of the story she crafts. Thus "story" is not a bad word for Bone, whose ability to resist, as she explains to us, was, from the very beginning, as a storyteller. As noted in the previous chapter, events in *Father Fucker* that the narrator did not witness herself and her mother's "stories" are clearly distinguished from Shizuko's "memories." This is not the case for the omniscient narrator of *Bastard out of Carolina*, who confidently re-creates conversations and events that she did not witness and only rarely qualifies information as secondhand.[16]

For example, Bone was not present when Glen Waddell, her future stepfather, first saw her mother, Anney, but Bone tells us he looked at Anney and said, "She an't no bigger than a girl" (11). We are privy to Glen's desire to share the Boatwright men's tough reputation and marry Anney, and Bone even tells us his thoughts: "He would have her, he told himself. He would marry Black Earle's baby sister, marry the whole Boatwright legend, shame his daddy and shock his brothers. He would carry a knife in his pocket and kill any man who dared touch her. Yes, he thought to himself, oh yes" (13). Bone does not indicate that she heard about this from Glen, her mother, or her Uncle Earle; she narrates it as part of her story. "Stories" and storytelling for Bone are not obstacles and dangers to be refuted. She revels in make-believe as a girl, and the practice of storytelling as survival connects the young Bone, who can captivate her cousins and friends with stories of gruesome murders, to the adult Bone, who is now the narrator of her own story. When Bone tells us that her future stepfather was attracted to her mother and attributes the above comment and thoughts to him, she foreshadows the sexual abuse by portraying Glen as a man whose fantasies involve both young girls and killing. Shizuko's stepfather's portrait remains more opaque, as we are never told his thoughts. His subjectivity does not matter for her (aside from a few comments about his love of military tunes and his "other" family); all that matters are its effects. Shizuko also rejects her mother's "stories" and takes control of her own "memories" by clearly identifying what she knows, how she knows it, and what she does not know. But Bone takes control of her story by rendering key players transparent, describing sometimes even their innermost thoughts, feelings, and motivations. Both Uchida and Allison write about childhood abuse in the form of autobiographical fiction, but storytelling is a practice Bone embraces and against which Shizuko struggles.

The narrators' attitudes toward "stories" are also inextricably linked to how their efforts as young storytellers are received. Whereas Shizuko's parents disapprove of her manga drawing and drive her Orphic expression underground, Bone's stories win her praise and popularity. It is not surprising that as Glen begins abusing Bone, he must further and further remove her from those who listen to her stories and their support. As discussed in the previous chapter, Shizuko describes the experience of being isolated from the outside world and subjected to her stepfather's constant surveillance. In *Bastard out of Carolina*, Bone recounts how she suffered increasingly frequent and violent abuse as her family was taken away from the watchful eyes of an extended family community and into a state of isolation. The catalyst for this move comes in the novel's first scene of abuse.

When Anney and Glen marry in the spring of 1956, Anney is already pregnant. Bone recounts Glen leaving her and her younger sister, Reese, in the car to wait outside the hospital while their mother is in labor. He later returns to the car and sexually assaults Bone, who is approximately seven years old at the time, while Reese sleeps in the back seat. Bone recalls being "too afraid to cry, or shake, or wiggle, too afraid to move at all":

> He pushed my skirt to the side and slid his left hand down between my legs, up against my cotton panties. He began to rock me then, between his stomach and his wrist, his fingers fumbling at his britches.
>
> It made me afraid, his big hand between my legs and his eyes glittering in the dim light. He started talking again, telling me Mama was going to be all right, that he loved me, that we were all going to be so happy. Happy. His hand was hard, the ridge of his wristbone pushing in and hurting me. I looked straight ahead through the windshield, too afraid to cry, or shake, or wiggle, too afraid to move at all.
>
> He kept saying, "It's gonna be all right." He kept rocking me, breathing through his mouth and staring straight ahead. I could see his reflection in the windshield. Dawn began to filter through the trees, making everything bright and cold. His hand dug in further. He was holding himself in his fingers. I knew what it was under his hand. I'd seen my cousins naked, laughing, shaking their things and joking, but this was a mystery, scary and hard. His sweat running down his arms to my skin smelled strong and nasty. He grunted, squeezed my thighs between his arm and his legs. His chin

pressed down on my head and his hips pushed at the same time. He was hurting me, hurting me! (46–47)

Glen returns to the hospital after sexually abusing Bone, and when he comes back out to the car, he informs Bone and Reese that their mother has lost the baby and will not be able to have any more children. Bone had been sitting in the car, "feeling the soreness," and trying to figure out whether or not the abuse had really happened, but when she sees him, she is unable to dismiss it as a bad dream. She "looked into that face and knew it had not been a dream" (48). Back at their house, Bone tries to seek comfort by sitting in her mother's lap, but her mother, presumably despondent over having miscarried, does not respond to her.

Bone describes being instructed as to how she should behave around her mother by her aunt Raylene, whose words—however unintentionally—discourage Bone from trying to tell what happened in the car. " 'Your mama's gonna need a little time,' she told me. 'Then she's gonna need you more than she ever has. When a woman loses a baby, she needs to know that her other babies are well and happy. You be happy for her, Bone. You let your mama know you are happy so she can heal her heart' " (49). Immediately after this first experience of sexual abuse, Bone is thus told to be "happy" for her mother's sake. She must put her mother's "healing" ahead of her own feelings, which is, in effect, an admonition to repress (even if an unintentional one). After Bone describes the initial abuse and Raylene's instructions, she tells the reader about Glen's decision to move the family away from the Boatwrights, away from the comfort of affiliation and the family whose love had made Bone feel safe. I have heard many activists and professionals in abuse-prevention communities in Japan and the U.S. express the belief that if there is, indeed, a rise in the occurrence of child abuse, such an increase cannot be divorced from the rise of the nuclear family and removal of children from larger, extended community or extended family involvement. Their premise (that the privacy and relative isolation of nuclear families can make abuse harder to detect and thus prevent) is born out in the sequence of events Bone describes, which explicitly connects the escalation of abuse that ensues to Glen's efforts to isolate the family:

He found a house over by the JC Penney mill near the railroad tracks and came back home to announce we were moving. Aunt Alma was outraged he'd take us so far away, but Mama just nodded and asked Raylene to help her pack.

"It'll be all right," she told Reese and me.

Glen put his arms around Mama and glared at Aunt Alma. "We don't need nobody else," he whispered. "We'll do just fine on our own." (49–50)

Concomitant with the isolation, for Glen, is a rhetoric of ownership and control reminiscent of Shizuko's stepfather, and Bone recalls him repeating, "I'm your daddy now" and "You're mine now" (51). The term of address ("Daddy") "sounded funny" to Bone, who, like Shizuko in *Father Fucker*, relates enforced terms of address to the ever escalating violent abuse.

Although he refers to both Bone and Reese as "his girls," his treatment of the two girls is notably different, as is the case in *Father Fucker*. As explained in the previous chapter, Shizuko's younger sister, Chie, is not subjected to violent or sexual abuse in *Father Fucker*, and Chie's role as the "good daughter" is depicted in contrast to Shizuko's "bad" qualities, which their mother often compares to behavior she associates with Shizuko's biological father. In *Bastard out of Carolina*, the sisters' contrasting experiences are also connected to their biological fathers. Bone knows very little about her father, whereas Reese's father, the idealized Lyle Parsons, died tragically when his truck crashed after hitting a "rain-slicked patch of oil" on the highway. Anney talks about Lyle, but she never tells any stories about Bone's father. Reese has a picture of Lyle, but no one kept pictures of Bone's father. Reese's other grandparents (the Parsonses) are not Bone's, and Reese has the romanticized story of a father who was good, gentle, and loving. Lyle died and left behind mourning relatives, while Bone's father was "run out of town." Bone describes yearning for a father of her own and hoping to find him in Glen even after he has begun abusing her and moved them away from the Boatwright relatives: "I remembered those moments in the hospital parking lot like a bad dream, hazy and shadowed. When Daddy Glen looked at me, I saw no sign that he ever thought about [the abuse] at all. Maybe it had not happened. Maybe he really did love us. I wanted him to love us. I wanted to be able to love him. I wanted him to pick me up gently and tell Mama again how much he loved us all. I wanted to be locked with Reese in the safe circle of their arms" (51–52). Bone expresses the confusion the abused child experiences when she, as Herman explains, "must find a way to preserve a sense of trust in people who are untrustworthy."[17] Herman describes how an abused child's efforts to see an abusive parent as loving and trustworthy can lead that child to "develop highly idealized images of at least one parent."

If the idealized parent is the abuser, the child's rage can be displaced onto the non-offending parent, and if the idealized parent is the non-offending parent, the child can view that parent's failure to protect her as a result of her own "unworthiness."[18] Although Bone does, for a short time, hope for the best with Glen, the extent of the abuse eventually makes it impossible for her to cling to the fantasy that he will become the father for whom she longs. Her idealization of her mother, on the other hand, continues even up to the moment of narration, when she is an adult looking back on what Glen did to her and what her mother failed to prevent. In contrast to Shizuko's depiction of her mother, Bone describes her mother in very sympathetic terms—even though some readers may find Anney's failure to remove Bone from the danger to be morally objectionable, complicit, or otherwise problematic.

Bone's yearning for a father of her own and for a safe family is later expressed as jealousy when she visits "Reese's daddy's people" who live in the wealthy hillside area that overlooks Greenville. Bone sees a safety she longs for in the Parsonses' world, but when she explains why she is "jealous of Reese for having Mrs. Parsons as a grandmother," she focuses on the trappings of class difference. She compares Mrs. Parsons, who "looked like a granny you'd read about or see in a movie" and who wore long-sleeved dresses, to Anney's mother, who "wore sleeveless print dresses that showed the sides of her loose white breasts and hitched up on her hips." Mrs. Parsons spoke about the pain of losing a child "while shelling peas into a galvanized bucket," but Bone's granny would "get so mad she'd start throwing furniture out the screen door." Bone compares the two grannies according to appearance, temperament, and manners, and she makes her middle-class aspirations clear when she concludes, "I loved Granny, but I imagine Mrs. Parsons might be a better choice for a grandmother, and sometimes when we went to visit I'd pretend she was mine" (55). An unvoiced question as to whether she might not be abused in a "better" (more affluent, "pure" white, etc.) family underwrites Bone's comparisons, which exacerbates the text's "friendliness" to stereotypes about where abuse is most likely to occur as much as it reflects Bone's internalization of those myths.

Reese has the fabulous stories about Lyle and the Parsonses, and Bone describes Reese as enjoying being compared to her daddy. But whereas Reese has "another family" and could choose to imagine a different life and identity for herself, Bone has only Anney, Glen, and the Boatwrights. Despite Bone's jealousy and longings for a family like the Parsonses, she does not portray Reese as cruel or indifferent, as Shizuko does in her depictions of Chie. Nonetheless, as Bone is gradually assigned the role of "bad daughter" by Glen, Reese responds accordingly. One day the two girls are playing after school and run into the house unaware that Glen is also at home. Glen catches Bone, whom he calls a "bitch," and prepares to be beat her with his belt, saying, "I've waited a long time to do this, too long" (106). Glen drags Bone to the bathroom and beats her until Anney comes home and screams at him to stop. Although Anney's initial response is to intervene and express anger at Glen, in a scene all too familiar to readers of *Father Fucker*, she then turns to Bone and asks, "Baby, what did you do? What did you do?" And Reese, who had been playing with Bone but who had not been targeted for a beating, responds in similar fashion, warning Bone, "You made him mad. . . . You better be careful" (107–8). Although Bone maintains a sympathetic view of both her mother and sister in ways that Shizuko does not, we see here how both Anney and Reese bend and adapt to Glen's story. That is to say, they accept the possibility that Bone *could* do something—that any child could—to warrant abuse or to avoid it. Bone reflects on how unfair these terms were, "There was no way I could be careful enough, no way to keep Daddy Glen from exploding into rage" (108).

What she could do was fantasize a world in which she had power; she could craft and control stories of how "things" might be better or, at least, different. In her stories, her "badness"—the reason Glen cites as his excuse for beating her and that she accepts as somehow true—is a source of power. She devises a "mean sisters game" to play with a cousin and Reese. In this game, the mean sisters of Johnny Yuma, Francis Marion, and Bat Masterson "do everything their brothers do. Only they do it first and fastest and meanest" (212–13). The game is met with tremendous enthusiasm, and Bone recalls how becoming Jim Bowie's mean sister and playing with a butcher knife allowed her to imagine killing Glen: "I practiced sticking Aunt Alma's knife into the porch and listened to boys cursing in the backyard. I was mean, I decided. I was mean and vicious, and all I really wanted to be doing was sticking that knife in Daddy Glen. . . . I played mean sisters for all I was worth" (213). Bone's rage finds its release in creative play and storytelling. She recalls regaling her cousins with other violent stories of murder and dismemberment.

Storytelling as an outlet for anger spills over into her school life, as well, and after she starts at a new school, she creates a whole new story about who she is in response to what she perceives as her teacher's "contempt" and low expectations of her. Bone senses that she is "trash" in her teacher's eyes, and when called on to introduce herself, Bone says her name is Roseanne Carter and that she is from Atlanta. She remembers everyone believing her "big-city stories" (and famous name) and how she enjoyed the popularity her storytelling provided. Before her enrollment records arrive at the school, Bone's family moves again, and she uses her real name at the next school. Bone says she did not know why she lied and called herself Roseanne Carter at the time, but as an adult narrator, she gives the reader many opportunities to see how "lying" and storytelling provided a means of creatively escaping painful realities. Her childhood "lies" communicated feeling states that could not be directly expressed. As she explains:

> My stories were full of boys and girls gruesomely raped and murdered, babies cooked in pots of boiling beans, vampires and soldiers and long razor-sharp knives. Witches cut off the heads of children and grown-ups. Gangs of women rode on motorcycles and set fire to people's houses. The ground opened and green-black lizard tongues shot up to pull people down. I got to be very popular as a baby-sitter; everyone was quiet and well-behaved while I told stories, their eyes fixed on my face in a way that made me feel like one of my own witches casting a spell. (119)

Bone tells us that she frequently had daydreams and imagined that she was powerful and important. For example, she imagines groups of people watching Glen beat and rape her and describes how these fantasies make her feel "wonderful": "In my imagination I was proud and defiant. I'd stare back at him with my teeth set, making no sound at all, no shameful scream, no begging" (112). Any sign of weakness, of being vulnerable, which in fact she is, or of reacting to the pain out loud are "shameful" for the young Bone and not part of the defiant self, the "mean sister," she crafts. Later on she expresses her desire to transcend the weakness and isolation through religion and her friend (and perhaps alter ego) Shannon Pearl, whose family is heavily involved in Christian revivals and the traveling gospel circuit. Bone remembers being drawn to the idea that there was a struggle between good and evil, between salvation and damnation, and she describes feeling like the center of attention when she went to churches or revivals because there she was, the not-yet-saved soul whom everyone in the congregation wanted to snare. There, she was wanted:

> There was something heady and enthralling about being the object of all that attention. It was like singing gospel on the television with the audience following your every breath. I could not resist it.
>
> I came close to being saved about fourteen different times—fourteen different Sundays in fourteen different Baptist churches. I didn't fake my indecision, the teary-eyed intensity and open-mouthed confusion that overtook me when the preacher turned his glance on me. . . . I wanted, I wanted, I wanted something—Jesus or God or orange blossom scent or dark chocolate terror in my throat. Something hurt me, ached in me. . . .

The magic I knew was supposed to wash over me with Jesus' blood was absent, the moment cold and empty. I would stumble out into the sunshine guiltily, still unsaved, and go on to a new church the next Sunday. . . .

I bit my lip and went back to reading the Book of Revelation, taking comfort in the hope of the apocalypse, God's retribution on the wicked. I liked Revelations, loved the Whore of Babylon and the promised rivers of blood and fire. It struck me like gospel music, it promised vindication. (151–52)

Bone meets Shannon Pearl, the daughter of a Baptist revival talent agent and Christian bookstore manager, at school and is immediately fascinated by the slight, pale girl with reddish eyes. Like Bone, Shannon tells horrible stories, "Most of which were about the gruesome deaths of innocent children" (157). In Shannon, Bone meets her storytelling match, and Shannon's stories, filled with many details of mutilations and gore, mesmerize Bone, who was accustomed to being the mesmerizer of other children. And like Bone's, Shannon's tales of horror belie her own isolation and pain. Shannon also wants to seek revenge and to be mean and strong, to lash out at those who ridicule and mistreat her. Bone describes how Shannon "spent most of her time brooding on punishments either she or God would visit on them" (157–58). For both Bone and Shannon, the prospect of salvation and redemption, which Christianity guarantees them, is overpowered by the appeal of judgment and righteous revenge.

Awaiting Bone when she momentarily escapes the violence she endures at home is Shannon's world of Baptist revivals. The truths of that world are equally harsh, and Bone and Shannon learn to navigate the dangers of the "gospel circuit" tents. Alcohol abuse, battery, and sexual assault, although not described in these terms, abound wherever Bone and Shannon look when backstage at a revival, yet Bone recalls that these truths "never seemed to register with Mr. and Mrs. Pearl" (163). Their failure to see the "unChristian" backstage world was, for Bone, linked to their ability to stay out of harm's reach. She wonders, "Maybe Jesus shielded their eyes the way he kept old Shadrach, Meshach, and Abednego safe in the fiery furnace. Certainly sin didn't touch them the way it did Shannon and me. Both of us had to learn to walk carefully backstage, with all those hands reaching out to stroke our thighs and pinch the nipples we barely had" (163).

As is the case for Shizuko, Bone is subjected to sexual assault when she ventures outside her home; but whereas for Shizuko being molested in the record store, for example, only reinforces her belief that she is "bad," for Bone being groped at a revival is an obstacle, a hurdle she and Shannon can "carefully" learn to clear. The abuse at home is, however, much more confusing for Bone, and she wonders what was wrong with her that "made" Glen hurt her (190). Not all of the backstage dangers, however, could be avoided, as Bone describes when recounting the nausea that overwhelmed her when she and Shannon sat under the stage one day. They crawled out from beneath the stage for air, and a man who saw Shannon exclaimed that she was the "ugliest thing" he had ever seen. Bone began to yell at him until Mrs. Pearl came out from around the tent. Mrs. Pearl complimented the man, a singer, and tried to quiet Shannon and Bone. Looking at Shannon's anger-filled expression and thinking of her own equally compelling reasons to be angry, Bone imagines her own happy ending to the lives she and Shannon are enduring. "If there was a God, then there would be justice. If there was justice, then Shannon and I would make them all burn" (166). God is not the agent of divine justice for Bone; she and Shannon would have the power to "make them all burn." In Bone's story, they would have the power to exact revenge and mete out justice, with God on their side, but it would be their own rage and power that would vanquish "them" in the end.

A Berserker Rage of One's Own

Bone's early attempts at storytelling and seeking refuge in religious fantasies of rescue and judgment do not immunize her from the psychological effects of sexual abuse evident in Shizuko's narrative. For example, Bone describes moments of dissociation while being raped by Glen, such as when she recalls feeling like she "had passed out briefly" and remembers how "red and black dots swam up toward the ceiling and back down toward [her]" (286). Her dream life also reflects her waking fears, as is evident in her dream of hands reaching around doorframes and mattresses and her description of feeling dread and "fear in [her] like a river, like the ice-dark blue of [Glen's eyes]" (70). Seared into the narrator's memory is the image of Glen's face. She describes his eyes as "dark and empty" or "icy blue" and indicative of his "berserker rage" and the "whirlwind" unleashed whenever he abuses her. She explains how Glen's "face would pink up and his hands would shake and his neck would start to work, the muscles ridging up and throbbing" (100). Here, she tells what she could not describe when it was happening. She explains that Glen never needed to instruct her not to talk to Anney about the abuse by focusing on her own inability to find the words: "He never had to say it. I did not know how to tell anyone what I felt, what scared me and shamed me and still made me stand, unmoving and desperate, while he rubbed against me and ground his face into my neck. I could not tell Mama. I would not have known how to explain why I stood there and let him touch me" (109). This description does not, however, speak to another critical reason for her silence: the fear of Glen's violence. The myth of consent so clearly present in Shizuko's narration also slips into Bone's recollection of events in this passage when she allows for the possibility that she could have "let" Glen (who not only sexually assaulted but routinely beat her) abuse her.

While staying with her aunt Ruth, who was very ill, Bone, then ten years old, is asked directly whether or not Glen has ever "messed with her" sexually, and Bone describes how this was, for her, an unanswerable question at the time:

> I searched Aunt Ruth's face carefully. I knew what she meant, the thing men did to women. I knew what the act was supposed to be, I'd read about it, heard the joke. "What's a South Carolina virgin? 'At's a ten-year-old can run fast." He hadn't done that. Had he? I felt my tongue pushing against the back of my teeth. Aunt Ruth's cheeks got brighter pink, almost red. I dropped my head.
>
> "No," I whispered. I remembered his hands sliding over my body, under my blouse, down my shorts, across my backside, the calluses scratching my skin, his breath hard and fast above me as he pulled me tighter and tighter against him, the sound of his belt pulling through the loops of his pants in the damp stillness of the bathroom. I shuddered.
>
> "No," I whispered. "He just looks at me hard. Grabs me sometimes. Shakes me." I hesitated, looking up at her flushed, sunken cheeks. "You know, when I'm bad." Tell her I thought. Tell her all of it. Tell her. "But the way he looks at me, the way he twists his hands when he looks at me, it scares me, Auntie. He scares me." (124)

Ruth, in asking this question, follows up on Bone's earlier comment, made in passing, that she thinks Glen hates her. Ruth initiates a conversation that Bone is not able to pursue, a conversation for which she has not learned the language. Emotional, linguistic, and situational constraints limit the possibilities any ten-year-old in such a situation would have to translate what she sees, thinks, feels, and experiences into words. Unlike a toddler, who cannot speak at all about feelings, a ten-year-old may appear capable of sustaining a dialogue, but, as James Garbarino and Frances M. Stott explain, "Words are not always the means that children are most comfortable using to raise problems and concerns."[19] Ruth's response to Bone in this scene (which is to ask, "What we gonna do with you?") is characteristic of how unprepared and incompetent we often are when it comes to creating opportunities for children to communicate abuse or other traumatic experiences (even when we are well intentioned or attempting to attend to a child's best interest). Ruth's question is impossible to answer, as Bone shows us, because although Bone is close to Ruth and in a relatively comfortable and familiar setting, Ruth does not respond in a way that allows the dialogue to unfold. Rather, she holds Bone without explaining why she asked the question or without trying to get a fuller sense of what Bone meant by being grabbed and scared.

Even when her mother notices abuse-related injuries, Bone is unable to speak about the abuse, but she shares with us the process of sifting through the false interpretations (that she "made" Glen abuse her) to get at her own story. In an interview with Carolyn Megan, Dorothy Allison comments on how Bone's movement toward the truth and away from imposed distortions and misrepresentations is central to her survival. Allison explains, "The only thing that saves her are the stories, the ones that she needs to make for herself."[20] The stories Bone tells as a child are not directly stories about the truth of her experiences, but they consistently refer back to what is going on in her life—even if only in contrast. Bone lets us know that it was too daunting and too unexplainable to connect even the physical signs of abuse to her own story out loud: "To say anything would mean trying to tell her everything, to describe those times when he held me tight to his belly and called me sweet names I did not want to hear. I remained silent, stubborn, resentful, and collected my bruises as if they were unavoidable. There were lumps at the back of my head, not swellings of flesh and tissue but rumpled ridges of bone. My big toes went flat and wide, broken within a few months of each other when I smashed into doorjambs, running while looking back over my shoulder" (111). Not being able to tell or having the words to communicate her experience makes the telling of other stories even more critical to Bone's survival, as can be inferred from the considerable attention to her youthful storytelling throughout the novel. In taking control of her story and its characters as the adult narrator and moving as close as possible to the previously unspoken trauma, Bone now reclaims her life story, giving it her own interpretations much as she reinterpreted the legendary outlaw stories to highlight the "mean sisters" she invented.

Bone tells us a great deal about Glen, who (unlike Shizuko's stepfather) is assigned motivations for his extreme cruelty. Bone locates the source of his anger in other faces, the faces she sees when visiting Glen's parents' home. Bone shares two different pictures, what she calls "movie images," of Glen— one of him screaming at her, "his neck bright red with rage," and the other of Glen at "his daddy's house with his head hanging down and his mouth so soft spit shone on the lower lip" (100). Glen, in Bone's account, is the angry son of a well-to-do family that sees him as a failure. She tells us that Glen's father owns a dairy, where he "hired and fired men like [Bone's] mother's brothers," and Glen's brothers are lawyers and dentists who live in nice houses, while Glen is fired from job after job. She describes how Glen is humiliated by his father, who frequently "delivered his lecture on all the things Glen had done wrong in his long life of failure and disappointment" (99). Bone provides the reader with ample reason to think that the feelings of frustration, shame, and anger that Glen does not express to his family are twisted and redirected at Bone, who is weaker and unable to defend herself. For example, in one scene, after beating Bone, Glen lies to Anney, saying that Bone provoked his anger by calling him a bastard and telling him he would "never be her daddy." And almost as if it were unrelated, he adds, "And—oh, God, Anney! They laid me off today. Just put me out without a care" (107). Bone gives us her account of the beating prior to relating this conversation between her mother and Glen, creating a window into the dimensions of Glen's frustrations and their brutal expression.

Bone's portrayal of Glen's motivations for abusing her are told from the vantage point of the adult narrator and not the abused girl. In discussing this distinction, it is helpful to refer back to the first chapter and the dilemma Donna Nagata argues survivors and those who seek to represent the experiences of survivors face—that is, the dual risks of overemphasizing the victimization and thereby minimizing the strength of the survivor and of overemphasizing the survival strengths and thus minimizing the trauma. The dangers of seeing Glen and Bone as equals in competition for Anney's attention, which can easily arise if we overemphasize Bone's strengths and power as a creative and intelligent little girl, correspond to the "with" (sex "with" my stepfather) that haunts Shizuko as she tells us about her painful past. Bone may tell us "there was always a reason" for Glen's violence, but she also explains that she knew she had not "done" anything to provoke his attacks.

But without a "reason" or an explanation, Bone has no means of organizing her experiences. Repeatedly having been told that she was bad, the young Bone understands her life according to the only terms available to her, locating her agency, her "badness" that "made" Glen abuse her, in her core being, in who she is, telling us she once felt "it was just me, the fact of my life, who I was in his eyes and mine. I was evil. Of course I was" (110). Bone's identification of a "bad self," one that allows her to explain the suffering she endures, is not unique. Assigning such false agency where no agency is possible has been a practice even among some "experts" who have encountered and attempted to explain the inner life of the abused child. Examples of professional attempts to hold the child accountable and explain away the abuse can even be found in the work of D. W. Winnicott, a preeminent psychoanalyst whose groundbreaking theories on "play" and culture might at first suggest a greater understanding of childhood dependency.

In discussing the case of a fourteen-year-old patient, Winnicott, for example, recalls learning that the girl had been sexually abused at age four. He tells us, "From the age of twelve she became rather heavy, languid, and quiet, and developed a leucorrheic vaginal discharge," and he discusses her "symptoms," such as nail biting, that could not be attributed to a "physical illness." Before concluding that the girl's "leucorrhea" was the result of sexual fantasies and dreams, Winnicott sexualizes her, portraying her as a proto–Lolita, who, at four, had brought on the abuse. He writes, "In this case there is no doubt that the incident was to some extent brought about by the child and the state she was in at the time, developing as she was in an extrovert way and always somewhat excited."[21] Positing "extroversion" as so powerful a force in a four-year-old child that it could "bring about" victimization blames the child for who she is, much in the same way that Bone blames her "evil" self for what she sees as the "fact of her life." It is not surprising that when the young patient visited Winnicott again when she was eighteen and later as an adult mother, he found that she was suffering from "more definitely psychiatric" complaints, the lingering effects of that which his initial analysis failed to address and distorted. Winnicott is not alone in his astigmatic view of sexual abuse; similar examples abound throughout the history of clinical psychoanalytic literature as many contemporary researchers, such as Herman, have shown.

Herman also contends that the "existential task" of the abused child is compounded by children's own tendency to see themselves as active agents in the abuse. She writes, "Though she perceives herself to be abandoned to a power without mercy, she must find a way to preserve hope and meaning. The alternative is utter despair, something no child can bear."[22] Thus, Herman explains, it is easier to accept that they are to blame than to find fault in their abusive parents, and a child such as Bone develops the "double self" and "takes the evil of the abuser into herself and thereby preserves her primary attachments to her parents."[23] The formation of the "double" or "bad" self does not necessarily, however, thwart a child's wishes to be "good" and earn her way out of the abuse, and Herman notes that the "good" and "bad" selves (the "debased" and "exalted" selves) an abused child may construct are therefore not easily integrated. This Manichean inner life of the child makes it hard for her to comprehend ambivalence outside herself, as well. That is to say, just as she sees herself as "good" or "bad," she organizes the outside world according to the same standards and thus experiences confusion when faced with the reality of ambivalence. In attempting to express these feelings to an uninformed clinician, a child may in fact present attitudes that reinforce the lie that she is somehow to blame.

If we read Bone's youthful storytelling as a valiant attempt to bypass the censoring forces, both internal and external, that would otherwise strangle her attempts to speak out, then we confront the failure of the adults around her to "listen to" and understand her stories. Garbarino and Stott, who address how unprepared many adults are to hear children's stories in their study *What Children Can Tell Us*, explain, "Storytelling allows children to distance themselves from frightening or unacceptable emotions by attributing them to characters in their stories. When either external prohibitions or internal inhibitions forbid children to acknowledge or express their feelings or discuss the events in their lives, the characters, be they people or animals, can do, say, think, or feel much that a child would not be allowed."[24] The hateful revenge of a "mean sister" or gruesome stories of death and dismemberment that Bone shares with her attentive cousins and friends are, in effect, translations of her own story, the one that she does not tell until she grows up to be the narrator of our story, the one that speaks to her experience without the distance Bat Masterson's sister once provided. Allison herself, in her book *Skin*, tells us that much the same could be said of her own use of "Bone" to say what Allison once could not: "By the time I taught myself the basics of storytelling on the page, I knew there was only one story that would haunt me until I understood how to tell it—the complicated, painful story of how my mama had, and had not saved me as a girl. Writing *Bastard out of Carolina* became, ultimately, the way to claim my family's pride and tragedy, and the embattled sexuality I had fashioned on a base of violence and abuse."[25] In so doing, Allison reconfigures the distortions that made her (and Bone) feel "strange" and "evil" into the story of what happened to her as Bone, the story Allison "had to" tell. Just as discovery in the novel brings the abuse to an end, Allison's "discovery" and recovery of her story undo the lies that "haunted" her. Or, as she writes in the opening lines of chapter 18 of *Bastard out of Carolina*, "Things come apart so easily when they have been held together by lies" (248).

The apparent ease with which Glen's stranglehold on Bone's early years is undone, however, belies the difficulty Bone faces even as the abuse comes to light. Keeping Allison's words regarding her own need to write the novel in mind, we find countless examples of how daunting a task this must have been; we see it in the seemingly never-ending series of obstacles that Bone faces. After Aunt Raylene sees dried blood in Bone's underwear and discovers that Bone is being abused, she calls in Bone's Boatwright uncles who exact their own violent justice on Glen. Anney refuses her sister's offer of a place to stay and moves her girls to a small apartment. Bone looks to Anney in the following days for comfort, but Anney does not talk to Bone, and Bone is left to suffer in silence as her sister angrily protests the lack of a television and other comforts that were left behind at the home where they had lived with Glen. Bone grows increasingly enraged as she endures the anger of her mother and sister, which is directed at her in the aftermath of Raylene's discovery. Reese, for example, tells Bone that Anney is frustrated and does not know "what to do" with Bone, adding, "I wouldn't want Mama to be mad at me the way she's been mad at you" (260). Like Winnicott's fourteen-year-old patient, Bone is cast as the agent of her own misfortune and pain. Biting her fingernails in anticipation of the return to Glen that she sees as inevitable, Bone wonders whether Anney still loves her and what might be awaiting her when—not "if"—they all go "back to Daddy Glen" (261).

Bone's fears prove prophetic when Glen later comes to Aunt Alma's house, where Bone is staying, and catches her alone. Initially commenting on her changing appearance and how she would soon be "breaking some man's heart just 'cause [she] can," Glen proceeds to try bullying Bone into convincing Anney to return to him (281). Bone tells him that Anney can go, but that she refuses to live with him ever again, at which point Glen insists, "You're not even thirteen years old, girl. You don't say what you do. I'm your daddy. I say what you do" (282). Glen shakes Bone, telling her that she is the cause of all their problems and vows to kill her if Anney refuses to come back. Throwing her, kicking her, calling her a "little cunt" and a "goddam little bastard," Glen then rapes Bone on the front porch:

"You're not going anywhere." He laughed. "You think you're so grown up. You think you're so big and bad, saying no to me. Let's see how big you are, how grown." He spread what was left of my blouse and ripped at the zipper on my pants, pulling them down my thighs as my left hand groped to hold them. I tried to kick, but I was pinned. Tears were streaming down my face, but I wasn't crying. I was cursing him.

"Damn you! Damn you! Damn you! *God will damn you!*" . . ."You'll shut up. I'll shut you up. I'll teach you. . . . You little cunt. I should have done this a long time ago. You've always wanted it. Don't tell me you don't."

Following the description of the rape, Bone describes looking up to see her mother moving toward them. Anney's initial response—the screams and objects she throws at Glen and her desire to take Bone to the hospital—are quickly followed by a familiar shift. Bone watches her mother turn to comfort Glen— and not her. "Could she love me and still hold him like that? I let my head fall back. I did not want to see this. I wanted Travis's shotgun, or my sharp killing hook. I wanted everything to stop, the world to end, anything, but not to lie bleeding while she held him and cried" (291). The same mother—to whom Bone looked for justice but who instead said, "Bone, be more careful" (112) and asked her "how could you do that" (111) when Glen had beaten the girl years before—at this point makes her unwillingness or inability to act on her daughter's behalf painfully clear. When Bone was still eight and nine years old, we are told, Anney saw only what she could "afford to notice" (66). As Anney turns her back on Bone in this scene, and later when she ultimately leaves Bone behind and runs away to "California or Florida maybe" with Glen, we learn how very little Anney can, in the end, "afford to notice." It is, indeed, difficult to reconcile this final abandonment with the fleeting and ephemeral moments when Anney goes to great lengths to defy Glen and protect her daughters, such as when she leaves the house (presumably prostituting herself) to make money for food so she can feed her daughters, who had eaten only crackers and ketchup earlier that day. Anney has no difficulty in expressing her anger at Glen when he does not provide her children with food, and she defies (and, according to local logic, emasculates) him by doing what he should but does not. But when confronted with the extent of the sexual abuse, Anney's limits as a caregiver are made apparent.

Storytelling may indeed be the only method of defense against stories such as those Bone is told by her mother and others, the stories that require her not to be so stubborn or sass back (10). Bone recalls, "Mama told me I should show

[Glen] that I loved him." But Bone, unable to fulfill this role or be "good enough" to avoid Glen's violence, is in effect framed. Regardless of how hard she may try to be "good enough," she cannot succeed within the family fiction Glen maintains, a fiction based on his claim that "that child ain't never gonna love me" (62). Bone is told to be "careful," to obey and be "good," but as she recounts her childhood years, we see that no amount of care or obedience could win her safety. Her hopes and the abuse are at odds, and the site where they cannot meet, the impossible space, is precisely where Bone is left in the end after her mother and Glen are gone. Her story, then, comes from that impossible space in which Bone struggles against the role that she is supposed to, but cannot, play.

Henry Giroux offers an approach to understanding struggles such as Bone's. He writes, "Bearing witness always implicates one in the past and gives rise to conditions that govern how youth act and are acted upon within a myriad of public sites, cultures, and institutions. . . . Witnessing and testimony, translated here, mean listening to the stories of others as part of a broader responsibility to engage the present as an ethical response to the narratives of the past."[26] Such a "broader responsibility" can be assumed by readers of Father Fucker and Bastard out of Carolina who go beyond merely reflecting on the specific traumas suffered by the fictional Shizuko and Bone and foster a greater attentiveness to the countless ways in which many children today are living in states of daily trauma —in their homes, group homes, schools, "correctional" institutions, the military, shelters, or elsewhere on the streets and in our lives. If we see these two narratives of fictional historical pasts as points of departure for better understanding the experiences of many youth and the origins of their rage, we inevitably confront problems of a more troubling magnitude. At the same time, however, we also open up possibilities for engaging in a practice of learning as potentially transformative—not simply for ourselves as readers of fiction, but for the communities in which we live, communities in which abused children often turn up dead, addicted to drugs, institutionalized, or murderous before we recognize or acknowledge the realities of their lives.

PART 2

The Message

If we make the wrong choice, then the danger is that we'll get hit again—that we'll be hit in a way that will be devastating from the standpoint of the United States.

—Dick Cheney, speaking of the 2004 presidential election,
Des Moines, Iowa, "Inside Politics," CNN, September 7, 2004

The parents of an 11-year-old girl are to take the extraordinary step of having her fitted with a microchip so that her movements can be traced if she is abducted. Danielle Duval will have the device implanted in her arm in the next few months. . . . [Danielle's mother said,] "Like us, Danielle needs to feel that she's safe at all times and could be located in a real emergency. I know nothing is ever 100% or foolproof, but we believe the microchip will go a long way towards protecting her."

—Jamie Wilson, *Guardian* (London), September 3, 2002

Don't push me 'cuz I'm close to the edge
I'm tryin' not to lose my head.

—Grandmaster Flash, "The Message," 1982

The second part of this book begins with the subject of fear. In the documentary film *Berkeley in the Sixties*, Bobby Seale, co-founder of the Black Panther Party, recalls the fearful reaction with which the Panthers were met when they began their armed patrols to prevent police brutality against the black population of Oakland, California. Specifically, Seale remembers the alarmed faces of white people confronted with this radical development: "They didn't need to say it. You could see it in their faces. Too many niggers with guns."[1] Seale interprets this fear as stemming from white people's awareness of historical and ongoing responsibility for the oppression of black people. Black Panthers armed with guns meant that the oppressed were prepared to fight back.

The Panther's patrols constituted a profound disruption of business as usual. By drawing on legal justifications associated with the "right to bear arms," they also forced conservative politicians into a corner. The politicians could either uphold the right of the Panthers to carry loaded guns in public or push through legislation to deny it. The swift move by state legislators, led by Republican Donald Mulford, to pass the Mulford Act (or so-called Panther Bill, designed to "de-weaponize" the Panthers), and Governor Ronald Reagan's enthusiastic signature, revealed the hierarchy of interests and values at play for the politicians and their constituencies. For Mulford, Reagan, and their peers, preventing even a small shift in race-based differential power outweighed defending the "right" to bear arms, a "right" in California that had included, until that time, the carrying of loaded guns in public.[2] The Panther Bill was thus fear-based legislation. The prospect of an armed black self-defense force was more frightening to white Californian society than any impact such a bill might have had on white people's ability to carry loaded guns. Of course, California's ruling white society already had a "militia" (the police and, under some circumstances, the National Guard) prepared to protect its interests and property, so the choice was in some ways overdetermined.

I begin with this anecdote because it raises a critical question: What does it say about one's relationship to another person or group if she believes that, if given the opportunity, that other person or group will hurt her? The Panthers approached their patrols with the premise that, if given the opportunity, the Oakland Police would hurt black people. Many white people believed that, if legally permitted to carry loaded guns, the Panthers would hurt them. The reasons why these two communities anticipated harm are fundamentally different, but any serious engagement with the aforementioned question in the case of the Panthers leads to the same trajectory of issues, which include white supremacy, multigenerational slavery, police abuse, and ongoing oppression. One's fears in this situation are shaped by one's relationship to and understanding of it. Another example would be the moment described in chapter 2 when Shizuko picks up the knife in the novel *Father Fucker*. What harm does Shizuko anticipate that leads her to take up the knife? What harm does her mother anticipate when she convinces Shizuko to put down the knife?

This introduction inaugurates what is in part 2 a sustained examination of how "youth violence" is manufactured, experienced, and understood in late-twentieth-century and early-twenty-first-century Japan and the United States. By exploring what harm youth anticipate and what harm we, as adult society, anticipate from youth, I hope to dispel many of the myths that have developed around representations of "juvenile crime" or "delinquency." This introduction also sets up a recurrent theme in part 2, which is that challenges to rights asserted, conferred, or assumed according to hierarchical relations (namely, "parental rights" and First World rights and privileges) must be disallowed, disavowed, vilified, and even outlawed to make those rights and privileges (at least appear) acceptable and sustainable. Finally, this introduction constitutes a conceptual bridge between the focus on the traumatic origins of some youth's rage in part 1—what prompts Shizuko to pick up the knife—and the engagement with when the knife is used and what happens next in part 2.

Situated in the tension between a moment of violation and the aftermath of a violent response to that violation, part 2 takes on questions that develop out of the apprehension that something violent will occur, that an attack is looming. The hyper-alertness, panic, fear, and desperation characteristic of that moment when one is "on edge" and anticipating the imminent blow presupposes some level of premonition, some familiarity with an advanced warning or signal that the attack is coming. I will begin by turning to a particular kind of apprehension associated with a guilty conscience—the fear of "chickens coming home to roost." This fear that the impending blow constitutes one's comeuppance is what Bobby Seale saw in the faces of white people and police looking back at him and the other armed Black Panthers.[3]

This fear is particularly pronounced in cases in which a fearful subject simultaneously recognizes and disavows her guilt, a situation that can produce confusing and contradictory responses, such as certain versions of the post–September 11 question, "Why do they hate us?" Often when this question was posed, the official answer was provided (they hate us because we love freedom and democracy) and further discussion was discouraged. The assertion that the escalating climate of fear developed out of an awareness (even if unconscious) of our collective participation and complicity in policies and practices that have oppressed and killed others and that "they hate us" because we hurt them (a view expressed immediately after September 11 by intellectuals such as Saskia Sassen, the late Susan Sontag, and, of course, Ward Churchill) was vociferously denounced as offensive by many self-identified leftists.[4] One common liberal criticism of the opinion that the September 11 attacks were brought on by U.S. foreign policy held that all violence is deplorable and that nothing could explain or justify the loss of lives in the Pentagon and World Trade Center. This response served to close off discussion that did not conform to the mass-mediated official modes of lamentation and memorializing or outrage.

As I will insist throughout part 2, regardless of whether one considers herself a pacifist, violent responses to violence do happen for a variety of reasons. Declaring them to be "bad" does little toward helping us understand how they happen or, even if only for purposes of sheer self-interest, how to prevent them from happening to us. Rather than, for example, treating the September 11 attacks and the wars on Afghanistan, Pakistan, and Iraq (or Black Panthers and Oakland Police) as equivalent, I want to shift the terms of these kinds of debates to the terrain of feeling states, especially enraged and fearful states, and to the subject of political (differential) power. By looking at how fear and (out)rage have been maintained as dominant national feeling states in recent years, we can better identify the socialization to which youth in Japan and the U.S. (and elsewhere) are being subjected and the experiences such socialization is producing. By looking closely at the differential power relationships that structure violent acts, we can open up room for theorizing remedies that are precluded when we avoid uncomfortable questions that might challenge the way we see ourselves in relation to youth and the rest of the world.

Often concurrent with the exhortation to be afraid is an equally compelling drive to numbness. Almost as if to manage the fear, people living in the U.S., for example, are encouraged to disappear in distractions: the latest episode of a popular television series, a shopping mall excursion, an Internet virtual world or social networking site, or any other (preferably consumer-based) activity that spares us from seeing or thinking about the materiality of suffering from which we might benefit and that, at the same time, serves commercial interests. When human suffering is overtly and inextricably linked to our own comforts or our very identity (as "Americans," for example), we rarely confront the evidence. Even when faced with obvious examples of suffering and profound inequality within the U.S., as was the case in the aftermath of Hurricane Katrina, the exhortation to look away can still trump the most irrefutable reality. Signs of war are especially scripted, muffled, airbrushed, or carefully kept away from the public theater other than those brief moments when we encounter photos from Abu Ghraib, for example, and are coached to respond as if they were aberrant, isolated, and perhaps for some, even justifiable.

This was made abundantly clear to me in the busy waiting room of a doctor's office on a winter afternoon in 2004. A woman, noticeably crying, entered the room and sat in the only available seat, which was across from another woman with a toddler. Both women were white and appeared to be in their late thirties or early forties. The woman with the toddler asked the crying woman if she was OK, and the crying woman replied, "I'm having a hard time. My only child, my son, just left for Iraq." The room was immediately tense with this introduction of the war and her affect into what was supposed to be a clinical (and thus "safe") space, and the body language of those near the crying woman grew rigid as they physically shifted away from her (as if she were scary or crazy). The woman with the child immediately closed off any possibility for further discussion with an oddly upbeat response, "You must be so proud. The army will be a great opportunity for him." The crying mother did not speak to her again.

This sort of reaction is necessary for the maintenance of unequal privilege, policies, and relationships. There can be no admission that privilege is maintained at certain people's expense, that some people's suffering does not matter because your comforts matter so much. To acknowledge that the war meant something painful for the crying mother (as opposed to an "opportunity" for her son) would involve introducing the complexity of the taboo subject of wartime suffering into the anonymity of waiting-room conversation. How would the woman with the toddler feel if her child were to have the "opportunity" to go to war in sixteen years? What kind of "opportunity" (and for whom) is the move into a work environment that may entail killing and being killed? Such questions could lead us to care about the crying mother, and if we begin to identify with her, how many more steps would it take until we began to sympathize with a crying parent in Iraq? We fear the crying woman in the waiting room who, in defiance of her prescribed role, announces that she is "having a hard time," because her "hard time" is not part of the sanctioned imaginary. The national state of fear, with its stock characters of who the "bad guys" are (never "us"), does not translate into a general acceptance and understanding of every fear or even fear writ large. We are allowed our fears and encouraged to express them, but only as long as we stay "on message."

In 2001, Amiri Baraka wrote "Somebody Blew Up America," which (after a short preamble) begins with the following lines:

> They say it's some terrorist,
> some barbaric
> A Rab,
> in Afghanistan
> It wasn't our American terrorists
> It wasn't the Klan or the Skin heads
> Or the them that blows up nigger
> Churches, or reincarnates us on Death Row.[5]

A year after Baraka wrote the poem, in the fall of 2002, people who probably had never heard of him before suddenly united in vocal criticism of him.[6] Their ire, provoked by a few lines that appeared later in the long poem, culminated in pressure on Governor Jim McGreevey to revoke Baraka's status as poet laureate of New Jersey. Because New Jersey had no guidelines in place for "firing" a poet laureate and Baraka refused to resign, considerable resources and time were spent on eliminating the position itself through legislative means. Baraka's support for reparations to the descendants of slaves and his long career of creatively representing the horrors of white supremacy in verse were not the focus of those who described his work as "hateful"—even though the familiar charges of "race baiting" and "anti-white propaganda" did emerge in some arguments for censure. Rather, his critics took issue with Baraka's posing of questions about what the U.S. and Israeli governments may have known about the September 11 attacks beforehand. The questions relating to Israel in particular were deemed anti–Semitic by many of his critics—even though Jews are among the many groups Baraka identifies as brutally oppressed in the same poem.

The anti-Baraka campaign extended from national publications to campus newspapers. Ward Connerly, the same public spokesperson for the repeal of affirmative action in California mentioned in chapter 1, described Baraka in an essay for the *Washington Times* published on October 11, 2002, as "one of America's premier haters" and "Somebody Blew Up America" as a "maniacal litany" of "ghetto facts." In an editorial for the *Stanford Review* published in October 2002, Joe Lonsdale (an undergraduate student at Stanford University at the time) described Amiri Baraka as a "buffoon" and a "clown," a "completely insane African American demagogue" whose "horrid stupidity, evilness, and utter foolishness" warranted a "violent death." Lonsdale also asserted that those who take offense at this characterization "deserve more than offense," leaving unstated what would constitute "more." Such incendiary language draws on stereotypical representations of African American men as sources of "foolish" entertainment and, to borrow John Dower's description of similarly troubling representations of the enemy in war, the lynch mob's "linguistic softening of the killing process."[7] Lonsdale's vitriol and resurrection of racist representational categories deflect attention away from the very poem he seeks to critique (yet never addresses in any detail). Much the same can be said of other anti-Baraka pieces that were published from that fall to the following spring.

In "Somebody Blew Up America," Baraka decries violent oppression perpetrated against many groups. Baraka poses questions about who has been responsible for a variety of historical and ongoing atrocities and injustices. Through a series of questions that begin with the word "who," he challenges readers to identify differential power relationships and the institutional and state policies that so often have left behind corpses of the poor, enslaved, and colonized, as well as those who have advocated for them. Some of the nearly 200 questions in the poem include:

Who killed the most niggers
Who killed the most Jews
Who killed the most Italians
Who killed the most Irish
Who killed the most Africans
Who killed the most Japanese
Who killed the most Latinos . . .
Who have the colonies
Who stole the most land . . .
Who own the oil
Who want more oil
Who told you what you think that later you find out a lie . . .
Who walked out of the Conference
    Against Racism . . .
Who put the Jews in ovens,
    and who helped them do it
Who said "America First"

and OK'd the yellow stars . . .
Who thought up "The Trail of Tears."

And the offending lines:

Who knew the World Trade Center was gonna get bombed
Who told 4000 Israeli workers at the Twin Towers
    to stay home that day
Why did Sharon stay away?

That these provocative questions appear in a poem as opposed to an op-ed piece in no way limits our ability to consider them critically. Nevertheless, Lonsdale's racist rhetoric and request that readers "consider" whether Baraka "deserves a violent death"—along with the uniform and repetitive-enough-to-seem-plagiarized scores of other attacks on Baraka—are obviously not simply about four lines in this long poem, no matter how controversial they may be.

Efforts to defend Baraka solely or even primarily on the basis of his right to free speech have run the risk of missing the reason for the attacks against him, as Ewuare Osayande has convincingly argued.[8] He writes:

> To approach this struggle as though it is just an issue of free speech doesn't do it justice. What we are dealing with here is larger than free speech. We are not dealing with one solitary individual's right to speak being violated. This is an issue of the repression of the collective speech, the collective history, the collective struggle of a people that has not just been censored but repressed. Truth is that, for Black folks in this country, speech ain't free anyway. It is costly. We pay a high price to speak—all too often our livelihood, if not our very lives."[9]

The U.S. government's targeting of a teenager, Sherman Austin, in 2002 further illustrates the limits and pitfalls in contemporary free-speech debates. Officially sentenced to federal prison for criminal intent in the distribution of bomb-making information, Austin was in fact selected for prosecution because of what Osayande calls the "collective speech, the collective history, the collective struggle." The "crime" for which Austin spent a year in federal prison served as a flimsy (if effective) cover for what the government actually sought to sanction, which was the political content of his website and his activism.

Sherman Austin's purported crime was the existence of web-based material that had been written by *someone else* and linked by *another youth* to a free-hosting area Austin provided from a server he ran for his own site, Raisethefist.com. Neither the other boy nor the original author of the offending material was ever charged with any crime. As is the case with many blogs, Indymedia sites, and other websites that offer open or self-publishing forums, Austin's site received comments and links from a variety of visitors. The other boy posted a link to his own website on Raisethefist.com, and that boy's website included a direct link to the "Reclaim Guide," a manual featuring instructions on how to build explosives. A link to yet another link would take visitors from Austin's site to the bomb-making information. Austin, the black son of a single white mother with no property, was imprisoned for violating 18 U.S. Code 842 (p)(2)(A) of 1997, a law sponsored by Senator Dianne Feinstein, a California Democrat, which makes it illegal to distribute information related to explosives *with the intent* to use that information in a "federal crime of violence." The question of intent was central in Austin's case.[10]

While it is not technically illegal to be an anarchist, Feinstein's law provided a means of using Austin's anarchist politics (as intent) as a basis to assign illegality to otherwise legal material (bomb-making instructions). In other words, the actions of another boy, the one who linked the verboten site to Austin's, served as sufficient grounds for Austin's imprisonment because Austin was a young black anarchist who had effectively reached a large international audience. He had not distributed or written the bomb-making information, activities the CIA, white-supremacist groups, and those who target abortion providers have pursued with impunity. As many of Austin's supporters at the time noted, books with bomb-making instructions also can be ordered online, and some groups with actual histories of violence include "how to" guides on carrying out assassinations on their websites. None of these groups or individuals had been charged under Feinstein's law, nor had those who distribute official (such as CIA-generated) information related to building explosives for the purpose of communicating (or even exposing) government policy. The judge in the case, Stephen V. Wilson (a Reagan appointee), indicated his hope that a harsh sentence would "send a message to other revolutionaries," making clear the political nature of the prosecution and sentencing of Austin in this case.[11]

The requirement of intent in Feinstein's law allows room for an incredible range of prosecutorial freedom to choose whose relationships to dangerous material (however tenuous or manufactured) can be interpreted as illegal. Sherman Austin provided federal prosecutors (and the judge) with the perfect test case for using this law, flexing new USA PATRIOT Act muscles, and assessing the deterrent effect a high-profile imprisonment might have on young activists. Not only was he young, black, an anarchist, and an activist, but he and his family lacked the financial resources to hire legal counsel. An institutional clumsiness (intentional or otherwise) with the technological aspects of the case helped to ensure that the fiction manufactured to explain Sherman's incarceration was removed enough from the pesky details of the truth as to seem, at least on paper, compelling and reasonable.

So what was so dangerous about this young person's website? Austin started running Raisethefist.com from a server in his bedroom when he was only sixteen years old. The site featured news and commentary related to the anti-globalization movement, police brutality, racism, sexism, and other issues related to social justice. In addition to news stories, information on anarchism, links, and music, the site offered visitors forums to share ideas and resources. The engaging design of the site and the opportunities it provided for young anarchists and activists to share ideas and organize protest actions attracted a heavy flow of visitors. By the time Austin was eighteen, his site also received regular hits from the U.S. Department of Justice and U.S. Department of Defense. I think it is safe to assume that the prospect of a successful, young, and organized black activist reaching large numbers of other youth with messages about, for example, the value of Black Panther–style community self-defense or the importance of showing up at international trade talks to voice dissent was enough to bring down the hammer.

Because the prosecution of Sherman Austin was based on the distribution of and intent behind text that was written and posted by someone else, efforts to defend him based solely on his right to free speech run the risk of conflating his political dissent with his relationship to the criminal material in question, the same logical flaw at the heart of the case against him. As Osayande has observed in Baraka's case, the free speech defense does not require that we actually engage the details of the charges leveled against Baraka's poem, only that we agree to tolerate its existence. For Osayande, this sort of defense is passive and, at worst, complicit in maintaining the power structures that continue to position voices such as Baraka's on the periphery. In the case of "Somebody Blew Up America," the questions themselves are tougher to engage than a facile defense of any poet's right to express herself freely. In Sherman Austin's case, they are inextricably linked to more than a century of state resources invested in the discrediting, incapacitating, and killing of anarchists, an issue I will address in chapter 6.

Ordering Fears

My primary concern here is thus not about defending Amiri Baraka or anyone else's right to free speech but about why "Somebody Blew Up America" attracted so much attention as a news item in the fall of 2002, a year after its initial release and a year before Sherman Austin began his one-year term in federal prison. What compelled so many politicians, lobbyists, news reporters, and journalists to focus so much time and energy on a poet and his poem? The answers to these questions require us to situate the controversy in its historical moment. In the summer of 2002 in the U.S., Amber Alerts and terror alerts occasionally interrupted television programming. "Nonspecific terrorist threats" to landmarks such as the Golden Gate Bridge (and eventually "orange" and "yellow" alerts) kept alive the fear that another attack could come at any time and anyplace as the nation was drawn closer to launching a full-scale invasion of Iraq, and people were urged to stay on guard and report any "suspicious" activities. The Amber Alert Plan (both an acronym for America's Missing: Broadcast Emergency Response and in reference to Amber Hagerman, a Texas girl who was abducted and murdered in 1996) began as a coordinated effort of the National Center for Missing and Exploited Children, local law-enforcement agencies, and other organizations in the fall of 2001 but was not adopted as a widespread practice until the late summer of 2002.

Increased public attention to the abduction of children contributed to many parents' fears for their children's safety as license-plate numbers of suspect vehicles flashed across highway signs, prompting motorists to scan for matching plates. The happy reunification of several abducted children with their families and the efficacy of the Amber Alert system are not subjects of my critique here. But the notion that children were more vulnerable to abduction by strangers at a time when such abductions were actually less common than they had been a decade earlier occupied a very specific and visible space in the mass media immediately before the one-year anniversary of the September 11 attacks, a focus that periodically deflected attention away from the drive to war on Iraq while maintaining combinations of fear and outrage as the dominant national feeling states.

In her study on the history and understanding of child abduction in the U.S., the historian Paula Fass underscored the pervasiveness of such fears, which were exploited long before the fall of 2002:

> The nightly news is full of children threatened by abduction and children lost to abductors. . . . As a society, we are haunted everywhere by pictures of abducted children in police stations, in newspapers, on television and posters, and on more homey objects like milk cartons. We have literally surrounded ourselves with reminders of our lost children, which serve as both cautions and come-ons, provoking anxiety and defining a cultural indulgence that exploits the very children we seek to protect. This seeming contradiction is, in fact, the result of how child kidnapping has been framed and evolved historically. . . . [Our] public representations do not channel our warm concern for children toward genuine protection and advocacy for their many needs; they substitute thrill for social commitment.[12]

Much the same could be said of Japan, where sensationalized images of threatened children are also ubiquitous while "social commitment" is sparse, inadequate, or simply disingenuous.

Even official data would suggest our fears are not well prioritized. For example, Federal Bureau of Investigation (FBI) data indicate that abductions of children by strangers in the U.S. were less frequent at the dawn of the twenty-first century than they had been in previous decades. The FBI estimates that there were 200–300 such cases each year during the 1980s, 134 in 1999, and 93 in 2000.[13] In Japan, the estimated numbers are even smaller (usually in the double digits unless data related to human trafficking and international child-custody-related abduction into Japan is included) even though abduction murders (such as the case of Kamitate Kana, which I discuss in chapter 5) generate considerable attention. By way of comparison, in San Mateo County, California, where the total population is roughly 700,000, more than 5,000 domestic child abuse cases were referred to the county in 2001. About 17 percent of these cases resulted in children being taken into state dependency.[14] Some consider this a relatively "good" rate in California, even though it constitutes a substantial increase from the 1,438 referred cases in 1994. The areas with the highest reported cases of abuse in San Mateo County were the cities of East Palo Alto and Redwood City. Because of social services' differential treatment of the poor and marginalized communities that are more highly concentrated in these cities, the data I have referenced are skewed, at best. In Japan, there were 17,275 child abuse reports for the entire nation in 2000.[15] This reflects an increase from approximately 5,000 in 1997.[16] Saitō Satoru, director of the Institute of

Family Functioning in Tokyo, said of the 1997 data, "These figures are just the tip of the iceberg."[17] Between 100 and 200 children are brought into the state's protective custody facilities each year in Japan—fewer than are taken into custody in San Mateo County. The vast majority of child abuse cases go unreported, and some cases referred to authorities result in a child's exposure to even greater harm.

Regardless of how one chooses to use and interpret the sort of data I list, she is likely to conclude that children in Japan and the U.S. are at greater risk of maltreatment in the home than at the hands of strangers.[18] Fass notes that some child abduction figures in the U.S. are "inflated" by the inclusion of abductions by parents, pointing to a blurring of distinctions between parents and strangers when the category of stranger is pronounced. A "complex social problem" (abductions by parents), she writes, is grafted onto a "heinous crime to portray child kidnapping as an even more common and therefore more terrifying occurrence."[19] Finally, Fass keenly observes, the focus on statistics "obscures the problem in a different way." She argues that the personal and individual horrors of actual abductions by strangers are lost in the broad-stroke representation of a huge social "plague": "The numbers are a cheat; only the children are real."[20]

It takes little investigative expertise to notice the biases that govern how different types of violence are assigned different meaning on the evening news. Even when a surveillance video of Madelyn Gorman Toogood, a white woman, beating her toddler daughter in a the parking lot of a department store in Indiana (after looking around to see if anyone was watching) was repeatedly aired on television news programs the same fall that the Baraka controversy broke, we were told over and over that we were all vulnerable to terrorist sleeper cells and strangers. The abusive mother provided an isolated spectacle, and her story was covered as if it were a rare glimpse into atavistic dysfunction, an exception to the "norm" and a brief distraction from the "War on Terror." Toogood did not represent the "real" America. Violence and perceived threats of violence, indeed, constitute the bulk of U.S. news programming, but the violence perpetrated by adult U.S. society (from the foreign policy of the White House to individual homes and parking lots, where violent abuse so often goes unreported and unnoticed) remains, for the most part, hidden behind the fiction that "we" are "good" and the "evil" resides elsewhere.

Even as the Bush-era mantras of "family values" and "personal responsibility" infiltrated local policymaking meetings of public school boards and state senates, the responsibilities of parents to love and care for their children seemed decidedly off-limits in public debates about cases involving actual children. Parental rights had eclipsed children's rights in ways we would never tolerate from a defense attorney advocating for the rights of the accused stranger, let alone the suspected terrorist. The government's case against the attorney Lynne Stewart is merely one example of how swiftly and completely categories of "good" and "evil" are invoked and reinforced and how rights discourse is tethered to the state's interest. According to the legal scholar Elaine Cassel, Lynne Stewart, the court-appointed defense attorney for Sheikh Omar Abdel-Rahman (who is serving a life sentence for "seditious conspiracy"), was arrested for allegedly facilitating communication between her client and his supporters.[21] Specifically, Stewart and the interpreter she used to communicate with Rahman, Mohamed Yousry, were charged with "aiding and abetting a terrorist organization." This was a high-profile case for former Attorney General John Ashcroft, who appeared on David Letterman's late-night television show the night of Stewart's arrest to, in Cassel's words, "assure viewers (and potential jurors, it seems) that the 'terrorist' lawyer was guilty as charged."[22] The government contended that Stewart had acted as a "front" by allowing Rahman to relay messages in Arabic through Yousry to his supporters. In 2005, Stewart was found guilty even though "she [had] never provided any financial support, weaponry—or any other concrete aid—for any act of terrorism." Indeed, as Cassel explains, "No act of terrorism is alleged to have resulted from her actions."[23] But because we are so successfully coached to fear the terrorist, it requires very little to convince us to transfer those fears to anyone who would represent the terrorist, even someone empowered or appointed by the courts to do so.

Likewise, American public sympathy evoked by stories of the events experienced and witnessed by the survivors of the September 11 attacks was not extended to the survivors of the subsequent U.S. bombings of Afghanistan. News coverage that increasingly privileges parent over stranger and the violent construction of "American" as mutually exclusive of "Arab" or "Muslim" has shaped much of the story of violence in the world as it has been represented to the U.S. public since 2001. Steven Salaita characterizes this type of storytelling as expressing a "sentiment that is widespread in the United States, one that attaches a proper American identity to racialized values and phenotypes."[24] Salaita is absolutely correct, and yet one cannot say that violence perpetrated by parents and "Americans" (whites) is not covered at all. In fact, certain incidents are covered at length, such as the Abu Ghraib prison abuse scandal, but they tend to be depicted as shockingly rare, somehow justifiable, or accidental, freak spectacles that do not represent the "real" United States. Such presentations are made possible by the elision of context and any mention of the differential power relations structuring acts of violence in our contemporary world. The next three chapters explore the elided contexts as they pertain to teenagers and young adults in Japan and the U.S., especially those for whom violence seems the only available means of expression.

CHAPTER 4

Engendering First World Fears:

The Teenager and the Terrorist

Reports of child abuse and youth violence such as the following were long-standing staples in the U.S. media by September 11, 2001. "Physicians noticed that the boy's body was covered in bruises and, suspecting he was a victim of child abuse, reported his condition. Upon questioning his parents, officials determined that he had been abused. Child protective services took the boy into protection in October last year, but he was later returned to his parents' care" (from an article titled, "Father Beats Three-Year-Old Son to Death," January 26, 2001). "A 19-year-old youth charged with playing a central role in the murder of another 19-year-old along with a group of friends, was slapped with a life sentence on Thursday" (from an article titled, "Teen Killer Gets Life Sentence," June 2, 2000). Despite increasing budget cuts in the area of social services, child protective agencies often would be the focus of criticism in reports such as the first, and the second story was only one of many used to "prove" the "epidemic" of youth violence. Both of these reports (slightly altered to remove proper nouns), however, appeared in the *Mainichi Shimbun* and refer to incidents that took place in Japan. Even now, similar stories can be found in the Japanese and U.S. mass media virtually any given week.

Japan and the U.S., two countries that long have been represented as antipodal—with the tired and overly generalized notions of the "group-oriented versus individualistic" or "repressed versus open" society stereotypes—are, as I will show, producing events, media stories, and even childhood experiences that are far more alike than some might feel comfortable acknowledging. Social problems such as child abuse, bullying, suicide, and "delinquency" are

regular topics in education journals in both countries (albeit problems sometimes expressed in different ways and assigned different meanings), and children in Japanese and U.S. juvenile halls describe remarkably predictable histories of childhood abuse and social discrimination. Perhaps most troubling,
official and popular discourse in both countries most often places the blame for
social problems squarely on young people themselves rather than on the adults
who model and perpetuate violence on a scale that renders the so-called epi-
demics of youth violence (and abductions by strangers) Lilliputian in comparison.

Some people in North America imagine Japan to be a fundamentally different place, a phenomenon that is reinforced by attitudes of unassailable
cultural uniqueness that shape conceptions of cultural and national identity for
some people who identify as Japanese. Rather than reducing this problem to
one of choosing sides in a "universalist–particularist" debate, I will make use
of a more context-driven approach that addresses specific realities of childhood experience in relation to specific distortions, fantasies, and ideals, such
as the notion that, "over there," life is radically different in ways that preclude
meaningful comparison. Indeed, many of the institutions and policies that
shape the experiences of youth in the U.S. affect youth elsewhere. For example,
the U.S. prison system exports its private arms of profit generation to places
such as South Africa, and the means and methods of sequestering and contain-
ing youth (and adults) have proved to be both lucrative and increasingly transnational.[1] In this chapter and throughout part 2 of this book, I hope to shed
light on how youth and means of "managing" youth are marketed, but also
what such economies mean to young people themselves—in the most demonstrable and material ways. Whether in the most private spaces, in the home, in
the classroom, on the streets, in the global marketplace, or through the war
system, the culture of child abuse is very much transnational.

Adult society tolerates organized state violence or hidden (or even suspected)
violence in the home with far greater ease than we tolerate the "unruly" and
"violent" teenager.[2] We permit our own nation's violence, or violence carried
out in our name or with our tax dollars, more easily than the violence of other
nations or peoples, particularly when that violence is directed at us or our
investments. Our collective discomfort with teenagers, like "terrorists," is
structured according to boundaries between "us" and "them," which we are to
believe are clearly delineable. This is particularly confounding in the case of the
former in that we all have been teenagers even if we may resist identification
with those labeled terrorists. Nonetheless, stories of dangerous youth are read-

ily deployable, and we rarely see teenagers as "cute" or "sweet" in the way that we might see toddlers, and, of course, many teens do not present themselves that way. This tendency has consequences that contribute to "youth violence."

When prospective foster or adoptive parents comb through the overflowing files of group homes (or other state or local agencies) for children, they are far less likely to invite a teenager home than to scoop up an adorable infant or toddler, a reality that is not lost on the "tweens" and teens who know they will be raised by a state that will, in general terms, "kick them to the curb" once they turn eighteen—as is also the case in Japan, where state support for foster youth is terminated when the child reaches eighteen. Any unwillingness to adopt children past their toddler years is often overshadowed by the misleading claim that there are no children to adopt in the U.S., one of many factors cited by those promoting international adoptions. There may be lengthy waiting lists and undesirable "trial" periods for infant adoptions in many places in the U.S., but this does not mean that there are not thousands of adoptable children who never find permanent homes in most U.S. cities and counties because they are seen as "too old" or "too challenging." The problems facing teenage "system kids," particularly those brought into state protective custody due to abuse, are compounded by our attitudes regarding youth, as one child advocate explained to the Los Angeles Times: "America has a lot of fears and confusion around young people in general. You put someone in foster care on top of that, and it perpetuates a myth that these are troubled children who did something wrong."[3] The gap between such a teenager's actual experience and many adults' perception that she or he is a "bad kid" obviously does not lend itself to better understanding, let alone the kind of systemic change necessary to provide these youth with more effective support and parenting.

The discursive terrain of "youth today" is riddled with such misunderstandings: misunderstood youth, misunderstood experience, and misunderstood cultures. Such misunderstandings are not necessarily new; nor is my identification of them groundbreaking. Many of us can recall negative reactions from adults to the music we enjoyed as teenagers, music that advocated political change or drug use, or even less provocative music that was nonetheless perceived as socially disruptive or simply too loud. My aim, however, is to venture beyond attributing various misunderstandings to a generation gap and instead address how certain misunderstandings are related, how they are enforced and maintained in a climate of fear, and the very material and often deadly effects of misunderstanding violence in the lives of real young people.

Although the mass media's obsession with young bodies and young dollars is undeniable in Japan and the U.S., rarely are the unscripted and unpackaged voices of real youth included in mass mediated discussions about or representations of violence and other social problems. Even when such discussions focus on "juvenile offenders," young soldiers, or young victims of violence, the opinions and experiences of actual young people are seldom taken as seriously as those of adult "experts" by (largely adult) audiences. This absence of the very subjects about whom so many discussions are generated is particularly telling in the case of "violent youth." The process of vilification is always made easier when the "villain" is absent or incapacitated, such as when young people are sequestered in juvenile halls or hospitals, where they are tranquilized and pacified—or turn up dead, as we have seen in recent cases involving the California Youth Authority—away from the view of a world that already dismisses the thoughts and feelings of the young as not fully formed, rational, or mature enough to warrant serious attention or engagement.[4] These youth have few means of talking back to a media or society that sees them as a problem. Therefore, they can be subjected to increasingly brutal and extreme forms of punishment without the general public's knowledge of what that entails.

Duc Ta, a teenage son of Vietnamese immigrant parents in California, was sentenced to thirty-five years to life in a state prison for adults because a passenger in a car he was driving fired a gun from that car. Duc was sixteen at the time, and no one was hurt, but because the passengers in his car were supposedly "gang members" and one of them fired a weapon, Duc was subjected to a "gang enhancement" sentencing clause.[5] Duc's story received some attention when he appeared in Leslie Neale's documentary Juvies (2004), and his sentence has since been reduced to eleven years to life.[6] There are many more like Duc whose stories are never heard while they suffer in adult prisons under draconian sentences. If legislation passed by the House and pending in the Senate at the time of writing proves successful, their numbers will skyrocket. The so-called Gang Deterrence and Community Protection Act (S.155), which is sponsored by Diane Feinstein, would place many more "gang-related" prosecutions under the jurisdiction of federal courts, a process that has already begun in earnest as many Salvadoran "gang" youth are considered "terrorists" working for al Qaeda.[7] Along with Adam Schiff's proposed H.R. 970 bill, Feinstein's legislation would increase the number of situations in which youth could face the death penalty and greatly broaden the range of activity that would make one subject to "mandatory minimum sentencing."[8] The effects of such bills would fall disproportionately on youth of color. In Juvies, The clinical psychologist and author Aaron Kipnis characterizes the sentencing of youth to adult prison as "a death sentence. It is a slow execution. It is gradual genocide." Kipnis's analysis is not hyperbolic when one considers who is being locked up in juvenile halls—and adult prisons—in the United States.

A rare example of a Juvenile Court judge who speaks out against the racist differential sentencing of youth in the U.S., Judge David Ramirez of Denver shared his observations with the organization Human Rights Watch, noting, "Minority youth are placed in the most restrictive, most punitive facilities. Sixty percent of those who are locked up are either African American or Hispanic, while those groups comprise only 30 percent of Colorado's population. The disparity is greater for juveniles sentenced as adults. In December 1996, 331 institutionalized juveniles had been sentenced as adults. Of that number 40 percent were Hispanic; 30 percent were African American; 22 percent were Anglo; one percent were Native American, and 7 percent were of unknown ethnic origin."[9] Once incarcerated, these youth face additional struggles, which run the gamut from personal health and safety concerns to access to books and classes. For youth with chronic health problems, juvenile hall and adult prison can be especially deadly. As one imprisoned fourteen-year-old in Colorado explains: "I'm not afraid of fights. I'm afraid that I will have an asthma attack when I'm locked in my room at night. There are only two staff, and the nurse leaves at two in the afternoon. The staff doesn't know anything about asthma."[10]

Such experiences are endemic in Japan and the United States. They are also entirely consistent with the already debilitating, isolating, and discouraging messages youth, especially the so-called at-risk youth of color, hear every day: "If you work a little harder, if you stop hanging out with the wrong crowd, if you show respect for authority, if you stay off drugs, if you get better grades, and if you show some personal responsibility, then maybe you can pull yourself out of your pattern of bad behavior and achieve something with your life." In the case of faith-based programs, a young person may be asked: "What do you think God wants you to change about yourself?" Imagine how different it would be to hear something like this: "There is nothing wrong with you. You don't need to be fixed. Something, multiple things, are wrong with society. What do you think is wrong with society? Based on your answer, what can you do to have the kind of life you want?"

It is not difficult to see which approach would be more effective, and yet the latter is so rarely taken. Before we can serve youth, we have to listen to and understand them, *on their terms*. From there, we can accomplish much more than if we tell young people what *we* think they should do or who *we* (or God) think they should be. This might sound like common sense, but those who work with the population that needs to be heard the most are often prevented from taking such an approach. In Iowa, as is the case throughout the U.S., that population is not hard to identify. In 2005, youth of color made up only approximately 8 percent of the overall youth population in Iowa, but they constituted a third of Iowa's incarcerated youth. In Iowa City, which prides itself on being a liberal bastion, black youth are arrested at nearly seven times the rate of white youth. Such data led the *Black Commentator* to rank Iowa as "the second worst place to be black" in the U.S. (after Wisconsin). Since that article was published, Iowa has been identified as having the highest disproportionate incarceration and suspension/expulsion rates in the U.S., and black Iowans statewide and regardless of age are incarcerated at more than eleven times the rate of whites.[11]

In the U.S., we have always harmed so-called at-risk youth of color and poor youth. Their intellectual lives in particular are severely neglected. They deal with daily stress that white youth and middle-class youth do not experience. Even in Cedar Rapids, Iowa, police helicopters patrol over "the black neighborhood." There are also no places to play or hang out that do not require money in this same neighborhood. Youth dance on the street and hang out in front of their houses, making the best out of the limited space available to them. Their sole space to play is not safe though, because police will make any youth considered "too deep" on the block disperse, and these "dispersals" can be violent, humiliating, and painful. Black youth in this neighborhood and many others are most often seen as in need of punishment or correction, criminalized from the get-go and seen as a problem, and that is certainly not conducive to anyone's intellectual or personal growth. Life is not so different for oppressed youth in Japan—especially those who are not perceived to be fully or "purely" Japanese, such as *zainichi* Korean, immigrant, and other minority youth. The patterns and structures of discrimination that impinge on marginalized youth's ability to move and grow leave them vulnerable to institutional abuse too horrible for many to believe.

Manufacturing Fear and Human Experimentation

> Most people say that they form their opinions from the media and that they believe juvenile crime is escalating. . . . Contrary to news coverage, violent juvenile crime has dropped 41 percent in recent years, but even though youth crime is down, media coverage of youth crime is up, generating more public fear.—*Juvies*, 2004

After each new high-profile incident involving youth and violence, whether in Japan or the U.S., the television pundits echo the now predictable refrain: "What is wrong with children today?" The terms of the debate are shaped by very different questions when young people describe the problem of violence in their lives. The following letter, which appeared in a nationally distributed newspaper published specifically for Japanese junior high school students in 1998, was written by a female ninth-grader in response to a series of highly publicized violent attacks by teenagers in Japan:

> My first thought was that a junior high school student just like me has murdered somebody again. I was shocked, but I also felt sympathy. It's strange for kids to be expected to live up to principles and standards that adults can't live up to. . . . We hear news stories about corrupt politicians and all sorts of unethical scandals. How can a society led by adults like that raise good kids?
>
> The truth is that kids are really good, kind, and warmhearted. But society is killing our great spirit little by little. I always think about how I don't want to grow up to be an adult like today's politicians. So I'm trying not to forget the goodness of my own feelings.
>
> It's not all the fault of adults, but I'd like them to understand that they do have some responsibility in this. After all, they are the ones making a society that leads people to crime. . . .
>
> Before they worry about banning the sale of knives or other weapons, they should work on fostering a better society. I want them to make a society where we can believe in something. But maybe this is just idealistic dreaming.[12]

Teenagers in the U.S. have reasons to express similar frustration—and they also have been told that their very understandable yearnings for better parenting by adult society are idealistic or simply cute or naive. As I explained in an essay published in the *Los Angeles Times* in December 2001, and as others have noted, the U.S.–North Atlantic Treaty Organization bombings of Yugoslavia that continued as President Bill Clinton urged American youth to solve problems "without resorting to violence" presented American teenagers who watched coverage of the bombings interlaced with footage of Columbine with ample room to question the division drawn between state-sanctioned violence by adults and violence in their schools and homes.[13] Such divisions are often reflected in the words we use to convey our understandings of what kind of violence is acceptable. For example, while the word "sanctions" has "a deceptively mild ring to it," as Richard Becker explains, "the sanctions imposed by the United Nations

Security Council on Yugoslavia, . . . a country of ten million people, cut off the country's economic lifeblood."[14] Becker's choice of words and oppositional metaphor underscore how different ways of seeing or understanding require different vocabularies.

The "Crisis in Kosovo" and the "Tragedy in Colorado," as they were named by CNN, have been followed by a long list of adults' acts of organized "responses" *qua* violence and "inexplicable" youth violence, such as the U.S. invasions, occupations, and bombings of Iraq and Afghanistan or Nathaniel Brazill's murder of his teacher, Barry Grunow, in 2000. (Brazill, who was thirteen at the time of the shooting, was tried as an adult and sentenced to twenty-eight years in prison.)[15] The voices of the incarcerated (from Guantánamo to the local juvenile hall) rarely if ever emerge in the nightly discussions of these issues on the television news. In fact, young people who kill disappear from view in a variety of ways. Dylan Klebold and Eric Harris, the Columbine shooters, are dead by their own hands (as are Jeff Weise, Seung-Hui Cho, and so many others). And countless other teens, the vast majority of whom are boys of color like Brazill, are on lockdown in juvenile halls, where their voices are muzzled by psychiatric medication and isolation from potential audiences. Meanwhile, those who have decided whose lives are expendable for the good of U.S. economic-military interest rest comfortably beyond the realm of what we consider ordinary legal responsibility. The savvy teenager in juvenile hall is left to wonder whether much of the violence of his or her parents' generation (at home or in the White House) is acceptable simply because "they say so." The terms according to which we define various debates affecting youth are in many ways crazy making, producing the very conditions that fuel the "inexplicable" violence we fear.

Manufacturing an ever heightening sense of fear is both good for business and good for government in Japan and the U.S., although the focus of our fears must be carefully and diligently tended to remain within certain bounds. Here again, staying "on message" is of paramount importance. For example, capitalizing on parents' fears that their children might be abducted has served as a convenient means of advancing the application of technology with the potential to harm the very children we purport to protect and generate substantial profit. We often refer to technological aids as "devices," a telling label for innovations that, no matter how ingenious or impressive, may also have the power to destroy, such as a "nuclear device." Among the many entries under the *Oxford English Dictionary*'s definition of "device" is the following: "Something devised or contrived for bringing about some end or result; an arrangement, plan, scheme, project, contrivance; an ingenious or clever expedient; often one of an underhand or evil character; a plot, stratagem, trick." The latter notion of a "plot" or "trick" might be particularly relevant to the introduction of Radio Frequency Identification Device (RFID) technology in the lives of children. A number of schools in Japan and the U.S. have already introduced the use of RFID chips as security measures.[16] RFID tagging has been promoted as a means of tracking the movement of students to ensure that children are where they are supposed to be, although many also acknowledge that the tags can be used to police "juvenile crime." We have yet to see whether this device that we are told will protect youth will, in fact, be used to "protect" us from them.

The tiny RFID chips currently used by some schools can be attached to items of clothing and "read" at wireless tracking points in much the same way that a bar code is scanned at a library or grocery store. In the event that a child is abducted, proponents of RFID tagging contend, he or she can be more easily located, an industry claim that is leading some parents to have their children fitted with RFID implants. This claim presumes the development of an RFID infrastructure with widespread tracking points that would support the reading of tags over a large area, something that is not currently in place. (It also does not allow for the possibility that an abductor might make use of the very technology to track and locate a child.) Playing on parents' fears about their children's safety and the very understandable desire to protect their children from possible harm can be lucrative, and significant profits stand to be made by firms engaged in RFID product development, such as Applied Digital Solutions (maker of the VeriChip) and Hitachi. As is the case with many new applications for technology, the long-term health effects of RFID chipping on humans are uncertain. A study conducted by Dow Chemical in 1996 was one of several that concluded that RFID chips contributed to or caused malignant tumors in lab mice and rats.[17] However, the buzz about RFID's possibilities as a tool for parents, law enforcement, and national security agencies has all but eclipsed discussions of possible adverse reactions to human tagging.

Here again, my concern is not so much the potential efficacy of RFID technology in reuniting an abducted child with her parents as with what RFID use says about how we organize and define our fears. If our children are most likely to be harmed anywhere, it is precisely in those places deemed "safe" by current RFID use practices—for example, in schools and homes. RFID plays into our tendency to fear the stranger (and the young person herself if she is considered "at risk" for criminal activity) more than the parent. RFID tagging's potential as a means of monitoring and policing target populations is not lost on those who would like to see it used that way. The collection and use of RFID data, in other words, can be determined by the group that gains access to retrieving the data transmitted by the device. It is not difficult to conceive of a wide range of applications that would appeal to law-enforcement agencies, advertising firms, government bodies, and even organized crime syndicates, such as those, ironically, engaged in the trafficking of children into the sex industry. And if their movements could be tracked, marginalized youth who are already subjected to racial or ethnic profiling and police surveillance could face greater intrusions on their freedom to move and participate in society, and victims of human trafficking placed in involuntary sweatshop or sex industry conditions could face even greater barriers to escaping. Savvy abductors could find ways around RFID even if tracking points become sufficiently widespread to make a child locatable. For example, attempts to locate and remove the device could put children at additional risk, and future anti-RFID technology could be used to thwart or disable a tag. RFID thus fits the larger pattern of deploying lucrative fears and obscuring fears for which powerful interests do not stand to profit.

Some are already calling for RFID-busting technology, the likelihood of which could mean that any RFID profits for "security" purposes may be short-lived. Richard Stallman, a leading advocate of free and open access to technology and founder of the GNU free operating system software, was among the participants at a conference on RFID technology held at the Massachusetts Institute of Technology (MIT) on November 15, 2003. At the end of the conference, which was sponsored by the MIT Computer Science and Artificial Intelligence Laboratory, Stallman issued a call to "develop, mass-produce and sell a very cheap RFID detector and locator." He went on to propose, "It need not be able to read any data of the RFID, though that would be a nice additional feature. The central feature is that you can precisely locate the RFIDs, if any, in something you just bought or anything in your possession [and] develop, mass-produce and sell a very cheap RFID destroyer, something that you can put near an RFID or aim at an RFID and make sure it will no longer respond at all."[18] Of course, the availability of such an "RFID destroyer," even if it effectively discouraged certain uses of RFID technology, would not in and of itself prevent continued experimentation with RFID or related tracking technology on vulnerable populations such as children. "Staying on message" when it comes to RFID technology means talking about combating child abduction, juvenile crime, and other officially recognized threats. The moral problems involved in testing technology on children are masked by the rhetoric of concern for their safety.[19]

For some HIV-positive black and Latino children brought into New York City's dependency system in recent years, adult society's willingness to subject them to human experimentation has had more devastating consequences. While medical experiments on people of color have a long and enduring history in the U.S., the story of the so-called Guinea Pig Kids of New York City is so completely at odds with the official fiction of the U.S. as a country that "leaves no child behind" that it may seem more like a frightening movie plot or flat-out fiction than a coordinated effort by the city's Administration of Children's Services (ACS), pharmaceutical firms such as GlaxoSmithKline, hospitals where the drug trials are conducted, and children's foster homes to make available vulnerable children as test subjects for medical research. The ability of an official state agency to remove children from homes and place them in institutions where they would be fed untested combinations of medication for research is possible because of the fiction that the medical protocols are beneficial, that they are "best for the children." In a nightmarish example of "doublespeak," the state's intervention on behalf of the children's "best interests" appears to have taken the form of medical abuse in this case, a reality that the ACS is claiming to "investigate" more fully now that the public has learned foster children were used for the medical trials through the 1980s and until at least 2002.

Because the ACS invoked the "privacy" interests of the foster children subjected to drug trials as grounds not to disclose significant details, the exact number of foster children involved and the number who died as a result of the testing are probably still unknown. Just as the stories of incarcerated youth are kept away from scrutiny, the stories of these sequestered children are carefully guarded secrets. "Privacy" is assigned meaning by those who have the power to define and determine when it matters and to whom. The "privacy" of the HIV-positive foster youth in New York City matters because of the corporate interests behind the drug trials, and the privacy of RFID-tagged youth is deemed of secondary importance because of the corporate and other interests that stand to benefit from their surveillance. In both cases, appeals are made to "what is best for the children"—their access to medicine and their safety from abductors, respectively.

Nonetheless, alarming data have surfaced. John Solomon writes that researchers at Columbia University Medical School and the New York Presbyterian Hospital had not obtained "proper consent, information and safeguards" for foster children used in the experiments.[20] Solomon also notes that the National Institutes of Health revealed that children in Illinois were used in similar experiments and that "more than 650" foster children had been subjected to the trials "since the late 1980s."[21] One might think this official corroboration would have made the "Guinea Pig Kids" story a headline-grabber across the country, but it did not. Although both RFID and the HIV drug trials are depicted as "best for the children," there are significant differences when it comes to the children involved, which relates to how and to what extent both stories circulate. Whereas affluent parents might choose to purchase implants for their children to keep them from harm, one would be hard pressed to find examples of parents offering their children up for risky pharmaceutical trials, a reality that is not lost on Vera Sherav of the Alliance for Human Research Protection, who appears in Jamie Doran's BBC documentary *Guinea Pig Kids*:

> You would not expect too many parents to volunteer their beloved children for such experiments. This means that if the researchers want to do the experiment on children, they are going to look for vulnerable children whom they can get. And when you have a city government agency accommodating them; that is the biggest betrayal of those children. . . . Why didn't they provide the children with the current best treatment? That's the question we have. Why did they expose them to risk and pain when they were helpless? Would they have done those experiments to their own children? I doubt it. . . . The city department created a panel, an ethics committee that approved the experiments that were conducted at Incarnation House [a non-profit medical facility and boarding home for HIV-positive children governed by Columbia University and the Catholic Archdiocese of New York]. There's only one pesky detail: The panelists all come from the hospitals that conduct the trials, so they all are stakeholders in saying that it was perfectly all right.[22]

Among the most confounding stories reported in *Guinea Pig Kids* is that of Jacklyn Hoerger, a pediatric nurse who worked at a foster-care site where HIV-positive children underwent the drug trials and who later decided to adopt two children with whom she had worked at that facility. After taking the children home and trying to care for them according to the research protocols, she noticed that their health only worsened. Hoerger describes taking the children off the experimental medication, at which point their health quickly improved, but once the ACS noticed that the children were no longer participating in the trials, the children were taken back into the foster-care system, where the protocol was resumed, and Hoerger was convicted of child abuse for not complying with the drug trials.[23]

The Orwellian circumlocutions necessary to depict attempts to care as "abuse" and dangerous experimentation as "care" are indicative of limits in the effectiveness of abuse prevention and intervention in the U.S. The very children who belong to communities subjected to the most police and social-service surveillance are the ones most easily sacrificed to potentially lethal "care" once in a system that, due in large part to gross public underfunding and defunding, forges ties with moneyed interests that make no bones about their focus on putting profits over children. In a country where countless self-help and recovery resources for survivors of abuse are manufactured for profit, it is perhaps telling that so few resources are directed to the elimination of childhood suffering and that so many resources are used to increase it.

Personal Responsibility

Manipulating language to deflect attention away from suffering in which we play a role (as taxpayers, consumers, etc.) is necessary for the maintenance of both the domestic and international hierarchies that bolster the governments of the U.S. and Japan. The phrase "personal responsibility" is surely familiar to many in both countries. For example, those in the U.S. who denounce welfare recipients as "lazy" often use the phrase. By not exercising "personal responsibility" and contributing to the workforce, those on welfare act as a drain on the economy, according to such critics. Similarly, members of historically oppressed communities who do not "pull themselves up by their own bootstraps" are responsible for any economic or social hardships they endure in this "land of opportunity." This pseudo-logic is easily translatable offshore, as is the case in arguments regarding how much Third World workers "benefit" from sweatshop wages. By virtue of our "largesse," in other words, poor people can obtain employment and we can purchase cheaper goods. This win–win situation in theory is quickly undone when one begins to examine the relationships that structure the dynamic (not to mention the material realities of life for the workers). Of course, for the rhetoric of "personal responsibility" to be compelling in any of these instances, one must conveniently leave out larger questions of responsibility, such as: Who benefits from a highly stratified society (or world) in which so many people cannot afford to pay rent or feed their families even when they work one or more full-time jobs? Who benefits when historical and ongoing oppression (within or across borders) is not addressed in the education system or workplace?

"Personal responsibility" was invoked in a particularly distorted fashion after three Japanese citizens were taken hostage in Iraq in 2004. Upon their release, the three hostages, the youngest of whom (eighteen-year-old Imai Noriaki) was attempting to study the effects of depleted uranium weapons, and their families were subjected to vicious attacks and harassment. Chief among the criticisms lobbed at the three was the claim that their actions in Iraq showed a lack of "personal responsibility." The three were in Iraq not as part of the Japanese contribution to the U.S. war and occupation efforts but to assist Iraqi people directly in defiance of the war. Government officials went as far as to demand that the three freed "anti–Japanese" rogues pay reparations for their repatriation expenses, an official response that was in keeping with the lack of official sympathy shown during their captivity: "Even as the kidnappers were still threatening to burn alive the three hostages, Yukio Takeuchi, a top official in the Foreign Ministry said of the three, 'When it comes to a matter of safety and life, I would like them to be aware of the basic principle of personal responsibility.' "[24] Like other young people who risk personal injury to express their solidarity with endangered and oppressed people, the hostages were aid workers and investigators who divested themselves of some of their First World privilege and entered a dangerous environment to combat suffering for which they felt at least partly responsible.

Yet their actions were roundly denounced as lacking "personal responsibility." Given the close relationship between government and media (in both Japan and the U.S.), this distortion was every bit as predictable as it was required. To allow the hostages their motivations would be to call into question Japan's participation in the war. One could argue that the Japanese government's fear of exposure to such criticism required that the "anti–Japanese" released hostages be the objects of public outrage. To express solidarity or sympathy with the hostages (or Iraqis) would be treasonous, just as was the responsibility the Japanese hostages personally felt to "them" and not "us."

The literary and cultural critic Naitō Chizuko maintains that the internalization of "us" versus "them" divisions of this type is as much a product of the Japanese emperor system as it is in the service of Japan's relationship to the United States. Naitō explains that the Japanese language itself was once considered to be to the "property" of the emperor and remains shaped by an emperor-centered structure, even though it has been conceptually reorganized since the onset of modernity. Even today, she posits, one "cannot help but be deeply affected by the structure of the emperor system." In other words, Naitō suggests what I would call a kind of emperor-lepsis, a socio-linguistic structure organized around an absent but central or genitive figure. Naitō explains how this "emperor-lepsis," or "passing" of the emperor system by omission, works:

> The emperor system structure that has lived on in the Japanese language is a structure that, at its center, is empty, nothing. And we are not supposed to question the meaning of that emptiness. The "Emperor" who is supposed to be at that center has turned into a kind of unspoken premise that, "if you are Japanese, anyone would know," and that feeling or sense that "any Japanese person would understand" has come to supplement "Him" in this structure. The feeling that "if you're Japanese, anyone would understand" is related to an exclusionary consciousness of nation or race and extends to exclude even those "incorrect Japanese" who don't try to understand that feeling.[25]

Naitō goes on to cite as an example former Prime Minister Koizumi Junichirō's references to the "friendship" between Japan and the U.S. when explaining why Japan supported U.S. war efforts. She asserts that this "friendship" is taken to be a given. The premises behind the "friendship" are left unexamined as obvious. The "obvious premise," she writes, "becomes the empty center and remains unchallenged" as one of the things "any Japanese would understand." Because the exhortation not to challenge the "empty center" is so effective and compelling, Naitō asserts, "People get the feeling that they more or less understand" and that "without knowing it, people who use the Japanese language are interpolated into this narrative structure, oblivious to the emperor system that makes it possible."[26]

The notion of an unchallengeable discursive space that demanded allegiance from any "correct" Japanese surely felt real to the three "incorrect Japanese" hostages as they confronted the backlash unleashed against them upon their release. Nowhere in the discussion of "personal responsibility" was there room to articulate and explain the horrors they had witnessed and experienced or the motivations that had led them to Iraq, because those experiences and motivations were off message. The renowned Japanese psychiatrist and trauma expert Saitō Satoru interviewed the three upon their return and, according to the New York Times, said that "the stress they were enduring now was 'much heavier' than what they endured during their captivity in Iraq." Furthermore:

> Asked to name their three most stressful moments, the former hostages told him, in ascending order: the moment when they were kidnapped on

their way to Baghdad, the knife-wielding incident, and the moment they watched a television show the morning after their return here and realized Japan's anger with them. "Let's say the knife incident, which lasted about 10 minutes, ranks 10 on a stress level," Saito said in an interview at his clinic Thursday. "After they came back to Japan and saw the morning news show, their stress level ranked 12."[27]

Nonetheless, one of the three, Takato Nahoko, indicated that the stress brought on by the public criticism only deepened her commitment to her very different understanding of "personal responsibility." Takato made clear her plans to return to Iraq to continue her aid work and told reporters that "she and the government didn't see eye to eye on exactly what 'personal responsibility' meant."[28]

The story Takato offers regarding her early life and motivations is very much in keeping with the response to trauma (described in chapter 1) that compels some people to make helping others their life's work:

> People still wonder why Takato risked her life to help the street children of Iraq. Quite simply, she saw herself in those children, she said in an interview after the Tokyo news conference. The kids, some as young as elementary school age, smoking cigarettes and inhaling paint thinner from dawn until dusk, reminded her of her own youth. As a child, Takato was a troublemaker who started smoking at 12, got hooked on paint thinner at 13 and soon afterward tried hashish. It wasn't until she moved to metropolitan Tokyo to attend university that she began to get an idea of what she wanted to do with her life.[29]

Socialization to identify with the powerful, the aggressor, and the strong requires that youth on drugs and "subversives" who identify with the suffering of the weak be cast as deviant, inappropriate, and, if necessary, criminal. The outrage directed at someone like Takato is proportional to the threat such a person represents to the fiction that "we" as the powerful may not be the "good guys" after all.

In an essay that appeared in the *New York Times* shortly after the hostages were released, Norimitsu Onishi makes an interesting observation regarding this phenomenon, one that transcends the specific way in which he may have intended it: "The former hostages' transgression was to ignore a government advisory against traveling to Iraq. But their sin, in a vertical society that likes to think of itself as classless, was to defy what people call here *okami*, or, literally, 'what is higher.' "[30] *Okami*, as will be addressed at length in chapter 6, is also a way to refer to the emperor, and one can argue that the three former hostages were in contravention of their roles as imperial subjects, not necessarily or exclusively a Japanese one given Japan's support role in relation to a larger empire in the Iraq war. The top-down ordering of a society in which certain lives are assigned greater value than others certainly complicates the meaning of "personal responsibility" when uttered by those near the top toward those at the bottom or those who attempt to advocate for those at or near the bottom.

On the Virtues of Treason

Throughout this chapter, I have described ways in which we are encouraged to be afraid and outraged, provided that our fear and outrage are directed at appropriate targets—provided that we stay on message in word and deed. We anticipate further terrorism without considering ways in which we might prevent inciting it, and we anticipate youth violence while subjecting some youth to conditions that can fuel violence. Our optic enables our outrage at those who speak or act in ways that indicate we may, in fact, be manufacturing the terrorism and youth violence we fear. The precariousness of these formulations is etched into our collective consciousness, a wellspring of anxiety that keeps us on edge. We know something is wrong, but if we accept the notion that we are always and invariably "the good guys," we limit our ability to decipher what that something is and can only wait for the blow to come. There is a kind of desperation to the moment I have attempted to flesh out in this chapter thus far. To be so afraid of questions that one would eliminate a poet's honorary position, to describe aid work in a war zone as "irresponsible," to implant a device in a child's arm, or to be so unnerved by a child's wish for better behavior on the part of adults that one condescendingly dismisses her as "overly idealistic" might be understood as panic responses. The more tenaciously we cling to narratives that refuse us any identity other than that of "the good guys," the more warranted our fear and panic become. In other words, by disallowing uncomfortable self-reflection, we almost make certain that someone else will do that "reflecting" for us.

In chapter 1, I argued that poetry and fiction provide a unique vehicle through which stories of traumatic suffering can be expressed, especially when such stories are denied a space to emerge in everyday discourse. Much the same can be said of dissent. When dissent is increasingly discouraged (or even criminalized), art offers one way for the officially prohibited or unpopular to find expression.[31] Expressing empathy for "the enemy" is particularly risky. One example of such risky artistic dissent is a song written in response to an earlier hostage crisis. On April 22 (April 23 in Japan), 1997, the four-month takeover of the Japanese Embassy in Lima by the Tupac Amaru Revolutionary Army (MRTA) came to a dramatic end as Peruvian Special Forces burst into the building, killing all of the rebels, including Nestor Cerpa, who was assumed to be the popular insurgent leader. All but one of seventy-two hostages survived the Peruvian government's "rescue" mission. In recent years, we have learned that at least eight of the rebels surrendered to the military forces but were shot, execution-style, from behind.[32] The singer and songwriter Nakajima Miyuki released the song "4.2.3." (in reference to April 23) one year after the Peruvian government's siege of the embassy. The song, which recounts Nakajima's reaction to the end of the hostage crisis, takes issue with a kind of cultural or national chauvinism that deems the lives of those identified as "us" as mattering more than the lives of "them."

The lyrics refer to Japanese television reporters' celebrations of the safe release of the Japanese hostages even as downed guerrilla fighters were shown being carried out on stretchers. At the end of the song, she sings: "This country is dangerous. / We commit the same mistakes again and again / all the while saying we hope for peace. / It doesn't seem to matter how cold-hearted we can be / when it comes to things we don't call 'Japanese.' "[33] Calling into question what it means to value only "one's own" or the very category "one's own," Nakajima's song connects public responses of relief (over the safety of what she describes as "Japanese they didn't even know") to the Japanese government, the mass media, and nationalism. Nakajima has been a regular figure on New Year's special television singing programs and in other very mainstream musical events. While many of the songs she sings on such occasions may incorporate similar themes, the explicit political commentary underwriting "4. 2. 3." more or less guaranteed that it would not make the corporate play list or be used to help ring in a new year.

Nakajima was not alone in expressing profound discomfort about that day at the time. Subcomandante Marcos, the Zapatistas' spokesperson, and others noted that the MRTA had been negotiating a peaceful resolution with the administration of Peruvian President Alberto Fujimori even as Fujimori was planning the military action to end the dispute. However, Nakajima's song focuses on the subjectivity of Japanese viewers, of a general public that accepted so easily the story of "dangerous rebels" as threats to "good Japanese." To engage seriously the question of why the MRTA would choose to take over the Japanese

Embassy would, after all, require some uncomfortable reflection. What role did Japan play in the conditions the MRTA found objectionable? By reducing their concerns to the catchall category of "communist" (read, "bad") and by focusing on "human interest" stories involving the released hostages, the media made it easier for the messier questions of motive to be overlooked. Coaxed into the false sense of security that we are always right, we are inevitably shocked by the desperate attempts of others to tell us otherwise; such acts are "inexplicable," according to the interpretive models with which we are familiar. In the formulaic official and mass-mediated versions of events, we can only be the victims and the heroes. Like the MRTA, kids who lash out to say we, as adult society, are hurting them are all too easily written off as menaces, as "lost causes," as "crazy."

The two strands of the terrorist and the teenage killer are woven together into a fictional exploration of the Japanese Embassy takeover in Hoshino Tomoyuki's novella *Uragiri Nikki* (The Treason Diaries; 1998).[34] Lima is the setting for *The Treason Diaries*, the story of Yukinori, the son of a Japanese father and Japanese American mother who ends up living in exile in Peru after murdering his teacher in Japan when he is sixteen years old. In Peru, Yukinori oscillates between attempting to shed his national identity by, for example, refusing to speak Japanese, and living in a dissociative fantasy world in which time, place, and even self can disappear. His embattled relationship to Japan and desire to disappear, both of which stem from childhood feelings of abandonment and alienation, culminate in his assumption of the role of "traitor" (traitor to nation, race, and family). Five years after he arrives in Peru, Yukinori is assisting the MRTA ("Maruta" in the novella) in the embassy takeover: "Yukinori was assigned to spy on the hostages. On December 17, when the Ambassador was hosting a gala in honor of the emperor's birthday, a rocket bomb was fired into the courtyard behind the embassy. That was the cue for Yukinori and Kiyoto, who had snuck in disguised as waiters, to quickly remove their white overcoats and try to pass as guests and pretend to be pushed around by the masked insurgents rushing in through the hole that had been made in the wall."[35] Hoshino's insertion of two Japanese characters as Maruta operatives passing as waiters is not without precedent. Released hostages reported that several Japanese rebel supporters, including "two ersatz waiters," might have been working with the MRTA rebels.[36]

In the novella, Yukinori's memories of the teacher he killed collapse into his experience of the present when the government sends in the Special Forces. Amid the chaos, he sees a vision of three corpses bound together by thread-like "blood veins." The bodies are Yukinori's own and those of Kiyoto, the other Japanese Maruta sympathizer, and the teacher Yukinori had stabbed to death back in Japan. In Yukinori's hallucination, he and Kiyoto, who are about to be killed by the Peruvian Special Forces, are iconic victims along with the woman Yukinori himself killed. To explain how Yukinori comes to link the three, even while he says that he himself does not understand it, I will describe Hoshino's portrait of Yukinori and how the young man remembers his parents and the murder of his teacher, as well as who Kiyoto is.

Yukinori is born in the U.S. to the Japanese American lover of a Japanese man who runs away to Japan to avoid parenthood. Almost immediately after giving birth, the mother takes Yukinori to Japan and leaves him there with the father who did not want him, and that is where Yukinori remains until he is sixteen. When he reflects on killing his teacher, Yukinori ends up talking not about her but about his parents and his rage directed at them, particularly his father. He recalls looking at the bleeding body of his teacher and seeing in her the mother whose face he cannot even remember—and, more pointedly, regretting not having killed his father instead. Yukinori's rage toward his parents cannot be contained and eventually spills out into a blanket condemnation of Japanese and American adult societies as "the enemy."

Yukinori is presented with a theory to explain his rage when he meets Kiyoto, who also left Japan for Peru after committing murder; Kiyoto killed two younger children, a detail that clearly evokes the Sakakibara murders, which took place in that same spring of 1997 and will be discussed at length in the next chapter. For Kiyoto, "exile" in Peru is not punitive; it is, rather, a personal choice and an opportunity. Kiyoto tells Yukinori that he decided against living in the U.S. and came to Peru instead on a mission to "change society." When Yukinori asks Kiyoto why he chose Peru, Kiyoto expresses his understanding of how people like the two of them can experience and accomplish more in Peru than they can in Japan or the U.S.

Kiyoto describes himself as having been repelled out of bounds (hajikareta) and Peru as "a country repelled out of bounds" (hajikareta kuni), a place where people who have been cast off or repelled can band together.[37] Kiyoto argues that there is no possibility for out-of-bounds people to form a community and organize in Japan. Peru, Kiyoto believes, offers an alternative to Japan that the U.S. does not. The U.S., as more "in bounds" than the "out-of-bounds" Third World, cannot give the traumatized, criminalized, and ostracized of the First World an escape route, according to Kiyoto. Kiyoto also decries Japan as a place where the hajikareta are not accepted. Peru, he tells Yukinori, can give them such a chance. It is the "promised land" for the disenfranchised, the oppressed, and the cast aside. These ideas and words are new to Yukinori, and he feels reborn after hearing them.

The faulty premise on which Kiyoto's theory is built—that First World defectors and runaways can escape and find "their own" in the Third World—does not prevent the young men from taking up arms with Maruta. The First World experiences that engendered their rage do not go away, but they also, obviously, do not translate into full participation in and appreciation of the Maruta revolution. The sources of Yukinori's dissociative rage and Maruta's political rage are still too different, even though they intersect here and there. Put simply, Yukinori wants to kill his parents, to hold them responsible in death for his suffering, to abolish his family line, and to make Japanese adults bleed. At one point, for example, he fantasizes about dropping an atomic bomb on Japan and using a machine gun to riddle his father's body with holes. Maruta, like its real-life counterpart, is motivated by a desire to end the neoliberal economic policies that structure Peru's dependence on Japan and the U.S. There is a globalized component to Yukinori's rage, as well. His very existence is interstitial, bound up in the relationship between two First World nations, Japan and the U.S., the countries of his parents, and the possibilities for movement between them. His last days are played out in a country where the policies of those two nations interlock and are deeply felt. The MRTA also sees itself as having been born of First World incursions into Third World local economies and daily life.

The Diaries of a Race Traitor

Kiyoto writes a "treason diary," which is reminiscent of some of the Sakakibara boy's writings and which Kiyoto says he intends to publish. Yukinori also keeps a diary in which he records his thoughts about killing his teacher, Michiko Sensei. Sometimes, we are told, Yukinori would write about the murder all day long, and each time he rewrites the story of the murder, he remembers and incorporates new details. The murder of Michiko Sensei is another key feature of this novel likely to remind readers of headline news stories, particularly the killing of a teacher by her eighth-grade student in January 1998, one of a spate of so-called butterfly-knife incidents involving youth. In fact, we cannot forget such real-life stories as we read the repetitions of Yukinori's murder—or, more accurately, his memories of the murder—which he constantly revisits, revises, and replays.

After stabbing Michiko Sensei to death, Yukinori escapes to Peru undercover. His father makes the arrangements and procures a false passport, telling Yukinori that by sparing him incarceration in Japan, he is absolving himself of all paternal responsibility once and for all, that from that point onward they no longer have any bond. Kiyoto, on the other hand, claims responsibility for his crimes and actually serves time in a juvenile hall. Because (like the Sakakibara boy), Kiyoto was such a reviled and feared figure whose identity was known, his parents insisted that he leave Japan upon his release. They said he could never lead a "normal" life in Japan. Kiyoto agrees only under the condition that he will go to Peru.

Kiyoto tells Yukinori that he chose Peru because he had heard rumors that Yukinori, another infamous killer teen, was there. Yukinori questions this story because Kiyoto also claims some connection to the underground Maoist Kiseki-ha ("Shining Red" Faction, an obvious allusion to both the Sendero Luminoso [Shining Path] and Japanese Red Army Faction)—hence, the desire to "change society." Kiyoto is also involved in a plan to blow up the emperor's residence in Japan. While not explicitly stated, the timing of the embassy takeover to coincide with a celebration of the emperor's birthday and this detail about a plot against the emperor evoke speculations that arose at the time regarding the possibility that the Japanese Red Army did play a role in the siege of the Japanese Embassy in Peru. These details also hark back to what I described earlier as "emperor-lepsis" and Naitō's notion of the emperor as the "empty center." While rarely mentioned, the emperor's presence is nonetheless central throughout and, in a sense, generates the plot of *The Treason Diaries*. In other words, he is what Naitō calls the "unspoken given."

In *The Treason Diaries*, the anti-emperor system and anti-neoliberal threads merge, appropriately, on a college campus, where Kiyoto introduces Yukinori to radicals with names like Abraham Cerpa (Nestor Cerpa was the real leader of the Tupac Amaru killed at the embassy), Mary Heidegger, and Kisaragi Gilvanio, members of a collective that trains in martial arts and allies itself with Maruta in efforts to end global poverty and discrimination. Japanese-language study is central to their training. Kiyoto leads the revolutionary language drills, calling out, "Down with Neo-Liberalism (*Datō shinjiyūshugi*)!," and the others repeat the phrase back to him. "Where is your house, Abraham?" "My house is the world" (*Watashi no uchi wa sekai desu*). The marijuana-smoking Kisaragi, also a pseudonym adopted by a character in Hoshino's novel *Lonely Hearts Killer*, takes on this old Japanese name for the second month, she says, so that her real identity will not be known. Mary is Canadian and perhaps vaguely reminiscent of Lori Berenson, a U.S. citizen who was convicted of treason in Peru (under a

Fujimori-era court) and is currently serving a twenty-year sentence for allegedly having aided the MRTA, a charge she continues to deny.[38]

Abraham Cerpa attempts to recruit Yukinori, and Kiyoto tells Yukinori that after the embassy action, they will sneak into Japan with the help of comrades to attack the emperor's palace. Kiyoto implores Yukinori to agree because all those living on the margins, especially those of mixed heritage, should form an alliance to topple the oppressors, who are, of course, the white ruling class of North America and Europe and the ruling class of Japan. By this point, after a night of drugs, sex, and political education, Yukinori agrees to join the revolution against global poverty and discrimination and soon after feels it no longer matters whether he writes in his diary in Spanish or Japanese, suggesting that even his relationship to language has been opened up by revolutionary internationalism.

The detail about Kiyoto's status as a Japanese underground revolutionary is subject to doubt. Kiyoto, who had beaten to death the two young children back in Japan, might also be Kiyoto the revolutionary traitor to Japan. He could also be a savvy poser who has created such an identity to become part of the movement. Yukinori and others are easily swayed by Kiyoto's fluent rhetoric and charismatic personality. He could be using Maruta. After all, Yukinori tells us that in the critical moments of the embassy siege, Kiyoto passes the Maruta false information. He could be an agent provocateur. The CIA is in the story too. But Yukinori does not seem to care whether Kiyoto lies to him about his reasons for being in Peru or not. His feelings for Kiyoto, whom he sometimes wants to kill, and his decision to join the rebels are more personal. For Yukinori, his act of rebellion against the very country he left is motivated by a highly personal rage, the feeling that gnaws at him in the form of an urge to stab or beat up people throughout the story, and that is the rage he feels toward his father. As he anticipates his death or execution at the behest of Japan for his final act of disobedience, Yukinori imagines his father's flesh embedded in the carnage and rubble around him. Almost as if to scream out, "You made me what I am," Yukinori invokes his father and Japan throughout.

While in the end Maruta's goals are not achieved, Yukinori's are in a sense, because he believes his own death will precipitate the (at least symbolic) death of his father. The clue for this reading appears early on when Yukinori says he wants to stab his father to stop a kind of hereditary disease, something "unclean" that Yukinori believes his father passes on. However, Yukinori also says that this alone would not be enough to end the cycle, that he wants to kill his father's parents, their parents, and continuing back through the line of his ancestors until the entire family line is eliminated. If not, he thinks he should kill himself as a kind of preemptive strike against the line's future. What more radical act can the "race traitor" perform than commit suicide, than to sabotage the continuation of the "race" through one's own body? Yukinori sees "no way out" of what ails him other than the destruction of this family line. He realizes that killing his teacher was a "mistake" not in the sense that he regrets it, but in the sense that it did not achieve that goal. Becoming a traitor and risking his life in an act of defiance against the nation of his father, however, does.

In her discussion of literature written in Japanese and the emperor system, Naitō issues a call to novelists. "Of course, as long as it is written in Japanese," she writes, "one cannot be completely free of the emperor system, but it is necessary to take it on consciously in order to resist the myriad forms of discrimination this structure produces in contemporary culture and society."[39] I see Hoshino as taking up Naitō's call by questioning that "which any Japanese should understand"—whether in his novels challenging the emperor system itself or, as is the case in *The Treason Diaries*, in the notion that youth violence is beyond the realm of our understanding and thus not our responsibility, that the "inexplicability" of youth violence is a "given." This is played out most dramatically in the final passage of the novel when Yukinori, for a moment, feels like he and Kiyoto have actually taken over everything with their presence, that they are "omnipresent" even as everything is falling apart. Perhaps we might think of this as a brief, albeit imaginary, fulfillment of different patricidal fantasies that find expression, however fleetingly, in a shared moment of violent resistance against father figures: Yukinori's own father and the emperor of Japan.

Hoshino thus brings together headline news stories, that which is familiar to "every Japanese," and combines them in such as way as to recast the teen killer as an ally of the Third World "terrorist." Both figures, the "terrorist" and the "teen," may evoke fears related to the maintenance of First World security, but Hoshino's story in effect places them in the same "army." We might thus consider the possibility that Hoshino's patricidal fiction is also directed at a literary "father"—at Mishima Yukio, who created "inexplicably" and "sensationally" bad children, some of whom engage political causes, and who was himself a devout defender of the emperor system. The post-nationalist, post-patriarchal desire (and its attendant treasonous, patricidal rage) one finds in Hoshino's novels speak to, about, and for subjectivities that can find little or no accommodation in the structures of nationness or patriarchy that have framed fiction such as Mishima's. One could even say that these desires seek to destroy, to render obsolete those very structures of nation and patriarchy. There is a certain irony, thus, that Hoshino was awarded the Mishima Prize in Fiction.

Hoshino and another prominent postwar novelist, the Nobel laureate Ōe Kenzaburō, share anti-nationalist and anti-militarist sensibilities, as is evident in an interview the younger writer gave to a British newspaper for an article on Ōe:

> Ōe is very independent, says [the editor of the literary journal Gunzō], adding: "For people like Shintaro Ishihara, the conservative, pro-military governor of Tokyo, Ōe is a pain in the ass." But for Tomoyuki Hoshino, a novelist in his 30s and winner of the Yukio Mishima Prize in 2000, he exemplifies commitment. "It's high time we look back to the era after the war," he says. "My generation has to take up the themes Ōe has been wrestling with." Hoshino sees Ōe as rewriting the political works of his youth in light of the "rise of extreme nationalism and yearnings for militarism." He believes literature can act against that future by shedding light on the psychology of those who want to be engulfed in it.[40]

Times are different, so it does not play out in simple analogy, but like writers in earlier points in history who have "given voice" to a generation (such as those who expressed the vacuity and humiliations of immediate postwar Japan), Hoshino brings to his writing inchoate and "dispersed" voices of youth or cries of youth that find no avenues of expression within the commercially mediated venues available in contemporary Japan—or are found only as fragments here and there in the media. Hoshino's is also a significant presence in the contemporary Japanese literary scene. For example, a novella of his appears alongside a piece by Ōe in the New Year's special issue of the literary journal Gunzō in 2005. And in January 2006, the preeminent literary journal Bungei released a special issue dedicated to Hoshino and his work. Hoshino's fiction is often characterized by critics and readers as "difficult," which I take to mean his plots are sufficiently layered and complex so as to preclude a quick or simply "fun" read. They are decidedly uncomfortable works. (Much the same can be said of Ōe's early works.) Relevant to any discussion of what makes Hoshino's writing distinct is the question of subjectivity, a core concept in modern Japanese literary criticism. Hoshino's views reveal why, in part, his depictions of youth violence diverge so much from the ubiquitous sensationalized narratives.

Subjectivity's, or shutaisei's, purported proprietary hold on the modern Japanese novel has been widely asserted by celebrated literary theorists such as Karatani Kōjin. In a journal entry on his website in January 2005, Hoshino takes up the question of shutaisei through a critique of what he calls *naimen no mondai*, or "the problem of interiority"—of what lies beneath the surface. Responding to well-known "postmodern" and "post-structuralist" characterizations of Japan as a surface society and Japanese culture as one of forms and exterior concerns—I assume he is thinking of Roland Barthes here—Hoshino writes that he finds this configuration to be an easy way out of examining intersubjectivity, the impact we have *in relationship with* others. In other words, he asserts that while an emphasis on surface forms may be comforting for the illusion it offers of inner life as contained—as private or even hidden—it actually serves to deflect attention away from the messier and even brutal manifestations of interconnectedness.

In our conversations, Hoshino has elaborated on this by saying an obsession with interiority brings out what he calls the most "grotesque" in Japanese society—everything from Internet suicide pacts to the vilification of the Japanese aid workers who were taken hostage in Iraq. Hoshino's primary concern is that a reverence for "subjectivity" actually serves the state's interest. This is particularly significant when it comes to the subjectivities of youth. We often think of young people as "empty" and waiting to be filled with the knowledge or experience that will move them closer to adulthood. Because we already see them as empty, it is relatively easy for us to impose our own interpretations on them, to create subjectivities for them. What, then, are we to make of these meanings we assign to adolescent subjectivity? And how might we reinterpret the subjectivity of the "teenage menace"?

CHAPTER 5

"Killer Kids" and "Cutters"

The emotional state of the chronically abused child ranges from a
baseline of unease, through intermediate states of anxiety and dys-
phoria, to extremes of panic, fury, and despair. . . . This emotional
state . . . cannot be terminated by ordinary means of self-soothing.
Abused children discover at some point that the feeling can be
most effectively terminated by a major jolt to the body. The most
dramatic method of achieving this result is through the deliberate
infliction of injury.

—Judith Herman, *Trauma and Recovery*, 108–9

Most Americans absolutely refuse to give up their right to inflict
pain on their children.

—Salim Muwakkil, *Chicago Tribune*, September 25, 2000

A Generation on the Verge

Whether we are in Japan or the U.S., we are routinely encouraged to
internalize the fear of the teenage menace. In this chapter, I not
only examine media accounts of youth violence, but also apply the
same interpretive and analytical skills to the writings of actual young people
that we might apply to media, literary, professional, or official adult discourse.
Looking at how young people describe their own feelings and experiences can
reveal much of what gets left out of the master narratives of youth violence that
shape so much journalism and even public policy in contemporary Japan and

the U.S. In other words, the different stories youths tell often reveal gaps or inconsistencies in our own. Central to my discussion will be a recognition of the complex interplay in the relationships among individual experience, available means for self-expression, and the social and cultural climates (from the home to the streets) that both limit and determine how young people see themselves and their lives in larger social and community contexts. As is the case in the U.S., the fear of violent teenage boys in Japan shows up in everything from television news programming to public policy and political campaigns. We might think of this fear as a constitutive feature of modern and contemporary consumer societies, where it is continually shaped and reinforced by what I earlier described as a culture (or cultures) of child abuse. In this chapter, I will discuss specific representations of violent teenagers taken from media and literature produced in Japan and the U.S. Because the representational and discursive impinge on and affect the subjectivities and experiences of those who are the objects of news media reporting, my coupling of media and literary analysis with actual cases is ultimately a necessary one.

To introduce my discussion of the violent teenage boy as he emerges in corporate media and the adult imagination in contemporary Japan, I will turn to the opening sequence of the movie *Go* (2001), directed by Yukisada Isao (and based on the novel and *manga* of the same name by Kazuki Kaneshiro), which depicts the struggles of a *zainichi* (North) Korean (Korean Japanese or Korean "Resident of Japan") teen who copes, sometimes violently, with his experiences of abuse and discrimination. The film begins with the protagonist (Sugihara) on a basketball court with a group of other boys who do not pass the ball to him and, eventually, throw the ball at him aggressively. After making an impressive basket, Sugihara attacks the boys who have been deriding him. What is interesting about this episode is Sugihara's narration. He begins by reciting what might be described as a relevant vocabulary list: *minzoku* (race, people, nation), *sokoku* (homeland), *kokka* (state, country, nation), *tanitsu* (unity), *aikoku* (beloved country, love for a country, patriotism), *tōitsu* (unification, oneness), *dōhō* (brethren, countrymen), and so on, culminating in the final words in the list, *konketsu* (miscegenation), *junketsu* (pure blood), and *danketsu* (union, solidarity). Sugihara intones this chant-like list (with occasional comments about the absurdity or disgusting nature of the words) as we watch the other boys taunt him on the court. After completing his list, Sugihara tells the audience that he was "born in Japan" and sees himself as "no different from a Japanese person," but that from the perspective of the other boys he is "zainichi" or "resident (Korean)," that last word being spoken not by Sugihara himself, but by the other boys (derogatorily) as they throw the ball at him. After making the basket, Sugihara explains to us that he then "lost it," at which point he proceeds to attack the other boys.

Kireru (the intransitive form of "to cut") is the word he uses to describe the moment when he is no longer able or willing to contain his rage, the word that signifies the moment of resistance, when he lashes out against the oppression signified by his vocabulary list. In the late 1990s, this slang term used by many Japanese youth made its way into mainstream public discourse, and it now appears with regularity in serious newsmagazines, television programs, and heated boardroom meetings. "Kireru" is not a new word, but the novel use of "kireru" in reference to a particular kind of feeling state is an inflection of recent generations of Japanese youth. Perhaps the closest equivalents to this expression in English would be "to snap" or "to lose it," but neither of these phrases captures the violent tenor of a term that draws on the image of cutting or slicing, a verb that casts its subject as someone whose anger and frustration have cut through the layers of socialization that keep members of a society "in check" and composed. That some of the kids who are said to have "cut" in this way have committed violent crimes with knives only underscores the power of this expression in contemporary Japanese parlance.

Although the verb is often invoked to describe inexplicable or sudden and unprecedented violence, the kireru moment depicted in Go can be interpreted as a response to cumulative stress. The experiences and feelings leading up to it are represented, in shorthand, by the vocabulary list the protagonist recites to convey experiences of oppression, discrimination, exclusion, and rejection. He "loses it," but he does so for a reason, or for multiple reasons. Hoshino Tomoyuki's novel use of the verb hajiku (to snap or repel), and specifically of its passive form, hajikareru, in The Treason Diaries (discussed in the previous chapter) in place of the ubiquitous "kireru" connotes rejection or exclusion. Hoshino's use of "hajiku" thus invokes the very causality elided in most mainstream uses of "kireru." The scene in Go contextually endows "losing it" with meaning, embedding the story of causes (social discrimination, bullying, etc.) in the kireru moment. This is the meaning of "kireru" I will explore to complicate the myth of teenage violence as simply inexplicable and to challenge the complacent and formulaic invocation of the "inexplicable" as a means of forestalling understanding and intervention.

At the same time that "kireru" was becoming a buzzword in mainstream Japanese media, the verb "to cut" was also being reconfigured to describe another behavior associated with "troubled youth" in the United States. Although the act of self-mutilation itself is not new, a growing awareness and interest in how and why many children cut themselves or otherwise deliberately harm themselves gave rise to the buzzword "cutters," an umbrella label for those who use knives, razors, or other sharp objects to cut their own bodies, carve words into their limbs, or mutilate body parts. As has been the case with the word "kireru," "cutter" has been used by everyone from daytime talk-show hosts to clinicians and academics to describe what is often portrayed as a relatively new phenomenon or an unprecedented epidemic. Chief among the many works to address "cutters" is Marilee Strong's A Bright Red Scream, in which the testimonies of "cutters" are discussed along with the works of leading psychologists and researchers to map out the dimensions and origins of self-mutilation.[1] Despite the increased attention to this social problem, Strong observes that adults frequently respond to "cutting" in ways that further aggravate or encourage the behavior. She writes, "[Some adults] overreact and police their kids, only driving their symptoms further underground. Other parents under-react, dismissing the cuts, bruises, and broken bones as melo-drama—'teenage bullshit,' as one cutter's father described it."[2] To engage in any meaningful discussion of kids who "cut"—literally and figuratively—one must address the complex interplay in the relationships among individual experience, available means for self-expression, and social and cultural conditions. Such conversations are perhaps made more difficult by the tendency among many young people who have been abused and subsequently engaged in violent acts directed at themselves or others to see themselves as in control and respon-sible for their actions, a tendency adult society is all too eager to endorse.

An abused youth who becomes a "juvenile criminal" may embrace a sense of inner "badness" (as if something inherent in her could explain both the abuse and her own run-ins with law enforcement or other subsequent problems), which typifies the widely documented phenomenon of the "double self" con-structed by abused children. Judith Herman has described the double self as stemming from the abused child's need to understand and justify traumatic experience when complete dissociation cannot be achieved. Herman writes that the child "seizes upon [the explanation of innate badness] early and clings to it tenaciously."[3] She further explains that this construction has enduring conse-quences: "Self-blame is congruent with the normal thoughts of early child-hood, in which the self is taken as the reference point for all events. It is congruent with the thought processes of traumatized people of all ages, who search for faults in their own behavior in an effort to make sense out of what has happened to them. In the environment of chronic abuse, however, neither time nor experience provide any corrective for this tendency toward self-blame; rather it is continually reinforced."[4] The world outside, from parents to publishers, readily subscribes to, if not determines, the beliefs of children who hold themselves responsible via such psychological adaptations.

Politicians who claim that theirs is the truly pro-child agenda appeal to public sympathy and pity, but they also rely on spreading fear, such as the fear of teenagers and dangers beyond the mythic safety of the home. In the U.S., for example, groups such as Focus on the Family, based in Colorado Springs, tap into white middle-class racism and homophobia when it warns that, if we fail to espouse its particular model of family values to guide public policy from the classroom to the realm of social services, society will be overrun by same-sex parents, "welfare queens," and the growing mass of teenage "super-predators" (as they have been described by juvenile crime "experts" such as the often cited John Dilulio, who has worked at the Brookings Institution, Princeton University, and the University of Pennsylvania; briefly led the Bush administration's Office of Faith-Based and Community Initiatives; and is credited with coining the term "super-predator," although he has since recanted his position). This would then force an apparently besieged heterosexual, adult, white, and Christian middle class to accept the distribution of condoms at schools and a social safety net that "rewards" single mothers, all of which somehow are linked to the breakdown of "American society" and to teenage killers.

Visions of "the family" as the institution capable of remedying violent or other social problems overlook how families serve as the very grounds where violent behavior is often learned and reinforced. "Family values" discourse such as that produced by Focus on the Family rarely lists familial abuse or the patriarchal nuclear family among the determining or contributing factors of violent behavior. Recognizing the widespread reality of child abuse and its relationship to juvenile violence is at odds with the belief in the primacy of "parental rights" held by such groups, and therefore the less common (though equally horrible) abductions and murders of children by strangers become a focal point for fear-baiting, distorting the reality that parents are a far greater threat to the lives of children than strangers or even other kids.

Profiling Predators

On April 16, 1998, evening news programs throughout Japan began what would be a week of extensive coverage of the death of Kamitate Kana, a second-grader in Iwate Prefecture. The seven-year-old child's body was discovered in the woods by a gas station attendant and later identified by her father, ending nine days of hope that the missing girl would return home. The palpable relief when the perpetrator was found to be a stranger was offset by the discomfort in the voices of news anchors who went on to describe the man, Sakagami Hisayuki, as a well-liked father living in the same community only four hundred meters from the Kamitate family. As is the case in the U.S., the face of the killer is not supposed to be the face of a parent, a neighbor, a teacher, a coach, or even a friend. We want our killers to be young men without children and, preferably, very different from ourselves—of a different class background, a different race, a different religion, or any difference that removes them from the realm of the familiar.

Above all in Japan today, the general public wants "child killers" to be "foreign." On November 22, 2005, the body of another seven-year-old was discovered in Hiroshima in a cardboard box. The little girl had been raped and strangled to death. A woman reported having seen the girl with a *henna gaijin* (strange foreigner).[5] Before long, photos of the Peruvian Juan Carlos Pizarro Yagi, in his thirties, were everywhere. He was indicted, and a "foreigner crime" panic dominated much of the mass media. The photo of Yagi accompanying print and television reports showed the close-up, unshaven face of a swarthy man with dark bags under his eyes. The public had the face to which it could attach its fears, and prosecutors began pushing for a death sentence. Debate as to whether Yagi was "simply" Peruvian or a Peruvian of Japanese ancestry and even controversy surrounding his real name lent added drama to the story of a "foreign menace" preying on Japanese girls. Unlike the case involving Saka-gami, the case of "Carlos" (as he was called by the mass media) fulfilled and fueled the public's and state's desires.

The familiar and familial positioning of "home" as safe and "outside" as dangerous characterized much of how the horrors of domestic violence and crimes against children were sometimes depicted as foreign (primarily U.S.) problems in Japanese popular culture in the last decade of the twentieth century. Okazaki Kyoko's popular manga *End of the World* (1992), which is set in "some state" in the U.S., begins with a young woman, Eleanor, discovering the bodies of her murdered parents, who, it turns out, were killed by Eleanor's sister, Molly, and stepbrother, Elias, or "Ease" for short. While on the lam, Molly and Elias, both of whom were abused by their parents, resort to prostitution and robbery to survive. The America in Okazaki's *End of the World* is not unlike that of Oliver Stone's *Natural Born Killers*—a seedy and high-speed killing field populated by the disaffected and traumatized and filled with violence and danger. While hiding out in the desert, Molly and Elias have sex, and the following morning he asks her, "Was I better than Dad?" She responds by telling him to "drop dead," and he then shoots himself in the head.[6] That a Japanese comic book released in 1992 about juvenile criminals, abuse, murder, and suicide would be set in the U.S. should not be surprising—nor, perhaps, should its popularity. The use of the U.S. and gun violence both places the story at a distance and reinforces notions of "America" as a place where domestic violence and crime are played out on a massive and grotesque stage. However, Okazaki's manga was also published at a time when local "human interest" stories of child abuse, sexual violence, and murder were beginning to appear with considerable frequency on news programs and talk shows in Japan.

The years immediately leading up to *End of the World* saw the courageous testimony of Korean "comfort women" who came forward with stories of how they had been sexually enslaved by the Japanese military in the Second World War, the serial killings of young girls in 1990 by a man who was widely reported to have been a regular consumer of violent and pornographic videos and magazines, and the highly publicized gang rape and murder in 1989 of a teenage girl whose dead body was placed in concrete by her male, high school student kidnappers.[7] The reality of violence—and sexual violence in particular—could no longer be as effectively denied, even though it continued to be seen as rare, shocking, or historical. What appeared to many Japanese to be a steady escalation of crimes committed by and against children set the stage for the current debates about the prevalence of child abuse in Japan and how best to punish juvenile offenders. From the very outset, the two issues of abuse and youth violence were linked by proximity, if not by the kind of causal logic I explore in this chapter.

As is the case in the U.S., where school shootings and daily reporting on youth violence continue to shape our images of young people, headlines about "kids killing kids" have become a mainstay in Japanese media and general public discourse in recent years. Beginning as early as March 1985 with the story of a nineteen-year-old in Yokohama who beat his mother to death, a perceived "boom" in "killer kid incidents" gradually took hold of the public imagination. That same year in April, a high school student in Chiba fatally stabbed her younger brother; in July, a group of middle school boys strangled a female ninth-grader to death with her underwear; and in August, a fifteen-year-old in Hokkaido killed his grandmother. The Japanese media learned that ratings and sales can soar with stories of violent youth offenders, and in the years since 1985 youth violence has made headlines with ever greater frequency.

A simultaneous fascination and repulsion in response to violent behavior in children is by no means a phenomenon unique to the 1980s, 1990s, and today. Indeed, today's image of the heartless and methodical teen killer in Japan has antecedents. Even at the level of representation, in other words, this figure is not new. While recent stories of teen killers and super-predators are often framed as evidence of something wrong with today's youth, something that marks them as different from earlier generations, the parents and grandparents of these youth grew up with their own images of teen killers. Occasionally, these histories are acknowledged, as was the case when Yū Miri's 1998 novel about youth violence, *Gold Rush*, was published. The promotional band around the original Japanese hardcover edition asked, "Why would a fourteen-year-old kill?" Underneath this question were three years and corresponding book titles:

1956: Mishima Yukio, *The Temple of the Golden Pavilion*
1980: Murakami Ryū, *Coin Locker Babies*
1998: Yū Miri, *Gold Rush*

At the same time that we might be encouraged to see certain representations of youth violence as new, therefore, we are also periodically reminded—here for the purpose of assigning Yū Miri a place in a literary lineage—that we have seen this sort of thing before.

Kinkakuji (The Temple of the Golden Pavilion) is not the only work by Mishima to engage this subject. In 1963, Mishima published *Gogo no eiko* (The Sailor Who Fell from Grace with the Sea), a story about a small group of boys whose violent preoccupations and acts are depicted in ways my students often say seem quite contemporary. The boys in Mishima's story are relatively unsupervised, and a few of them come from "broken homes." They are also depicted as unusually bright. For example, the leader of the group, whose frequently empty home serves as the boys' meeting place, is introduced as a "solitary boy" who "read at thirteen every book in the house and was always bored."[8] As part of the main character's initiation into the group, he must kill a cat. The protagonist, Noboru, approaches his initiation rite with determination and a studied "cold heart," and after he beats the cat, the "chief" mutilates and dissects the corpse. My students concur that this scene is unforgettable, the most powerful image in the book. Thus, I was surely not the only person in November 2001 to recall this scene when cats were found hanging by nooses, dismembered and brutalized, in different places in Japan—or whenever I hear similar stories or see cat-killing episodes in films or television programs, such as the television drama *Seija no kōshin* (When the Saints Go Marching In; 1998).

Mishima's detailed representation of the brutal killing concludes with Noboru's elation over his successful "graduation":

> Noboru had withstood the ordeal from beginning to end. Now his half-dazed brain envisioned the warmth of the scattered viscera and the pools of blood in the gutted belly finding wholeness and perfection in the rapture of the dead kitten's large languid soul. The liver, limp beside the corpse, became a soft peninsula, the squashed heart a little sun, the reeled-out bowels a white atoll, and the blood in the belly the tepid waters of a tropical sea. Death has transfigured the kitten into a perfect, autonomous world.
>
> *I killed it all by myself*—a distant hand reached into Noboru's dream and awarded him a snow-white certificate of merit—*I can do anything, no matter how awful.*[9]

Mishima suggests that the boys' "evil" is hard for adults to detect because of our over-attachment to and willingness to believe in childhood "innocence." The picture of intergenerational conflict Mishima presents is thus rendered in stark contrasts: The adults are naive and assume children to be pure-hearted and tender, whereas the children are cynical and malicious in their intent to do harm.

Mishima's adult vision of the remorselessness and ever escalating capacity for violence displayed by the young teenagers, who, we are to assume, kill Noboru's stepfather at the end of the novel, has anticipated and probably affected patterns of representation in more recent Japanese fiction, as well. Leaving aside the historical markers that make Mishima's novel particular to Japan in the early 1960s (of which there are many), it is safe to note that the descriptions of the boys' acts and feelings have since been thoroughly troped (perhaps in part because certain social conditions that lend themselves to anxieties over youth violence were already present when Mishima wrote). While this is not to argue that Mishima invented our fear of the teenage menace, he certainly contributed to the direction of its development, providing a kind of stock vocabulary or scenario.[10] For example, teenage "super-predators" have been similarly portrayed (albeit with somewhat more attentiveness to the traumatic origins of youth violence) in Murakami Ryū's *Coin Locker Babies* (1980), Sakurai Ami's *14* (1997), and Yū Miri's *Gold Rush* (1998), all of which feature lengthy descriptions of young boys engaged in shocking acts of gruesome violence.

In May 2000, a week of nonstop youth violence yet again was the subject of headline news stories in Japan—beginning with reports of a seventeen-year-old who was arrested for stabbing a sixty-five-year-old woman to death to experience what it was like to kill, according to police, and another seventeen-year-old who hijacked a bus and held the passengers hostage. The ensuing violent crimes, all committed by other seventeen-year-olds, gave the media and public pause as they asked themselves why so many teens of the same age were doing such things. Another seventeen-year-old attacked an elderly couple with a hammer, and two seventeen-year-old girls were arrested for holding a twenty-four-year-old woman hostage, torturing her, and cutting off her ears. Public discourse in response to such events has long centered on the problem of "today's youth" and the incomprehensible disregard for human life that is said to characterize this new generation, but now there seemed to be a particular age, a generational epicenter. In popular media, the Japanese novelist Morita Ryūji and others were quick to identify the connection between the seventeen-year-olds in 2000 and the fourteen-year-old boy who, three years earlier, had catapulted the issue of youth violence to the forefront of public discourse in what remains the most often discussed case of youth violence in recent Japanese history, the defining incident, which I will discuss at length later in the chapter.

The seventeen-year-old of today, Morita and other observers explained, was the fourteen-year-old who terrified us back then, and their parents are the same age as the notorious leader of the Aum Shinrikyo cult, Asahara Shoko, whose followers carried out the Sarin attack in a Tokyo subway. If the viral strain that had been shaking the security of a nation convinced of its safety could be located in particular age groups, then perhaps it could be contained. The isolation of the problem offered a false sense of understanding that comforted an audience bombarded with images of the bus jacking, the photo spreads and news footage that seemed too horrible, too foreign, to be true. It also reduced the specificity of each youth and each situation to a singular image—or, at least, a generic one that could accommodate different props in different settings. For example, pictures of heavily armed police squads encircling the bus, which was hijacked by a boy armed with a knife on the San'yō Expressway in northern Kyūshū and driven to Hiroshima, were plastered across magazine covers and displayed over the heads of news anchors. The boy took hostages, killing a sixty-eight-year-old woman. The four-hour standoff with police was a media event much like what we in the U.S. watched in "real time," as it happened, at

Columbine High School in Littleton, Colorado. The event became so much a part of the national consciousness that Iwai Shunji's internationally successful movie *Riri Shu Shu no Subete* (All about Lily Chou-Chou; 2001), about trauma and youth violence, includes several scenes in which characters watch the bus jacking unfold on television. News anchors recounted how inside the bus, the boy had a knife pointed at a ten-year-old girl. A passenger who escaped told police and reporters that the teenager, one of the passengers, suddenly "snapped" or "lost it" (*totsuzen kireta*) as the bus drove through Saga Prefecture and took out a knife.

In a three-part special series in the *Asahi Shimbun* dedicated to the boy who had stabbed the elderly woman to death, the teenage perpetrator's "broken home" and obsession with videogames were cited as if to explain his actions. The absence of his biological mother and the psychological impact of prolonged use of violent videogames offered simple explanations: This is what happens when parents divorce; this is what happens when mothers abandon their children; the poor father must have worked so hard to raise the boy without a wife. "Expert" and celebrity commentators echoed such opinions on talk shows, news programs, and evening specials. Having brutally stabbed the elderly woman forty times in the neck and face, struck her in the head, and reportedly explained that since he wanted to see what it felt like to kill someone, he had chosen an elderly victim, because "it didn't seem right to kill someone who had a future," the boy offered the public the image of a coldhearted superpredator for which they longed:

> He was born in Nagoya, and his parents, both teachers, divorced when he was one year old. He moved with his father to his grandmother's house. His grandmother took on the role of mother. He called his grandmother "Mom" until entering middle school. While in the fourth grade, he was asked by his grandmother whether or not he wanted to meet his real mother. The boy replied, "I don't want to meet her."
>
> In an evaluation, the boy's middle school homeroom teacher wrote, "I never sensed any loneliness stemming from his family circumstances." . . . Even when his close friends smoked cigarettes and drank alcohol, he didn't follow suit. "He didn't get swayed by people. He had convictions," according to a classmate.
>
> He left his textbooks at school. His grandmother said, "I rarely saw him studying at home." He played video games at the television every day. On weekends, class activity days, and holidays, he would start before noon

and continue playing straight through for seven hours. [A former] middle school teacher, his grandfather would say, "If you want to go to a top university, you'd better study two or three hours," to which the boy lightheartedly replied, "I can't do that that much! The key is the power to concentrate."

Nevertheless, the boy's grades were good. . . .

He was clearheaded and logical. Confident, cool, and composed. That personality even showed through during the incident. The reason he chose a housewife (64) he'd never met was because he "thought it wasn't right [to kill] a young person with a future." "I was aiming for the perfect crime," he said in his affidavit.

When he trespassed on her property and confronted the housewife, he wavered for just a moment, thinking about how murder was wrong and that he should stop. He stabbed her in forty different places, killing her.[11]

References to videogames and broken homes offer tenuous—if reassuring—evidence for those seeking to distance themselves from the boy and his family. But newspaper reporters also cited classmates and neighbors who referred to the boy in question in very positive terms, describing him as a "normal kid," and thereby contributing to another common image of the young generation as a mass of time bombs waiting to explode where and when one least expects. As if to guarantee public fear, which invariably boosts sales and ratings, many newspapers and television news programs also reported on juvenile crime statistics (the latest and widely reported data at the time being that, in 1999, 207 minors had committed murders in Japan) to "verify" the boom in violence among Japan's youngest generations and foretell even greater danger to come.

The attempt to isolate the problem of "juvenile crime" in a particular age group was, of course, untenable as soon as it was advanced. With each report of an older or younger youth killing, other theories had to be reinvoked and reasserted. Even the assurance that this was a "boy problem" required amending when, for example, an eleven-year-old girl cut a classmate's throat with a paper cutter, killing her, in June 2004. And it could not be reduced to simply a knife problem, either. A nineteen-year-old killed his parents with free weights in November 2004. One of the most highly publicized post-1998 cases involved a twelve-year-old stripping a four-year-old and then throwing him off the roof of a parking structure in Nagasaki on July 1, 2003. The twelve-year-old (an honors student) conformed to the pattern of the "quiet, good kid," which resurrected the "ticking time bomb" theory. However, in the days following the four-year-old boy's death, reporters and police began to consider whether the twelve-year-old might have been responsible for a series of nearby molesta-tions in recent months; it could no longer be a "bullying gone awry" story. Significantly and predictably, the types of experiences that would lead a twelve-year-old to sexually assault younger children were not prominent themes of inquiry.

The seemingly daily barrage of headline-grabbing incidents involving "kids killing kids," such as those reported between January and March 1998, for example, have fostered antipathy and fear among some Japanese adults toward the younger generations. In January, an eighth-grader in Tochigi Prefecture stabbed and killed his English teacher with a butterfly knife, and a male high school freshman described as an "average kid" attacked a female classmate in Yamanashi.[12] In February, two middle school students held up two other youths with knives, a ninth-grader in Aichi assaulted another youth with an air gun, another ninth-grader attacked a Tokyo police officer with a butterfly knife in an attempt to get the officer's gun, yet another ninth-grader was arrested for trying to hold up a post office with a kitchen knife to get money to leave the country, and an eighth-grader in Fukushima robbed a grocery-store customer at knife-point—reportedly to get money for comic books. Then, in March, a seventh-grader in Saitama attacked a classmate with a butterfly knife, and a boy in Nagoya who had been severely bullied fought back against his tormentor, stabbing him to death. Each of these stories was a featured lead-in on nation-wide television news programs, and the months and years since then have been filled with similar breaking news stories that keep adults' fears about the young generation very much on center stage. The public perception of an unprece-dented problem of growing proportions is indisputable and continues largely unabated today.

Not merely a safely distanced fictional locale for End of the World, the U.S. is also a place where changing attitudes and perceptions about apparent "booms" in youth and violence are being forged against tenacious beliefs in the "rights" of parents. The cover of the first Time magazine published after Eric Harris and Dylan Klebold killed twelve classmates and a teacher before taking their own lives on April 20, 1999, at Columbine High School in Littleton featured photo-graphs of the two boys and the headline: "The Monsters Next Door." Many other magazines and newspapers used the less interpretive one-word headline, "Why?" The discussions and debates in the aftermath of the televised "Tragedy in Colorado" (covered along with the "Crisis in Kosovo") focused on what are now seen as the predictable causes of youth violence in contemporary U.S.

society: violent movies (*The Matrix* and *The Basketball Diaries*), violent videogames (*Doom* and *Mortal Kombat*—but never military-recruiting videogames such as *America's Army*), and violent music (Marilyn Manson and gangsta rap); the availability of handguns and other assault weapons; and the failure of parents, school officials, and law enforcement to identify and "discipline" potentially violent youth.[13]

When Harris's and Klebold's parents were discussed as perhaps responsible for their children's actions, their failure to "discipline" or take notice of the boys' bomb-making activities at home were cited as evidence. But "experts" and pundits on CNN, MSNBC, and the other networks devoted most of their analyses to blaming Hollywood, blaming the National Rifle Association, and, in many cases, blaming the "boys as monsters" for what happened in Littleton. In all of the attention directed at answering the "why" question, rarely was the question raised (however unanswerable it may be, given the very limited information we have regarding the home lives of Harris and Klebold) that strikes to the heart of understanding what happened in Littleton. On April 22, 1999, however, Alvin Poussaint, the esteemed professor of psychiatry and dean of the Harvard Medical School, spoke to CNN and opened up this very line of inquiry, a line that was quickly evaded by a return to the predictable and comforting discussions of the videogame *Doom* and the film *The Matrix*. Poussaint said, "We don't know what the home life of these young people [Harris and Klebold] was all about. . . . We do know children who are rejected and abused at home, who are struck a lot, can have the tendency to grow up to be very violent adults."

Poussaint's comment, softened as it was, was not what CNN—or, perhaps, most of the U.S.—wanted to hear. Much more comforting was Jefferson County Sheriff John P. Stone, who appeared over and over again on MSNBC, CNN, and other news channels portraying the boys as coldhearted killers. Stone said in an interview aired throughout the day of April 21 on MSNBC: "It appears they just went in guns blazing. There's games, Satanic death music, and even some of the movies coming out put romance into these kinds of things. It's disturbing as a law enforcement officer and as a parent. We've got a couple sick minds here." To pathologize the boys as "sick" or demonize them as "monsters" is to provide non-answers. This allows us to avoid the more threatening questions, such as Poussaint's, that not only invite litigation from the besmirched parents but also bring us face-to-face with our collective complicity.[14] Mike Males lays out this significant discrepancy in attention paid to possible causes in the Columbine shootings:

For those who claim videogames made 'em do it, a theory all the rage now and coming into vogue when Klebold and Harris made their video, the latter says to the camera: "It's going to be like fucking *Doom*. Tick tick tick tick . . . Ha! That fucking shotgun is straight out of *Doom*." That one is quoted a lot. No one in today's "personal responsibility" climate seems inclined to blame family abuses, but just in case Klebold throws in a sop: "You made me what I am," he railed at his extended family. "You added to the rage." Don't look for that to be quoted.[15]

Six months after pictures of Eric Harris and Dylan Klebold appeared in every mainstream newsmagazine and newspaper in the U.S., the tide was turning, according to Lisa Belkin, who, in an article for the *New York Times Magazine*, announced that "the push to hold parents responsible for mass murder committed by offspring has taken on the mantle of a movement."[16] Belkin took as evidence the lawsuits filed against the parents of the young shooters by some parents of victims of the killings in Pearl, Mississippi; Paducah, Kentucky; Jonesboro, Arkansas; Springfield, Oregon; and Littleton, Colorado. The suits against the Harrises and Klebolds, Belkin, notes, are for "negligence and wrongful death under tort law." Nowhere in Belkin's article are the words "child abuse" mentioned; they remain far beyond the scope of what can be safely theorized in print. She writes that the Harrises and Klebolds are being singled out in the lawsuits for not protecting society from their children, a far cry from the kind of lawsuit (or conversation) that might be built on questions such as those posed by Poussaint.

The "paradox" here, as explained by Belkin and her sources, is that, on the one hand, there is the opinion that juvenile killers should be tried as adults, and on the other, that their parents should be tried. The yearning for a legal victory, for a monetary award to assist those whose lives have been ripped apart by tragic violence, is expressed in ways that do not disrupt the familiar logic that parents must mold and discipline their children, who are prone to all sorts of evil without firm (and, if necessary, brutal) moral instruction. While it is safe for a reporter or a justifiably outraged and grieving parent who lost a child in the Columbine shootings to claim that parents must discipline their children, there is still little room to say that it is parental "discipline" or other emotional, sexual, or psychological abuse or neglect that, in fact, can engender violence. To do so would be to defame the character of the parents of the boys who in death are routinely demonized.

Concurrent with the awareness among most of those working directly with young people who have committed violent crimes that the one common denominator that links every violent youth is a history of some form of child abuse or social discrimination has been the lambasting of the "abuse excuse." That is to say, while more information (about how abuse and trauma can fuel violent behavior in some young people) has come to light, a reactionary backlash holding children responsible for violent behavior has successfully shaped much mainstream public discourse about the nature and origins of youth violence. Childhood trauma is seen as more improbable than other motives for youth violence (such as greed, inherent evil, or an innate pathology), further restricting the space through which survivor discourse can emerge in relation to discussions of youth violence. The constellation of images that have come to mark the problem teenager (whether Mishima's cat-killing gang of boys or media portraits of Harris and Klebold) reinforce young people's tendency to blame themselves. The aberrant monsters are inherently bad. Some of them even tell us so. And when they do try to convince us otherwise, we respond by rebuking them for shirking responsibility or for indulging in "playing the victim." By locating the problem inside the mind, heart, or soul of the violent youth in this way, we can overlook the coercive control we exercise over the minds of children.

Just as the series of school killings in the U.S. continue to send shockwaves in the form of lawsuits, "zero tolerance" school policies, and enhanced security measures, Japan is reeling from the defining incident that catapulted the problem of "today's violent youth" onto the center stage of public discourse, eclipsing government scandals, international news, and stock market developments. Along with ensuing incidents, this case was used as justification for amendments made in 2000 to the Juvenile Criminal Code of 1949. In May 1997, the head of a boy named Hase Jun was found outside a school's entrance gate in Kobe.[17] Two handwritten notes were stuffed into the eleven-year-old's mouth. The handwriting was uniform and even, as if the characters had been written against the edge of a ruler, which police and reporters took as a sign that the killer was attempting to disguise his handwriting. Although the initial suspect profiles by the police described an adult male killer, the perpetrator, charged in early July, turned out to be only three years older than the victim, as well as the older brother of one of Jun's playmates.

The struggle to explain why a child would kill another child continues to return to this incident. Some analysts inaugurated what by now has become the commonplace association between violent behavior and videogames by pointing out that the boy was born in the same year that the popular Nintendo home videogame console went on the market. Kids who spend hours in front of a game such as *Biohazard* simply have no feelings, no humanity, according to such theories; such children become extensions of a violent virtual world and no longer fully human. Some analysts have focused on how the boy's writing style is reminiscent of the vocabulary of video role-playing games, and others, drawing on the boy's own words in his letters, have seen the education system as ultimately responsible.

More often than not, however, discussions of the "Sakakibara" boy focused on how incomprehensible his actions were. His parents were often objects of pity and sympathy, especially in interviews conducted with people on the street to assess public reactions to the crimes. Reporters told us the boy's parents had worked hard (like other parents) to make a good home for their three sons, doing everything they could to provide the best educational opportunities. Their oldest son was a "regular" kid, a "normal boy," the parents insisted, as did others who knew him. He was a good boy, thoughtful, sweet, and sensitive, which made the following letter sent to a newspaper in Kobe, in which he claimed responsibility for the murder of Hase Jun in the idyllic "New Town" district of carefully planned and uniformly groomed neighborhoods, subject to a wide array of speculation regarding "split" or "multiple" personality disorders that might offer some explanation for what seemed to come out of nowhere.[18]

To the Kobe Newspaper

The TV happened to be on the other day as I was leaving, and I heard the reporter mispronounce my name and call me "Onibara."

There is no greater disrespect than having one's very name mispronounced. The characters I used to sign my name were not a coded message, riddle, or even alternate reading. I am no liar. I am the real deal. That's been my name from the moment I came into existence, and what I'd want to do was decided from the start. Still, sadly, I have no nationality. I've never had anyone call me by my name until now. Maybe if I had been able to be myself since birth, I wouldn't have had to do things like leave the severed head in front of the junior high school's main gate. I thought about doing it, caught everyone unaware, and was able to thoroughly enjoy the act of murder. As for going to the trouble of getting the public's attention, my life has been and will continue to be a transparent one. All I ask is that you recognize me as another human being who occupies the same space and that this transparent existence of mine is the product of the compulsory education system and the society it creates. I have not forgotten to seek my revenge on that which has spawned me.

Yet if it were simply a matter of revenge, I'd only be letting the great burden I have endured until now fall from my shoulders, and there'd be nothing to gain. I discussed this matter with only one person, a friend who like myself leads a solitary and transparent existence. When I did so, he replied, "If you want to seek a meaningful revenge and not a pathetic one, you should do it in your own style, as your reason to live, and for a cause, and have fun with your revenge, committing murder like playing a game. If you do, it will not be about winning or losing, it will be more than that, and you will do more than make a new world for yourself." Moved to action by his words, I began my killing game.

Nevertheless, even now I don't know why I like to kill. All I can say is that I was scarred with this personality by nature. Only while I am killing can I be liberated from my constant hate and feel at ease. The pain of others is the only thing that can ease my pain.

One Last Word

You probably got the gist of what I have written here, but I have more than your average confidence in my own existence. That is why I cannot tolerate having my name misread or my existence denied. Even though it bothers me to watch what the police are up to, I relish knowing I've managed to fool them. Aren't they even trying to stop me? I'm risking my life in this game. If I am caught, they'll hang me. I can't go so far as to say that the police are also risking their lives, so they'll have to pursue me with more passion and mean it if they want to catch me. From now on, if my name is mispronounced even once or if anything else spoils things, I will destroy three vegetables a week. If you think I'm a kindergarten criminal who only kills children, you are very much mistaken.

I possess the power to kill a person two times.[19]

Perhaps some of these words sound familiar to those who remember sound bites from the media package Seung-Hui Cho sent to NBC (in which he says, "You forced me into a corner and gave me only one option. The decision was yours.") or Eric Harris's website entries and writings that were shown on U.S. news programs ("I HATE PEOPLE and they better fucking fear me if they know whats good for em" and "Fucking people with their rich snobby attitude thinking they are all high and mighty"). The letter by the boy who named himself Sakakibara, like the words of Cho and Harris, conveys rage and assigns blame.

Only the Clever Survive

In the letter and in a note stuffed in the mouth of Hase Jun's severed head, the boy used an original and dramatic nonstandard rendering of the surname Sakakibara, writing out the characters for "alcohol," "demon," and "rose." He used the given (or "first") name Seito, written with the characters for "disciple" or "saint" and "unbalanced." Much has been said of his choice of characters: the association of alcohol (which young generations may visualize as red wine) and roses to the color of blood, the use of supernatural images such as demons and saints, and the psychological implications of feeling unbalanced. Clearly, the thought behind the name (which might be rendered in English as "the Crazed Disciple of the Drunken Red Demon") and his reaction to its mispronunciation on the television point to its importance in his self-representation. The message he left in Hase's mouth includes taunts to the police, challenging them to "try and stop" him, and begins with the ominous threat: "Now the game begins" (Saa, geemu no hajimari desu). He also writes, "I want to see people die so much I can't stand it." Such claims were irreconcilable with the image of the "good" and "average" kid portrayed by those who knew the boy, and the gap between the boy's writing and the image of him portrayed by his parents, friends, and teachers remains a subject of considerable debate.

The boy was incarcerated at the Kanto "Medical" Juvenile Correctional Facility in Fuchu, western Tokyo, until he turned eighteen and entered a halfway house, or "correctional" school. In television, magazine, and newspaper venues, anonymous sources came forward with stories of the boy's fear of being struck after having been punished with beatings. The boy's experiences of childhood beatings were most concretely demonstrated to the public through his kindergarten records, which indicated his parents had told teachers they disciplined the boy by hitting him until he was three years old. While in the Kanto juvenile prison, he also reportedly developed a strong attachment to one of his counselors, whom he described as an idealized mother figure. Although such details pointing to childhood trauma in the boy's early years did emerge in many media reports, they were not pursued. The Japanese media, like their counterparts in the U.S., have found reporting on videogames, antisocial youth culture, and occasionally the school system to be more lucrative (and more acceptable). That the consumers of such information are for the most part adults, many of whom might also be parents, certainly affects the lack of public discourse on adult responsibility.

In March 2004, when it was announced that the Sakakibara boy (or "Youth A," as "juvenile offenders" are often designated) would be released in December and wanted to be a writer, Japanese Internet chat rooms, blogs, and message boards were filled with postings by young adults who had grown up with the story of this other youth and how he had, the story goes, affected the nation. The following responses were typical of the Internet postings I read regarding the boy's goal of becoming a writer: "Who'd wanna read his writing?" "Typical! Another annoying person will write a book." "I'd be scared to read it. What if I liked it or could understand what he was saying?" "I'm curious to see if there are answers." When he came off the monitored period of his probation in December 2004, these same chat rooms and blogs were replete with reported sightings or conjectures about his whereabouts. Continued interest in him has not gone unnoticed (and unfueled) by those who stand to profit from his story.

The money made off of the Sakakibara boy by publishers and news outlets has played a role in the attention to youth violence in the years since 1997.[20] Although it is still sometimes portrayed as a new problem, there are moments of retrospection when events from the 1980s, 1970s, and generations before, are acknowledged, but even then, the final analysis comes down not to discussions of increased reporting or changes in the politics of information but, rather, to what is seen as a uniquely generational crisis, a new breed of youth predisposed to disregard the lives of others. For example, news reports in early 1998 that described how three male junior high school students attacked two teachers at their school in Tochigi Prefecture drew on such adult paranoia of a sociopathic younger generation. This incident occurred at the Toyo Junior High School on February 24, after the three ninth-graders and five others had been writing essay assignments. When a teacher asked the students about a loud noise he had heard coming from the room, they refused to answer. The teacher took one of the students to another classroom in an attempt to get more information, and a second student kicked down that classroom door and attacked the teacher, and others joined in. Articles devoted to the story often cited police statistics, such as how in 1997, 2,263 Japanese youth between the ages of fourteen and twenty were convicted of murder or aggravated assault (or rape), double the number of convictions in 1993.

What could one conclude other than that there is something deeply wrong with young people today? After all, only a few weeks earlier, a teacher had been stabbed to death by a thirteen-year-old. The teacher, Kayoko Koshizuka, was killed by a boy with a butterfly knife on January 28, 1998, in a school hallway in another part of Tochigi. (This is the incident that appears to have inspired the character of Yukinori in Hoshino's *The Treason Diaries* discussed in the previous chapter.) The student was late to class, having been in the school infirmary. After the third-period class ended at approximately 11:45 A.M., his teacher had berated him in the hallway for having been late, and the boy stabbed her in the chest and back at least seven times with the four-inch blade of his butterfly knife. This particular incident was the first in a stream of "butterfly knife" murders, which, many analysts and "experts" contended, were inspired by a television show ("The Gift") starring the popular actor and singer Kimura Takuya (of the pop group SMAP), in which the lead character brandished a butterfly knife. Weekly magazines such as *Shūkan josei* (Weekly Woman's Magazine) included lengthy special reports on this and other knife incidents, and the verb "kireru" appeared throughout such articles to describe the boy's sudden violence. Headlines referred to how not even a year had passed since the Sakakibara murders, how once again the perpetrator was a middle school youth, and how schoolyards had become, as they are also described in the U.S., war zones.

Many Japanese women's magazines included commentaries on how critical it is for children to be able to express their feelings. Free educational materials (available in women's centers, clinics, schools, and other places mothers may frequent) such as the journal *Herushiitōku* (Healthy Talk) published by the Tokyo Department of Health and Human Services, feature regular articles on how to get along with one's teenage children. It is relatively easy to find essays in these materials about the dangers of hitting a child or the importance of strong listening skills. More typical of the "hard reporting" associated with "men's" newsmagazines, on the other hand, is an essay by Otsuka Eiji in a February 1998 issue of *Chūōkōron* (Central Review). Otsuka compares recent murders committed by youth to the incident in 1980 when the group of boys killed a girl and buried her in concrete.[21] Otsuka does not question why young people "snap" or "lose it" (*kireru*). Nor does his comparison extend beyond a listing of surface details. Rather, his focus is fixed on how mass-produced butterfly knives have taken on a fashionable accessory status, like "loose socks" and Nike basketball shoes. Otsuka and other writers whose essays appear in "hard news" periodicals only rarely venture beyond linking and listing incidents or asking general questions about the relationship between media violence and actual violence.

Some public intellectuals who addressed the topic in the late 1990s described Japanese youth as living in a thunderstorm, an environment that is supercharged with electricity and in which lightning can strike at any moment.

Such arguments hinge on the notion that this "electricity" must eventually find a release somehow, and when it does, although there may be a few identifiable factors, it will be random and ultimately unpredictable. This image of youth "on the verge" is certainly still one of the dominant representations of young people one finds in Japan today. Another theory, one that is by no means unique to contemporary Japan, holds that Japanese kids are out of control because society has abandoned corporal punishment. Those espousing this point of view contend that kids learn right and wrong physically and not intellectually— through beatings—and that kids properly disciplined this way do not disobey. One also finds countless discussions of how youth today are more selfish and stubborn, unable to control their desires.

What these dominant images of contemporary youth (as ready to snap, as needing to be beaten into obedience, and as unable to self-regulate) share is how markedly different they are from pictures that emerge when different questions are asked and when children themselves describe their own responses to youth violence. This holds true in Japan and the U.S. Daryl Payton, a student at Fairfax High School in Los Angeles, was among many young people interviewed around the U.S. in the wake of the Columbine shootings. When a reporter from KTLA asked Payton for his thoughts the day after the incident, he said, "I feel sorry for the people who did it, because something must have been going on in their lives for them to kill so many people like that."[22] Payton's immediate identification with the shooters and recognition that rage is not accidental or inexplicable was, however, not a sentiment widely echoed by adult analysts after the shootings in Littleton. Other young people, such as the Columbine student Sarah Neilsen, expressed concerns that the incident would lead to increased discrimination, and asked adults and other youth not to hold other kids, such as those associated with the "Trenchcoat Mafia," accountable for the actions of Harris and Klebold. "You shouldn't stereotype a whole group of kids just because a couple of kids snapped one day," she said to a reporter for KUSA in Denver the day after the incident. Perhaps most complex were comments from those who knew the boys well, such as Alejandra Marsh, also a member of the Trenchcoat Mafia group, who spoke to a KUSA reporter. She said, "I saw Dylan and Eric. I knew how sweet they were. They knew all this before they started doing this. They had studied things like that. They'd done paint ball almost like it was a real war situation. But they were great friends. They were some of the sweetest guys to know, but they had the ability in them to do this. And they chose to do it."[23] While explaining to viewers that the boys were "sweet" and good friends, Marsh also provides a way out for disturbed adults by invoking, in the end, the fiction of inner badness along with the logic of personal responsibility. The possible origins of any such a "criminal pathology" were once again a taboo space covered over by images of the boys as having had an inherent capacity for evil and made the choice to act on their evil thoughts.

Four months after the Sakakibara murders in Japan, an anonymous fourteen-year-old boy was quoted in the newsmagazine *Aera* as being heartened that the tragedy might motivate adults to think seriously about how ninth-graders feel and what life is like for them.[24] Many letters written by other Japanese youth to publications such as the *Asahi Elementary and Junior High School Student* newspapers expressed sympathy with the Sakakibara boy, even though the writers often qualified their reactions by asserting they would never go so far as to kill another person. The vocabulary youth have used to describe these shared feelings, typified by words such as *mukatsuku* (crazy making, annoying, or frustrating) and "kireru," is remarkably similar to the language of many youth in the U.S. who express frustration over the ways in which their lives are also characterized by feelings of profound agitation. As resounding as this call to be understood according to their own terms is, however, official adult discourse remains all too willing to discount, trivialize, and ignore those we so often purport to protect.

School Sucks

One of the popularly designated social "symptoms" of what ails today's youth in Japan is the rising demand for "free schools" and educational alternatives. Unlike the frequently religious or ideological debates surrounding home schooling in the U.S., public discussions of long-term school "absenteeism" (*futōkō*) in Japan focus on the ways in which the demands and pressures in the Japanese school system and its examination requirements are unbearable for many students. (The implementation of "results-oriented" education and high-stakes testing in the U.S. is now producing comparable effects.) Whereas home schooling emerged as a reaction by some parents in the U.S. to their perception of inadequate moral training or attention to the "basics" in public education, children studying at home in Japan are more often depicted as having been psychologically or intellectually unable to handle the demands of school. Predictably, conservative thinkers blame parents and children for shirking the hard work and discipline needed to succeed, but educational activists are also working on behalf of students, many of whom are often at risk for suicide and who cannot tolerate the very material stresses and dangers they often face at school.

Terawaki Ken, an educator and activist, provided one of the few dissenting voices in the alternative schooling and chronic truancy debates in the late 1990s, at the height of the panic over youth violence in Japan. In one essay, Terawaki observed that the unquestioned belief that children must attend school was contributing to a great deal of suffering among youth who did not feel like "normal" students or even "normal" kids.[25] He described a conference for educators held in Hiroshima in 1996 that was called in response to ijime (bully-ing)-related youth suicides (which have recently been in the news again in both Japan and the U.S.). The local school board and Parent–Teacher Association put up a big sign in red letters that read, "Your life is more important than anything else. When you feel like you don't want to go to school because of bullying or when you feel like you want to change schools, please talk to a nearby grownup right away. We adults will always be your strength." Soon after, there was a reply to this message posted up by a group of kids: "Please understand what it feels like to not want to go to school." Terawaki took this impromptu reply from the students as his starting point and asked parents and educators to do more than simply offer promises of support and to tell kids, instead, that if they feel as if it would be better to die than go to school, then they do not have to go to school. He added to this "treasonous" suggestion the caveat that it is incumbent on adults to make sure that a child can also return to school or change schools easily at any time after spending time away. Although this may seem like common sense, if one bears in mind the way in which grade advancement is contingent on rigorous rounds of testing, the obstacles to realizing this challenge are significant.

Terawaki argued that many adults have difficulty understanding what alter-native learning can be because the school system has been so thoroughly natu-ralized. This, he argued, extends beyond a failure to recognize readily available learning spaces such as libraries and the Internet to a highly codified relation-ship between educational background and social standing, a relationship that the novelist Murakami Ryū has elsewhere called an "outright lie."[26] Terawaki is suspicious of the biases revealed by comments such as "Kids today aren't as smart as they used to be," or "Kids today are not motivated to learn," because such comments invariably reveal an unwillingness to recognize the specific pressures children now face in schools. He believes that each child should have the opportunity to discover what she or he wants to be and wants to do, and that without feeling this freedom, some children are virtually forced into depression when they cannot "fit in," because all they hear from their parents and society is that everyone has to go to school or that it would be embarrassing if they did not go to school. Citing the limited number of counseling services available to kids and parents (out of the approximately 11,000 junior high schools in Japan, for example, only 1,065 had school counselors in January 1998), Terawaki laments how few alternatives there are and how even the available alternatives are rarely used. Of those children and parents who even know about alternatives, he explained, the stigma remains so great that few actually explore or create such options.

One of the many problems, in addition to bullying, contributing to some children's aversion to school in Japan is sexual abuse on school grounds. A seemingly endless list of incidents involving teachers' sexually abusing students has made this a familiar subject in the U.S., as well. Kadono Haruko's study *School Sexual Harassment* represents the growing attention to the dimensions and effects of this problem.[27] Kadono documents cases such as female students being forced to undress in front of male and female teachers who touch and comment on the girls' bodies.[28] She also provides written transcripts of interviews with children who were sexually or violently assaulted by teachers. One junior high school student and his friend, for example, were caught smoking in the bathroom by a physical education teacher who called in several other teachers. Together, the teachers beat the boys until they could no longer stand and their lips were bleeding. The physical education teacher then said, "If you have a problem with this, why not quit school?"[29] Interviews with children who were raped by teachers or whose teachers threatened or attempted to kill them are also discussed by Kadono, who asserts that the problem of safety in schools is as much, if not more, a result of adult (often criminal) misconduct than of children bullying other children.

Like many who attempt to shed light on the reality of assault in the lives of Japanese children, Kadono sees "school sexual harassment" as a distinctly Japanese problem, which she explains by drawing a comparison between ways of articulating resistance in Japanese and English. She argues that Japanese children in difficult situations have no word equivalent to the English "no" and are limited to phrases such as *yamete kudasai* (please stop) or *yamete* (stop). The more forceful command to stop, *yamero*, she elaborates, is usually considered "male" speech or otherwise insubordinate, and girls especially have difficulty using this expression. Thus, she claims, it is nearly impossible to work one's way out of linguistic hierarchies in moments of crisis due to what she sees as a fundamental peculiarity of the Japanese language itself.[30] It would be a mistake to write this comment off as inaccurate or naive simply because we know children in the U.S. would have a hard time (including having a hard time finding words) in the same situation. The way we name and understand a problem such as school sexual harassment is inextricably linked to the vocabularies available to us.

Kadono also argues against interpretations of adult men's sexual attraction to children as a natural, if unfortunate, part of reality, which she critiques as the invocation of "Lolicon," or the "Lolita complex," to justify the rape and sexual abuse of children. She takes issue with those who see Lolicon as a sickness or predisposition (which, she cautions, might lead us to pity perpetrators) instead of as a violation and argues that a "revolution" in the way Japanese adults view children is in order.[31] She points to the way many reacted to the news that a thirty-eight-year-old teacher had killed a twelve-year old student in Hiroshima in 1990. When it was learned that there had been rumors that the teacher had been raping the girl since the previous autumn, many concluded the teacher suffered from an obsessive "Lolicon." But, Kadono writes, at the same school two years earlier, another teacher had raped a student, which indicates what she contends is more likely an institutional and social climate that permits the gross abuse of authority and facilitates rape. She cites many other examples of teachers who have raped and, in some cases, killed students to suggest that such hostile and dangerous school climates are to blame because teachers hurt students when their environment and culture encourage them to do so.

Progressive analyses such as Kadono's were accompanied by a proliferation of popular narratives of abuse in schools, in the home, and in various institutions. The television drama *Seija no kōshin* (When the Saints Go Marching In; 1998), for example, was loosely based on an actual incident involving the violent and sexual abuse of thirty mentally disabled youth who were living and working (for less than the equivalent of $50 a week for full-time work) in a rehabilitative factory group home in Ibaraki. The drama, written by Nojima Shinji and starring an array of performers whose names read like a Who's Who of contemporary Japanese popular culture at the time, centers on a boy who learns to stand up for himself and others, and, in predictably melodramatic fashion, eventually forgive his abusers. One of the young protagonist's teenage companions, played by the celebrity sex symbol Hinagata Akiko, is raped by a factory owner in several scenes. Hinagata appears in various "fantasy" costumes in these scenes, and the plot involves many other enactments of precisely the kinds of exploitation the drama purports to decry. Tabloid renditions of similar tales of vulnerability and injustice were regularly featured in women's magazines while the drama aired. For example, the April 7 edition of *Shūkan Josei* featured a cover story about "the shocking truth of a real life 'When the Saints Go Marching In.' "[32] The two-page article describes the experiences of a twenty-year-old who was sexually abused by her father and two neighbors and who eventually was awarded monetary damages in a court settlement. The article begins with the qualification that "because of her mental handicap (*chiteki na shōgai*), she endured this suffering for eight years." The girl's father, according to the article, was fined (roughly $30,000) but not imprisoned, and the two other perpetrators were fined (approximately $20,000 each) only after her attorney convinced the judge that a mentally disabled person could be considered a reliable witness.

The Abuse and Recovery Industries

As was the case with stories of youth violence, stories about child abuse began to appear with increasing regularity in mainstream Japanese public discourse during the 1980s. A growing body of professional literature and comparative research challenged notions that child abuse was a foreign problem or misinterpreted "discipline" (*shitsuke*). Ikeda Yoshiko's landmark study of "twisted parent–child relations," *Child Abuse* (1987), launched a trend in comparative studies about violence against children that continues today.[33] At the same time, more adults who had been abused as children seemed to be speaking out about their experiences, and the media attention to "shocking" crimes was increasing. In this context, the image of Japan as a safe society became harder to uphold, even though there were still those, particularly those in positions of policymaking authority, who insisted that Japan is a "peaceful" country, free of the rampant violence plaguing the outside world and that, as Tokyo's Governor Ishihara Shintarō has notoriously suggested, foreigners and minorities are responsible for most crime.

The belief that contemporary Japanese national identity and a well-ordered, nonviolent society are inextricable is something against which survivor discourse, despite its commercial appeal, struggled in the final decades of the twentieth century. Nonetheless, only two years after the publication of *End of the World*, and one year after *Father Fucker* first appeared in print, a complex shift in attitudes toward children and violence was nonetheless becoming discernible in some bookstores, women's centers, and self-help groups. The manga artist Sasaya Nanae and the journalist Shiina Atsuko joined forces in September 1994 for what would be the first installment of their "documentary" comic book series *Kōritsuita me* (Frozen Watchfulness), which depicts actual cases of child abuse and the efforts of medical and social-service communities to intervene and respond to victims of violence, sexual abuse, and neglect. By 1996, their series filled two volumes.[34] Unlike the sensationalized story of Molly and Elias, which begins after the abuse that has led the teens to murder and lives as outlaws, *Frozen Watchfulness* shows the damage, the burns and bruises on young bodies, and takes as its subject the immediate and very material effects of child abuse, as well as the struggles facing those who tried to intervene, particularly medical doctors and social workers, in the 1990s.

In just a few years, the space through which stories by and about survivors of child abuse could emerge had been widened by a growing survivors movement, increased professional awareness, and rising ratings of daytime talk shows that took on the subject (as spectacle) to attract viewers. By 1998, translations of Judith Herman's *Trauma and Recovery* and Torey L. Hayden's popular novels about the abused children and those with severe needs with whom she had worked as a special education teacher in the U.S. were heavily promoted and featured in the windows of large bookstore chains, such as Kinokuniya, throughout Japan. And the success of literally hundreds of Japanese books on child abuse, trauma, and "AC" (the Japanese shorthand for "adult children," the meaning of which expanded in Japan to include not only the adult children of alcoholics but also any survivor of abusive or inadequate parenting) released between 1995 and 1996 alone proved to publishers and television networks that what had once been off-limits was now very profitable.

When I interviewed her in the late 1990s, Shiina Atsuko recalled how this shift had taken place in a relatively short time.[35] She explained that although she was interested in a wide range of social problems, including child abuse, in the mid-1980s, her editors were not: "Stories would arrive in the office about a child who died [from abuse] without anything being written up about it. [My editors] made the decision not to use this material. They told me to leave it alone. That's what caught my interest—that these stories were not being pursued. I thought about it on my own for a long time until I got the chance to review ten years of medical journals."[36] Shiina contacted doctors who had worked on twenty to thirty of the most egregious cases of abuse documented in medical journals, but only one doctor was willing to discuss the problem of child abuse with her at length, and he later contributed material for *Frozen Watchfulness*. Taking as her model the journalistic books on cancer and AIDS that had introduced information "into the Japanese home," Shiina launched her coffee-table book campaign to "raise the public's awareness of the reality of child abuse." Because "more people in Japan read manga than other types of books," she said, she contacted Sasaya Nanae, who agreed to collaborate with her on the project. The relative success of *Frozen Watchfulness* or the consciousness and recovery industries are, nevertheless, peripheral eruptions on a landscape that remains overshadowed by the corporations, institutions, and ensconced attitudes that play direct roles in the actual abuse of children.

It is this broader and more diffuse arena that Hoshino Tomoyuki takes on in his unflinching prose. Even when they only subtly line the edges of his fiction, politics, cultural mythologies, consumerism, globalization, education, technology, media, and militarism contribute to the suffering of his young characters. Left with the pain and rage, Hoshino's youth respond in violent and, to borrow his word, "grotesque" ways. Their desperation and "that which spawns it" are the focus of the next chapter, which looks to Hoshino's fiction to better understand the politics of youth "fighting back." His fiction considers more than "recovery" or "healing"; it demands we think about reparations, revolution, and the possibilities of non-cooperation and non-participation.

The Fiction of Hoshino Tomoyuki and Japanarchy 2K:

Lonely Hearts Revolution

I don't mean go out and get violent; but at the same time you
should never be nonviolent unless you run into some nonviolence.
I'm nonviolent with those who are nonviolent with me. But when
you drop that violence on me, then you've made me go insane,
and I'm not responsible for what I do.

—Malcolm X, "The Ballot or the Bullet," 1964

Persecute us! That's right, persecute us! Don't you know that for
every force there is a counterforce? Persecute us! Persecute us as
much as you wish. The old way is fighting the new—imperialism
versus anarchism. Go ahead: Take your piece of stick and try with
all your might to stop the onrush of the Sumida River.

—Kanno Sugako writing from prison before her execution, January 21, 1911

Responses to conditions of alienation and oppression include violence, both representational and real. We tend to identify these
responses according to categories of expression, scope, or discrete
aim—the drive-by or the school shooting, violence directed at the self or another, violence narrowly focused within the realm of interpersonal relationships, violent ideation or fantasy, the massacre or the assassination, and violent
attempts to redress material deprivation or social discrimination, just to name a
few. Added to this list, of course, is the category of violent direct action as a
form of protest or political action, the violence of one person's terrorist and

another person's freedom fighter. When many today think of "terrorism" in or related to Japan, the Aum Shinrikyo cult's Sarin gas attacks on the Tokyo subway system in 1995, are perhaps first and foremost in their minds. Fewer might recall the more classically "terrorist" Japanese Red Army (JRA) or United Red Army (URA) attacks on airports and corporate, military, and political sites around the world throughout the 1970s.[1] Unlike Aum members, who claimed the Sarin attacks would serve a spiritual purpose, the JRA's and URA's followers saw themselves as participating in a global revolution, making strategic hits on the capitalists and occupying ruling classes in the process.

Fewer still may think of Japanese anarchists, such as a small handful who dreamed of killing the emperor in the first decade of the twentieth century. However, it is precisely that legacy of Japanese anarchism that appears to be invoked in some calls to resistance in contemporary Japan, as well as in some literary explorations of political and social alternatives. For example, the recent fiction of the award-winning novelist Hoshino Tomoyuki might be described as literary Molotov cocktails often aimed directly at the Japanese state and the emperor system. Like the Molotov cocktail, Hoshino's fiction draws from that which is readily available but transforms the familiar (a glass bottle or potting soil) into something explosive and disruptive.

More than a century ago, the Japanese anarchist Kanno Sugako was sentenced to death for what was, in effect, a thought crime. Along with eleven others, she was found guilty of thinking about killing the emperor in 1910 and subsequently executed.[2] In the final years of the Meiji era, the Japanese state saw anarchists as terrorists, but Kanno and some of her fellow "conspirators" argued that only by ridding Japan of the emperor could a world without authoritarian differential power begin to grow. The anarchist desire for self-determination and autonomy in communities free of hierarchical divisions and state war mongering offered anti-capitalists and anti-imperialists in Japan and elsewhere a vision for an equitable society that was more radically anti-authoritarian than what socialists of the time imagined. Kanno seems to have understood that her anarchist writings and (thoughts) against the state put her at risk but felt that the possibilities of a world without hierarchical power was worth any such sacrifice on her part.

Similar stories from the annals of a global anarchist history (filled with names such as Emma Goldman, Mikhail Bakunin, Peter Kropotkin, Lucy Parsons, Ferdinando Nicola Sacco, and Bartolomeo Vanzetti) are not surprising; neither is a story of leftists resisting Japanese imperialism at the turn of the twentieth century. Only a few decades later, Kobayashi Takiji would be murdered by the military police for his "dangerous" fiction, which challenged imperialism and capitalism and depicted the desire to harm the emperor. Conventional wisdom in most scholarly circles holds that the emperor system was a problem in pre–Pacific War modern Japan. But what are we to make of an anti-authoritarianism and anti-imperialism predicated on a rejection of the emperor system in Japan today, at a time when the emperor is popularly understood by most in and outside Japan as a symbolic figure without political power? Why have recent novels by the celebrated authors Shimada Masahiko (The Endless Canon Trilogy, which features a character modeled on the current Princess Masako) and Hoshino Tomoyuki (Lonely Hearts Killer, which dramatizes events following the unexpected death of a fictional young emperor) taken on the emperor system? And perhaps most pointed, why are some anarchists in Japan calling, still, for an end to the emperor system? To better understand these questions, I will look at how Hoshino and some activists in contemporary Japan are turning to representational violence to expose the ways in which violent state policies elicit interpersonal brutality. At the heart of much of their work is a critique of the emperor system as more than symbolic in its reach into daily life.

First, to establish the place of the emperor system in contemporary anarchist protest in Japan, I will turn to an example of the longtime communiqué of choice for activists: the political poster or flyer. Throughout June and July 2004, a poster produced by the activist and punk musician Shiga Naoki appeared at various antiwar rallies in cities such as Nagoya and Tokyo. The anonymously produced photo was also posted on Independent Media Center Japan, part of the world-wide Independent Media Center (Indymedia) Network, and various activist websites. The split image of Emperor Akihito and Empress Michiko is accompanied by the slogan, "Dismantle (Kaitai) the Imperial House (Kōshitsu)." In the poster, Shiga at once calls attention to hereditary status and privilege as problems and violates the bodies of the royal couple, slicing them down the middle and pasting them together. Among all the placards and signs decrying the sending of Japan's Self-Defense Forces (SDF) to Iraq and the war itself, these anti-imperial signs perhaps seemed strange and even anachronistic to some, especially given the lack of say either royal figurehead had in whether or not Japan participated in the wars on Iraq and Afghanistan. After all, while the emperor carries out certain state-related rituals such as "investiture," his relationship to political decision making is largely accepted as nonexistent.[3] Michiko's relationship to the war and politics could seem even more removed.

What is left out of such causal reasoning are larger questions related to

Anonymous photograph of a poster produced by the activist and punk musician Shiga Naoki and distributed at antiwar rallies in Nagoya and Tokyo, June–July 2004; posted on Indymedia and activist websites.

patterns of affiliation. Kanno Sugako, even at a time when the emperor was more powerful, expressed no criticism of him as an individual and, in fact, claimed she considered him a decent man.[4] However, he represented the icon and pinnacle of a social system that deemed certain lives to be more important than others. While the lives of soldiers and workers were rendered expendable by an aggressively expansionist empire (and the lives of the colonized were seen as even less valuable), the emperor remained above and apart from the rest. By spilling his blood, Kanno and others hoped to show that he was human, that he would bleed, and that by making his humanity visible, they would trigger a collapse of the entire hierarchical and mythical system.[5] One might interpret a similar desire in Shiga's poster, produced almost one hundred years later.

Although he nowhere advocates or endorses killing the emperor (or anyone else), Hoshino Tomoyuki has also speculated about what might change if the Japanese emperor system were to be abolished, and these speculations underwrite his powerhouse novel *Ronrii Haatsu Kiraa* (Lonely Hearts Killer; 2004).[6] This novel invites a host of possible interpretive trajectories, and mine (which eschews, for example, the ample room provided for a pacifist reading) is merely one and by no means an exhaustive one or one that takes into consideration all of the many themes and threads Hoshino brings together. This novel begins with the death of a fictional young emperor and public reactions to his death, as they are related by mass media. The plot of the intricately detailed *Lonely Hearts*

Killer, when reduced to its most skeletal level, involves a story of national events on a grand stage (the emperor's death, the succession of his sister, the impact of climate change, and the rise of a new political leader), a story of private or individual events (the "love suicide" of two central characters that sparks an "era" of suicide pacts and murder-suicides), and a story of how the public's knowledge of both the "public" and "private" stories is shaped by the mass media. The mass media are implicated at each level of the plot in that news reporting on the emperor's death, for example, contributes to individual actions, and individual "incidents" are reported in relation to larger political developments, such as the enactment of martial law or the rise of a news celebrity to political office. In other words, the mass media truly mediate and make possible a complex and often morbid relationship between the most private and most public spaces in the fictional world Hoshino creates.

In a special issue of the literary journal *Bungei* dedicated to his work, Hoshino explains the question that led him to write the death of an emperor. While no longer as blasphemous an act as it could have been only two generations earlier, describing the death of an emperor remains largely off-limits in the world of Japanese literature. However, many young Japanese people, especially those who do not consider themselves nationalists, are baffled by any suggestion that the emperor is important (as either a positive or a negative figure). Hoshino's discussion addresses both of these tendencies: "After writing [*Lonely Hearts Killer*] my students and young writers asked me, 'We don't understand why you'd want to problematize the emperor. Is the emperor really that big of a presence in the lives of people over thirty?' I felt the same way when I was younger. But then I wondered what would happen to the people of Japan if right here and right now the emperor system were abolished?"

In a speech titled, "I of the Ambiguous Identity" (which evokes the title of Ōe Kenzaburō's Nobel laureate speech, "Japan, the Ambiguous, and Myself"), Hoshino offers the following elaboration on his creative decision-making process.

> I think of literature as an act of rebellion against [nationalist and other trends toward] unification. It offers the chance to describe the kind of world in which words scatter out and are filled with a range of new meanings. If not, words can only carry their officially prescribed meanings. And it becomes that much harder for the individual and for minorities to express themselves. We live in a time—and this is not limited to Japan—when fixed notions of identity, particularly identities associated with a people or race (that is to say, the new nationalisms) are being promoted by majorities. To

avoid being devoured by this, the individual and the minority must continue to speak their own words, and that, I believe, is the act called literature. If my novels are ambiguous or hard to interpret, I think it's because they are rebelling against the unification of identity.

The novel from which I'm about to read, *Lonely Hearts Killer*, explores the question of how an "identity without an identity" might be possible. I believe the existence of the emperor is supporting the identity of the Japanese majority at an unconscious level. They have yet to face their internal emptiness because it has been left to the emperor. If the emperor system were suddenly abolished and the emperor disappeared, wouldn't the Japanese majority that has given little thought to the emperor up until now feel quickly and unexpectedly as if they weren't themselves? And wouldn't they then resort to brutal aggression? I started writing the novel with that premise in mind.

I also wanted to show with this novel that, as I have already said, nationalism is supported by words, especially those words that attack the Other.[7]

Implicit in this speech is Hoshino's concern about how easily the "Japanese majority" throngs to nationalism and cultural chauvinism, a phenomenon he and others have likened to the rise of patriotism qua nationalism in the U.S. after September 11, 2001. Hoshino has implicated such First World nationalisms in the concurrent escalation of Islamic, Chinese, and Russian nationalism and commented that nothing frightens him more than the tyranny of majorities, of masses dedicated to exclusive and "unified" national or cultural identities. In one such discussion, he calls into question the long-term viability and merit of nation-states as organizing structures (a point of view that further links his concerns to those of anarchists).[8] The centrality of the emperor's symbolic value to nationalist identity takes shape in the escalation of violence and fear in *Lonely Hearts Killer*.

The end of the emperor system (and perhaps the nation) that Hoshino imagines in *Lonely Hearts Killer* is not a sudden occurrence. Rather, it takes place in stages, first with reports of the death of the young emperor, then with the unprecedented succession of his sister (a topical development, given the recent debates about female heirs in Japan's imperial house), and finally with provocative questions as to "what comes next" in a society defined and motivated by its fears. The "world without emperors" for which several characters yearn is full of possibilities, most of which are left "in progress" and unresolved when the novel ends. Early-twentieth-century anarchists also imagined the possibilities of a world without emperors. As Kanno Sugako and her colleagues believed, without one above and beyond society there would be no need for those below and outside. Many of today's anarchists in Japan are no less hopeful that the end of the emperor system would precipitate the end of differential power in all of its expressions. And their protests, which sometimes take the form of street party rallies, are expressly anti-authoritarian.

No Joking Matter

Advertised through flyers and Indymedia websites, a demonstration against the war on Iraq disrupted weekend activities in the streets of Nagoya and in Yaba Park on June 6, 2004. Organizing groups included anarchists, punks, war resisters, and the so-called Nagoya Heavy Drinking Brigade. Like the Reclaim the Streets (RTS) events in the U.K. and elsewhere, this demonstration was intended not only as a protest against the war, but also as a form of jubilant civil disobedience and prefigurative political expression. Naomi Klein explains the RTS's demands for "uncolonized space—for homes, for trees, for gathering, for dancing":

> It is one of the ironies of our age that now, when the street has become the hottest commodity in advertising culture, street culture itself in under siege. From New York to Vancouver to London, police crackdowns on graffiti, postering, panhandling, sidewalk art, squeegee kids, community gardening and food vendors are rapidly criminalizing everything that is truly street-level in the life of a city. . . . Since 1995, RTS has been hijacking busy streets, major intersections and even stretches of highway for spontaneous gatherings. In an instant, a crowd of seemingly impromptu partyers transforms a traffic artery into a surrealist playpen.[9]

Rebel revelers at such gatherings resist restrictions on the use of public space—or "the commons"—by breaking the very laws they find objectionable, classic civil disobedience. Related political messages are invariably brought into RTS and similar "happenings," as is evident in anti-corporate globalization posters and chants about the violent methods used to support the oil and automotive industries, proponents of labor rights, and precarity demonstrations one might find in such a street party qua protest.[10]

The protesters in Nagoya on June 6 hoped that the introduction of a party atmosphere would help them convey antiwar political messages, express their dissent, and have fun at the same time. This strategy (of using playful protest

and humor to make the message more appealing) is by no means unique to recent RTS or similar movements. One can look back to Abbie Hoffman and even
popular peasant revolts in mid-nineteenth-century Japan, such as the riots depicted in Imamura Shohei's celebrated film *Eijanaika* (1981). Like Imamura's fictional peasant protesters, the Nagoya youth incorporated music and dance into
their demonstrations. The use of humor to advance an antiwar message was
pronounced in demonstrations in urban areas of Japan earlier that year, in April,
when young women dressed in miniskirts and lingerie held placards indicating
that they refused to have sex with men who supported or participated in war.[11]
Their "sex strike," while certainly capturing the attention of passersby, remained
largely symbolic. While the same could be said of the street protest in Nagoya, the
demonstrators were struggling with a complex model of consciousness-raising,
humor, and direct action.

The struggle to develop effective forms of protest is ongoing. More and
more restrictions are placed on those who seek legal means (such as obtaining
permits) to protest, and the space allocated to permitted protests and demonstrations shrinks, often to the point of rendering protests invisible and inconsequential. Given the lack of media (at least, corporate media) coverage of the
impressive protests that nonetheless occur, the inevitable downplaying of the
numbers of protesters (by media and official sources), the ubiquitous police
presence (including as informants and infiltrators), and the purveyed image of
protesters as crazies, it is not surprising that an incredible amount of creativity
is channeled into organizing protest activities and developing props, posters,
and the like to make the message as appealing and noticeable as possible. In the
U.S., one of the better known contemporary groups to engage in playful protest
(at political conventions and Halliburton shareholder meetings, for example) is
the Ronald Reagan Home for the Criminally Insane based in San Francisco.[12]
Its guerrilla theater presentations of "Republicans Gone Wild" and "The
Weapons of Mass Destruction Psychic Hotline" occasionally have made the
news when marches and other protest actions have not.

This is not to say that protests today should be or are "all fun and games."
The seriousness of purpose with which many antiwar and anti-imperialist protesters approach demonstrations can also translate into serious tone and action. For example, prior to the Japanese government's deliberations on whether
or not to maintain a deployment of SDF troops in Iraq, protestors gathered in
Tokyo's Ebisu Park and in front of the prime minister's official residence on
December 5, 2004, to appeal for an immediate withdrawal. Speeches focused
on the heavy toll of the assault on Fallujah, in terms of both the dead and the

cultural devastation. Such rallies, in which protestors see themselves as speaking of and for the dead, while also perhaps being largely symbolic, convey a sense of urgency sometimes lost in more playful forms of protest. Protests in Saitama on November 7, 2004, were especially serious not only for the content of the demonstrators' antiwar messages. Reports began circulating soon after the protest began that someone had set off a homemade bomb outside the nearby Asaka SDF base. Two explosions were heard while Prime Minister Koizumi Junichirō was visiting the base for a celebration marking the fiftieth anniversary of the SDF. According to the *Mainichi Shimbun*, "radical guerrillas" were blamed.[13] Aside from a handful of very cursory reports, virtually no attention was paid to this bombing story. The identities of the "radical guerrillas" and the purpose of their actions disappeared with other unanswered questions almost as soon as the incident was reported. (Three years later, in February, U.S. Vice President Dick Cheney's visit to Japan inspired a similar bombing at a base near Tokyo, and this, too, received scant coverage.) In contemporary Japan, as we will see in the following example, as well, the mass media participate in (or abide by) a suppression of information related to certain protest actions.

In August 2005, a fifty-year-old woman brought her grievances as directly to Koizumi as she could. She approached his residence in a car. When she was unable to reach Koizumi, she began stabbing herself. The following was one of only a handful of news reports on this particular incident: "A woman driver tried to forcibly enter the prime minister's official residence on Tuesday and then stabbed herself when she was stopped by police, officials said. The woman slashed herself in the neck, abdomen and wrists as police tried to wrestle her from her car, police said. Police said the woman was a 50-year-old homemaker from Nagano City. About 20 to 30 handbills bearing slogans opposing Prime Minister Koizumi's government were found in the car, police said. Police riot squad officers and about 50 reporters were at the scene."[14] Despite the presence of reporters, the print and television media's attention to this event amounted to little more than such cursory descriptions. The limited information made it easier to dismiss the woman as "desperate" and "crazy," and the story quickly disappeared and was generally forgotten. Whether or not the woman survived the suicide attempt and what her handbills indicated about her grievances were not accorded even the slightest attention in the corporate and state mass media.

A sense of desperate urgency, of being "fed up" and outraged, underwrote all of the protest actions I have mentioned thus far and was particularly pronounced in the publicity for the protest in Nagoya on June 6. On one of the flyers distributed to advertise that protest, a man is pictured holding a black flag and preparing to leap or pounce. Next to him is the caption: "Enough already with this screwed-up world and screwed-up routine! We're setting off a screwy ruckus in response to the screwed-up way things are, and by and for the screwed." Admittedly, this translation is inadequate. The phrase I have translated as "screwed-up" is *roku demo nai*, an expression that connotes lack of value, purpose, and meaning. Likewise, what I call "ruckus" is referred to as a *bakuon demo* in the original. *Bakuon* is made up of the characters for "explosion" (as in bomb) and sound (as in music), and *demo* is short for "demonstration." The flyer included the following position statement:

> You bust your ass for measly wages. You can't find a job you want. You have no dreams, no hopes. And what's up with all these surveillance cameras? They are not just in convenience stores and banks. They're on street corners! And as if all that weren't bad enough, people are being killed for financial gain! People are being killed every day! Are you really OK with this? It's unbearable! And the indifference is the worst!
>
> In the name of the public good, they're cracking down on our freedom. They say we can't use the streets and the parks as we like? Hold on! Aren't they the people's streets and parks? Haven't they always belonged to the people? We will not be manipulated by the government and its kept mass media anymore! The flag? The national anthem? You're willing to die for the homeland? Please! We won't die for Koizumi, big corporations, or Dear America's business interests. Hell no! We hate what we hate. We'll decide how we live and how we die!
>
> More than 10,000 people have been killed in Iraq, and the killing continues! You call that "liberating" Iraq? This is no joke! Aggression is aggression. And it's only natural to resist aggression. Don't call resistance terrorism! Japan is contributing massive financial, material, and human resources to the American military; that's supporting the murder of "Iraqis." Withdraw the SDF now! No more support for war!
>
> Every day, the news is disgusting. Of course we're pissed off. But we need to do something with our anger, by any means necessary.

June 6 is a day for the screwed up and screwed over of the world to unite. Bring a drum, a pot, or a pan, or whatever else you'd like, and let's give the world an earful of our rage! No more places where they "manage" and "control" our freedom! Hell no! We'll sing, we'll yell, we'll dance in the streets!!

Free the Streets! Free the People!

The trajectory of issues espoused by some of the protesters included abolition of the SDF and the emperor system, characteristically anarchist positions.

Such views have been dismissed as overly idealistic, at best, by critics on the left and maligned as unpatriotic or terrorist by those on the right. Furthermore, the dominant cultures in the U.S. and Japan historically have portrayed, and continue to portray, anarchists as dangerous, immoral, and irresponsible. As Naitō Chizuko explains, news reporting on anarchists in the early twentieth century not only fostered fear of anti-establishment organizing, but also characterized anarchists as debauched and engaged in a scandalous "lifestyle." She cites many newspaper articles, one of which, "The Unseemly Habits of the Kashiwagi Anarchists," appeared in the June 25, 1907, issue of Tokyo's *Asahi Shimbun* and included the following "evidence" of anarchist dissolution:

Daily Activities

The usual suspects assemble for meetings, and thus their lifestyle involves having a good time. First, to throw out merely one example, one need only look to the time when Kanno Suga and Arahata lived together illicitly in a house in Kashiwagi. They would roll out of bed around ten o'clock in the morning and loaf around all day doing nothing. Before long, night would fall and suspicious-looking student-type fellows would throng into the house, reciting utterly subversive tunes, carrying on, stamping their feet, and debating every night until two or three in the morning.[15]

As Naitō elaborates, this anarchist "lifestyle" was depicted as an illness by the media.[16] Women engaged in the "lifestyle" were particularly lambasted as sexually deviant. If their personal lives were so unconventional and "sick," surely, as readers were led to believe, their political goals must be equally as twisted.

A similar campaign against anarchists is evident in recent U.S. news media. The policing of anarchists' activity and concomitant criticism of the behavior and values of anarchists have been particularly pronounced in the wake of September 11, 2001. For example, on the heels of a successful conference of young anarchists of color from across North America held in Detroit, law enforcement stepped up its efforts to intimidate and incarcerate these youths, who have been organizing more and more effectively in greater numbers. On November 15, 2003, police raided a benefit party at the office of the prison abolition group Critical Resistance in New York City hosted by local members of Antiauthoritarian and Anarchist People of Color (APOC), assaulting and arresting several of those in attendance even though no crime was being committed—other than one individual allegedly holding an open container of alcohol outside the event. With the exceptions of an interview with Maruyan Tiruchelvam, one of those who was assaulted, on *Democracy Now!* and some reports on Indymedia sites, this event went largely uncovered by media in the United States. As Tiruchelvam explained, several of the people who were assaulted by the police "did not get to go the hospital until after they were released," even though some of them had been seriously injured.[17]

Eric Lichtblau addresses police surveillance of anarchists in an article for the *New York Times* on November 23, 2003. He cites a confidential memorandum the FBI sent to law-enforcement agencies in October 2003 regarding the collection of "information" on antiwar activists. While the memo urges police to assist the bureau in the monitoring of all protest activities, it singles out "anarchists" and "extremist elements" as special subjects of "information gathering" efforts.[18] Concern over anarchist activity has not been limited to the FBI and police agencies. Liberal public intellectuals also malign anarchists, particularly anarchist youth, for what is perceived to be "extremism," "immaturity," and "irresponsibility." These attacks on anarchists are not unlike the characterizations of early-twentieth-century anarchists in Japan that Naitō describes, and they, too, follow a predictable formula: Anarchists are disgruntled and unruly youth in black who see protests as opportunities to engage in random violence and mayhem. Lamenting what they perceive to be immature attempts to discredit "appropriate" protest actions, many liberals and even some progressives contend that "these kids" should be policed. For example, in an editorial published in November 2003, Molly Ivins invokes the myth of the anarchist ne'er-do-well, writing, "These anarchists wear black masks and run around breaking store windows, a tactic that is not only a breach of the peace but also considerably less effective against GATT [the General Agreement on Tariffs and Trade] and NAFTA [the North American Free Trade Agreement] than singing 'Kumbayah.' "[19] Although presumably intended as part of a sustained joke about how unthreatening the peace movement is (hence, the hyperbolic reference to the song "Kumbaya"), this statement relies on the post–Seattle model of anarchist vilification (window-breaking kids in black). Ivins also asks, "Why doesn't the FBI infiltrate anarchist groups that are opposed to free trade agreements, instead of the peace move-ment?"[20] Ivins's question here reinforces the overdetermined myths about young anarchists and justifies the increasing police crackdown on anarchist youth as somehow unrelated to the rights of more "peaceful" and "mature" protestors to express dissent. It is also, of course, a question based on a false premise in that the FBI does place informants in anarchist groups that oppose free-trade agreements.

Leaving aside discussions about how many "violent" acts attributed to anar-chists in Seattle and elsewhere appear to have been carried out by undercover police-agent provocateurs (hardly anarchists), I would like to highlight what is conveniently left out of the fantasy image of young anarchists as immature or dissolute troublemakers: their ideological seriousness of purpose. Anarchists, as different as we may be in terms of our age, backgrounds, and specific concerns, tend to share a commitment to mutually rewarding relationships free of hierarchy and oppression or exploitation. Many of us do not believe that differential power is a given in life and that other patterns of relationship are already present, preferable, and worth sustaining. And despite what might be seen as more than a century of "anarchist bashing," anarchist anti-statism persists, as do other less obviously politicized forms of anti-authoritarianism. We might then conclude that the conditions inspiring anarchists' aspirations have not disappeared; nor has the urgency of such yearnings if anarchists are still willing to risk incurring personal injury and incarceration to make their views heard, to make their grievances visible. Making distinctions between anarchists and the peace movement writ large might be warranted in that many anarchists today continue to eschew the pacifism of peace movements in favor of a self-defense stance reminiscent of the Black Panther Party, the Japanese Red Army, the Weather Underground, the American Indian Movement, and even Kanno Sugako. Instead of using such distinctions to justify a differential standard in policing, however, we might consider how pacifism becomes inef-fectual, harmful, or even irrelevant.[21]

Regardless of whether one considers herself a pacifist or how one under-stands the role of violence in affecting political change, violent reactions to conditions of oppression, even those one may not perceive as such, do occur. Such violence often appears to have no relationship to political conditions, particularly when it is relayed to us via mass media. Violent acts committed by youth, for example, are rarely understood by those youth or society in general as responses to political conditions. As the two previous chapters indicate, such acts are more often deemed "inexplicable" or attributed to individual pathol-ogy. If we preach "personal responsibility" to youth and discourage them from criticizing society, we in effect may be writing our own death warrants, an idea that is not so far-fetched or merely polemical. When direct resistance is rendered impossible, when people of any age are prevented from seeing the mechanisms of their suffering or oppression (or someone else's), when they are prevented from developing a cogent and relevant alternative analysis (whether it be anarchist or something else), the results can be horrifying *because the rage still seeks an outlet, and in the absence of a direct and understandable target, the outcome is often mangled beyond recognition.* Hoshino Tomoyuki's novels zero in on precisely such mangled scenarios and explore both the social and political conditions that create them. In particular, *Lonely Hearts Killer* challenges readers who are not content with existing social or political conditions to build a meaningful alternative analysis. Hoshino achieves this not by producing didactic art or providing dogmatic answers. While he writes what might be characterized as "political" or "politicized" fiction, he is not a propagandist. Indeed, it warrants repeating that the reading that follows is only one of many possible interpretations of the fictional world he creates in *Lonely Hearts Killer*.

Chronicling the End of Days

If one were to compare Hoshino's fiction with that of other contemporary authors, perhaps one fitting comparison would be the work of Leslie Marmon Silko. Both writers foreground the ways in which political forces affect private lives, and both also produce complex and richly layered works that make intersubjectivity inescapable. For Hoshino and Silko, the adage that all life is interrelated and that oppression anywhere affects people everywhere is more than a "touchy-feely" theme; it is a fundamental organizing principle of reality. And neither writer avoids the messiest and most disturbing examples of global intersubjectivity. Suicides, murders, disappearances, and accidents are never self-contained or isolated incidents involving only a few (even when the toll on individuals is apparent). They are, instead, products of far-reaching and sometimes suppressed relationships that, in turn, produce widespread effects. Significantly, both writers turn to what might be termed the "supernatural" to represent some of the most buried or obscured relationships, but that is not to say that their works are not grounded in a concern for the material suffering of the living.

Lonely Hearts Killer, like Silko's *Almanac of the Dead*, might even be read as a creative diagnostic manual for what ails us. Both novels can be read as long and intricate preambles to better worlds that we, as readers, might imagine, and each novel sets the stage for what could be (or seems likely to be) the end of something big: the emperor system, Japan, the American century, or white supremacy. In Silko's epic saga, indigenous people, the poor, and the disaffected from across the Americas respond to signs that the prophesied disappearance of all things European from the hemisphere is at hand. She weaves together stories of white excess and brutality with indigenous organizing and resistance. She even delves into tensions within various anticolonial and insurgent factions that impede growing resistance movements. Hoshino tells of another "end of days"—that of the Japanese emperor system—and the rise of an underground organization engaged in the extralegal movement of people across national borders for vague and perhaps (depending on how one interprets several key passages) politically ambiguous purposes.

Borders of all sorts are significant in both *Almanac of the Dead* and *Lonely Hearts Killer*. They are arguably the most contested sites, what some characters seek to reinforce and others seek to destroy. National borders, for example, are of great concern to the governments in each novel, and considerable resources are invested in "securing" them. The U.S. government deploys troops to the U.S.-Mexican border to stave off the insurrection of the poor and indigenous in *Almanac of the Dead*, and wealthy elite on both sides of the border turn to private security contractors to protect themselves and their interests. In *Lonely Hearts Killer*, we also see glimpses of xenophobia and racism, directed most overtly at anyone or anything that seems Chinese, as well as a growing hostility toward the elderly and infirm that translates into a push for state-mandated euthanasia and official eugenics. The immigrant bashing in *Lonely Hearts Killer* gives way to utilitarian allowances for otherwise criminalized immigration. For example, a popular new prime minister enacts martial law and creates opportunities for foreigners to obtain citizenship if they serve in the military. (His simultaneous push for euthanasia to reduce the population of senior citizens prompts an exodus of the elderly abroad.) There are also characters, such as Mokuren in *Lonely Hearts Killer* and La Escapía in *Almanac of the Dead*, whose work involves defying border laws and moving people across national boundaries. In the chapter Silko titles "Imaginary Lines," the character of Calabazas describes borders as a matter of "belief": "We don't believe in boundaries. Borders. Nothing like that. We are here thousands of years before the first whites. We are here before maps or quit claims. We know where we belong on this earth."[22]

Anti-immigrant sentiment is always just beneath the surface in the world of *Lonely Hearts Killer*. It takes little (bad weather while one couple is dining in Chinatown, for example) for some characters to voice the undercurrent of superiority easily tapped by the majority of the society Hoshino depicts. When Mokuren, a woman with what some take to be a foreign-seeming name, takes out an advertisement in a newspaper to express her feelings about widespread fear of murder-suicides and declare her resolve not to kill anyone, the response is curiously fierce and often couched in terms of her perceived ethnic or cultural difference.[23] For example, Hoshino brings in one such voice through a professor of modern Asian history who responds to Mokuren's advertisement by publishing a letter that reads in part, "I do not know where you came from, but is it really that fun for you to bring your chaos to this Island Country? Right when we all came together as a people, proud and united in our stand and ready to defeat the threat to our security, you cut it short. . . . I am not saying go back to where you came from, but just keep to yourselves, do not bother us, and we'll leave you alone, too. It is customary in this country for people not to cause one another trouble. As long as you intend to stay here, I suggest you mind that custom" (198).

Mokuren's public rejection of the culture of fear gripping society in the "Island Country" is threatening, but the perception of her as an outsider seems enough to damn her—even though she grew up in the Island Country, as did many others whose names might seem "foreign." Mokuren, who lives in a remote mountain retreat, is tracked down and attacked by a member of a paramilitary organization called the South Kantō Community Watch. Both *Lonely Hearts Killer* and *Almanac of the Dead* feature central characters such as Mokuren whose lives and work involve risky border crossings. In the case of Silko's novel, the effects of changed borders on those already accustomed to moving freely across the land raises questions specific to the Americas. In *Lonely Heart's Killer*, Mokuren's family has ties to China (although neither China nor Japan is named as such, as I will explain later), and these ties to "the mainland" and vast network of connections in both countries enable her to operate an underground railroad of migrants between both places. Significantly, those who, like the professor, attack her in the press and on the Internet, as well as the paramilitary members, do not know this. Neither, apparently, does a close friend who lives with her. However, in the third and final chapter of the novel, when Mokuren herself is the narrator, she explains her work as follows:

> I find above-board job opportunities for those from the mainland looking for work on these islands and those from these islands who want to cross over to the mainland. Obviously, all the work involved in that process is

more than I can do on my own. People like me shuttle from here to there and there and back delivering human resources. The world's a big bathtub full of people, and our job is to stir it up . . .

Even though my role in the process is completely legal, after they cross, some of the people I place commit crimes. That's why the Feds have their eyes on me. I think they set up police surveillance at our mountain retreat so they could check on the comings and goings of myself and those close to me. . . .

I'm probably seen as a necessary evil on these islands, where fewer babies are being born, and on the mainland, too. Actually, I'm getting fat off [Prime Minister] Kishi Terujirō calling for foreigners to join the military and scaring the elderly overseas. That's not all. Kishi Terujirō is putting his own head in the noose. (239–40)

Her extralegal movement of people across borders can be read in many ways: as exploitative, *coyote*-style work or as a front for a growing political resistance, especially given the last sentence, to list just two possibilities.

My students enjoy debating many possible interpretations of what Mokuren "really does" precisely because Hoshino has left the reasons for her enterprise unclear and provided "evidence" that can support often very different readings, my favorite of which involves her providing the "retreat" as a training camp for revolutionaries who will take their positions in various industries and sectors (government, banking, media, etc.) to dismantle the entire social and political system of the Island Country. Indeed, many different types of people "stay" at the retreat, where they engage in activities that range from number crunching to physical training. A group of young men obsessed with "extreme" experiences could be "typical" young men, but they also could be Ruckus Society–type activists prepared to scale skyscrapers and tag subway stations. The room to speculate is sufficient to support very different conclusions. For example, an "arsenal of farming tools" purchased for the mountain retreat could be nothing more than what Mokuren and her friends need to tend their vegetable garden, but it could also be a crude self-defense kit. Mokuren's friend Kisaragi (also the name adopted by a character in *The Treason Diaries*) does not know about the farming tools, but she does know about public hostility toward the retreat and says, "We must be ready to defend ourselves by any means necessary." Mokuren herself, however, seems to disavow violence—at least, in the declaration "I Won't Kill," she pays to have published in a newspaper. This detail in the novel also lends itself to a range of interpretations, which can differ greatly among readers depending on the extent to which they read the paid advertisement as genuine and sincere or a secret message to insurgents.

In *Almanac of the Dead*, the revolutionary "migrant" underground's activities are made more explicit. For example, two sisters born in Mexico migrate as children to the North American Southwest, and they supply arms and other resources to indigenous people across the hemisphere. Nevertheless, both novels end with the possibilities and results of "treasonous" border crossings left open-ended. Readers are taken up to the moment when the "giants," as one character (Awa Gee) in *Almanac of the Dead* calls them, are about to fall, and the people are on the move.

Revolutionary Suicide

Lonely Hearts Killer is made up of three long chapters, each narrated by a different key character, and its multilayered and richly detailed plot leads in very unexpected directions. One theme that courses through the work as a whole is the disaffection and depression that can sneak up on those who benefit from the suffering of others they do not see, or choose not to see—the psychic gout brought on from "living too well." The symbiotic bond between consumption (of high-tech entertainment or a rare tea for example) and violence feeds off depression and yearning, because the drive to consume (to fill the sadness or overcome suffering) can never be sated, and the only way out of the resulting chronic disappointment, for more than a few characters, is violent death. The violent incidents Hoshino depicts are plausible extrapolations on the most nightmarish of the evening news, spectacles that deflect attention away from the conditions that produced them. And still, as will become increasingly apparent in the discussion that follows, Hoshino ensures that we cannot leave the world of his story with the sense that the violence was "inexplicable." Constantly calling attention to itself as a locus of suffering is the emperor system, and all of the violence somehow points to that system and what it represents, even when other identifiable political, social, and interpersonal exigencies are also involved.

The worldview I identify at work in *Lonely Hearts Killer* is notably consistent with the political theory of the Black Panther Party's co-founder Huey P. Newton, so much so that one could say Hoshino's novel plays out the kind of scenario Newton believed was inevitable. In the manifesto introducing his autobiography, *Revolutionary Suicide*, Newton argues for an approach to political resistance that complicates traditional understandings of violence, suicide, and martyrdom. Newton distinguishes what he calls "revolutionary suicide" from the loss of hope characteristic of suicidality among the oppressed, the latter being, according to Newton, ultimately in the interest of perpetuating existing differential power relations. (Put simply, if you are poor, black, and unhappy, white-supremacist society would rather have you kill yourself than challenge the conditions that make you poor and unhappy.) Newton complicates the conventional portrayal of the willingness of Black Panther Party members and other revolutionaries to risk incurring the wrath of state violence as suicidal not by rejecting the term, but by investing it with new meaning. He explains, "It is better to oppose the forces that would drive me to self-murder than to endure them."[24] Using the modifiers of his milieu, Newton posits that "revolutionary suicide," unlike "reactionary suicide," stems from a desire to live—not as the individual subject, but as the collective. This inflection allows room for Newton to see his efforts as part of a continuum, part of a sustained campaign for survival. His vision of revolution is therefore necessarily far-reaching in scope. He writes:

> [If] the Black Panthers symbolize the suicidal trend among Blacks, then the whole Third World is suicidal, because the Third World fully intends to resist and overcome the ruling class of the United States. If scholars wish to carry their analysis further, they must come to terms with that four-fifths of the world which is bent on wiping out the power of the empire. In those terms the Third World would be transformed from suicidal to homicidal, although homicide is the unlawful taking of life, and the Third World is involved only in defense. Is the coin then turned? Is the government of the United States suicidal? I think so.[25]

For Newton, "revolutionary suicide" is thus ultimately an expression of hope and, in his words, "not defeatist or fatalistic."

We can see both the fatalistic and the revolutionary in *Lonely Hearts Killer*, but perhaps no characterization of the need for political resistance posited by the novel as a whole would be more apt than Newton's assertion—even though (or "because," in Newton's terms) the setting is decidedly First World. The characters in *Lonely Hearts Killer* who might appear to suffer the most are comfortably middle-class young adults who have no sense of their own privilege, who, as one character (Inoue) explains, do not consider working for a living or worrying about how one will to be able to eat (let alone get a job) real concerns. Their middle-class disaffection fuels another kind of suicide, one that appears nihilistic on its face but speaks volumes about globalization, xenophobia, and political power. Japan (albeit unnamed as such) in Lonely Hearts Killer is, like Newton's United States, suicidal.

Here again, the parallels to Almanac of the Dead are striking. In both works, we see "senseless" violence among the apparent beneficiaries of First World privilege—the "middle class," university students, and so on. For example, in Lonely Hearts Killer, we find throughout the long second chapter examples of shocking suicide pacts and murder-suicides such as the following.

> At the peak of the rainy season, the corpses of two men were discovered inside a parked car in Aokigahara. Exhaust was running in through a hose. They were students at the same university in the city, where they apparently hung out quite a bit. They were holding hands, their wrists bound together by rope, and, in what appeared to be painful homemade tattoos, each had the name of the other etched into his arm with these words: "Chung-chi, Blood for Life" and "Kōsuke, Blood for Life." All the more horrifying, each had a couple hundred CC's of the other's blood, which was of a different type, injected into his own body. There was also evidence they'd taken narcotics. (118)

Mothers killing themselves and their children, children killing their parents and themselves, and couples committing "love suicides" fill much of the long second chapter. After the two young men in Aoikigahara die, the "rate of love suicides escalated with each passing day."

The inaugural event in the media's story of the "Love Suicide Era" is the murder-suicide of two young men (Inoue and Mikoto) who are vilified and later branded as "cultish" figures when copycat incidents and variations ensue. Despite what can be interpreted as vague political motivations in Inoue's and Mikoto's case, as well as hints of sociopolitical elements in some of the ensuing "incidents," it is not until the "love suicides" take on a more overtly political form that they are portrayed as a threat to national security. The media's changing labels for these "incidents" reflect the state's interest in stoking fear while purporting to fight the perceived trend as well as the impact the media's story of a "Love Suicide Era" has on individuals. For example, a thirty-three-year-old man, after more than a decade of failing the bar exam, integrates his interpretation of the "first" love suicide with his criticism of the legal system. Specifically, he invests new meaning in the call made by Inoue (one of the two to die in the "first" incident) for people to kill themselves and take at least one other person with them in death. He does so by choosing to kill a government figure and representative of the legal system, the minister of justice, before killing himself. The media brands this the first of the "assassination suicides" (136–38).

As the following passages illustrate, the "era" continues with new types of "love suicide" and concomitant political developments.

> The first indiscriminate love suicide occurred after Christmas near the end of December when the Communications Monitoring and Prevention of Subversive Activities Acts were revised. (140)

> The Chief Secretary of Cabinet proclaimed, "This is indiscriminate murder and a new breed of suicide terrorism. It differs from crimes of a personal nature such as love suicides." (141)

> The mass media didn't delve into the particulars of any case, but instead started to fill the airwaves with special features on how to avoid "personal terrorism." They offered friendly advice on avoiding rush hour trains, busy streets on weekends, and crowded places from which it could be hard to flee, and created stereotypical profiles of "dangerous types" to watch out for. There were also segments on how to use martial arts techniques and legal weapons to fend off attacks from suspicious characters. Every channel and every magazine tried to attract attention with more or less the same kinds of baseless predictions about how the economy looked better for next year and how that meant fewer people would want to die. And the commentators who enjoyed the most popularity were hawkish right-wingers who accused the government of "sitting around and doing nothing while the people's security and safety were in jeopardy."
>
> Along with deep chills, the dead of winter saw an increase in incidents branded with unfortunate labels like indiscriminate love suicide, random street killing-suicide, personal terrorism, and suicide-terrorism. There were seven more incidents in January and an even sharper rise in February, when there were eleven in the first two weeks alone and not a single day in the second half of the month without an incident. By that point, society was pretty much in a state of panic. The police increased their street presence all over the country to little effect, because it's simply not possible to prevent crimes when you don't know when and where they'll occur. (142–43)

Because the main characters are involved, to differing extents, in the "first" love suicide that sparked the era and because the media coverage of ensuing incidents is so integral to the plot, the brief "corrective" reading of the love-suicide trend Hoshino inserts in the story is at once jarring and pointed in its implicit criticism of mass-mediated (manufactured) crime trends in our own societies.

As explained in earlier chapters, the mass media can have a decisive role in the ordering and valencing of public fears, and Hoshino (a former journalist) draws attention to perspective and priorities in his fictionalized culture of fear through a brief description in the advertisement Mokuren takes out in the newspaper. She writes:

> "Please take a good look at reality. There is no mass destruction or carnage happening to justify the sensational use of expressions like 'survivor' or 'survival.' Since early April of last year, there have been a total of fifty-eight incidents of this [love-suicide] type. Slightly less than one hundred people have died. Of course, these are not merely numbers, but we have to examine the meaning we invest in them. After all, more people die in traffic accidents. If we set aside unnecessary fears, which lead to unnecessary panic, and look at this coolly and calmly, the chances of experiencing such an incident are very slim." (186)

Hoshino thus calls attention to the ways in which the mass media define and direct our fears and also, throughout the novel, raises troubling questions as to why certain types of violence (what is called "private" or "personal terrorism" in the novel) occur in contemporary consumer societies.

Once again, the parallels to Silko's work are striking and warrant mention. Near the end of *Almanac of the Dead*, which was published in 1991 (before the Columbine High School shootings), we find the following passage, which now might seem uncanny or prescient:

> "The enraged spirits haunted the dreams of society matrons in the suburbs of Houston and Chicago. The spirits had directed mothers from country club neighborhoods to pack the children in the car and drive off hundred-foot cliffs or into flooding rivers, leaving no note for husbands. A message to the psychiatrist says only, 'It is no use any longer.' They see no reason for their children or them to continue. The spirits whisper in the brains of loners, the crazed young white men with automatic rifles who slaughter crowds in shopping malls or school yards as casually as hunters shoot buffalo."[26]

In both novels, the citizens of a First World nation are gripped with fear, and both novels suggest that this fear is manufactured but also somehow indicative of a collectively guilty conscience, an awareness (however subconscious) that the enjoyment of comforts exacted from the suffering of others is not sustainable. The primary vehicle for stoking this fear and making it commercially and politically lucrative is the news media.

Fact, Fiction, and the News

Suicide, murder, and even "natural" death in Lonely Hearts Killer, as in the case of Hoshino's other works, come to us in the form of incidents. In his novella Suna no wakusei (Sand Planet), a fictional poisoning in a school lunchroom is compared to a real-life incident in Wakayama involving a woman who laced curry with arsenic at an outdoor festival. In chapter 4, I described Hoshino's use of a fictionalized takeover of the Japanese embassy in Peru by the MRTA as a vehicle for exploring yet another headline-news figure, the seemingly ubiquitous teen killer of the late 1990s. Although it is not uncommon to find fiction inspired by or drawn from the news, Hoshino foregrounds the presentation of "news," writing the reporting process (the framing, exaggerating, and flat-out misleading) into his fiction. This is perhaps nowhere as explicit as in the case of Yoshinobu, the main character in Sand Planet who is so caught up in the "news" he writes that readers are left at a loss as to where to find the line between "news" and "fiction."

Chronological time and actual events are displaced by the immediacy with which Yoshinobu experiences his own memories and fantasies. He begins to believe what he imagines as even "more real" than "reality": "Yoshinobu was overwhelmed by the reality of the article he'd written. He believed the words reflected on the monitor with all his heart and soul. He thought they were the absolute truth."[27] As I asserted in part 1, storytelling often functions as a way to make sense of trauma. (In Yoshinobu's case, the traumatic "incident" that motivates "telling" might be his father's death.) However, Yoshinobu, unlike Shizuko and Bone, surrenders totally to Orpha; the fragment overwhelms the whole. Orphic expression becomes a totalizing force in Yoshinobu's adult life, and he believes in the alternative worlds and stories it creates. Total reliance on Orpha precludes other opportunities for growth and awareness, and thus Yoshinobu's story is a tragic one.

Yoshinobu submits the article he believes (as if it were "the absolute truth") to his managing editor, who calls for a meeting. The editor tells Yoshinobu that "the content is OK" but the style is "too literary." When the editor says newspaper articles should be grounded in fact, Yoshinobu replies that is precisely what he had sought to achieve in writing the article.[28] This problem of what the editor considers "style" is integral to Yoshinobu's experience of the world. His progressive "breakdown" after the encounter with the editor culminates in a final, immobilizing descent into fantasy. "Frozen," Yoshinobu watches his story disintegrate as he reads another version, the version deemed fit to print in the newspaper.

Naitō Chizuko reminds us in the introduction to *Empires and Assassinations* that confusion such as Yoshinobu's is not without precedent.

> Stories pervade—everywhere. One could even say that stories are not only that which is written to be literary, but that which is routinely born out of an arrangement of words. For example, a storytelling quality is pronounced in the language the news media uses to relate certain kinds of incidents in ways that inspire in readers a desire to know.
>
> *The gap between her pedigree as an elite graduate of the private Keiō University and the reality of her life as a "woman of the night" is attracting attention to the murder of Ms.——, a 39 year old OL [office lady] at Tokyo Power whose body was discovered in an apartment in Tokyo's Shibuya District. What was the reason that led her to loiter around love hotels at night? (Shūkan Post, April 4, 1997)*
>
> *When news of this incident first broke, the top-tier elite Keiō graduate and Tokyo Power OL's nightlife as a street prostitute drew attention, and various media outlets, beginning with this publication, investigated the details of her mysterious personal life. (Shūkan Gendai, August 9, 1997)*
>
> These excerpts come from weekly news journal reports on the so-called Tokyo Power OL Incident of 1997. The victim was a woman, and the notion that this woman was a "top-tier elite OL" by day, but had a completely different face by night, was scrutinized repeatedly as a source of "attention" by the media. The reason why relates to the various particulars of this incident that lent themselves to it being narrated as a story.
>
> First and foremost, the mark of woman alone holds news value for its difference when both the sender and receiver of information are assumed to be male in the masculinized media world. Deviance from the norm or standard is more likely to pique curiosity, so it is desirable for a protagonist to have some distinguishing characteristic, scar, or differential negative in a story. Second of all, the extreme "gap" between her afternoons and evenings opens up a wide range for story development and promises of the depth so appealing in stories. The seeming endlessness of the story can raise the curiosity and expectations of readers higher and higher as they are drawn further

along for the ride. Third of all is her "mysterious personal life," which is imbued with sexual meaning. You want to know because it is "mysterious," and a sexual element is added to that desire, so the desire then multiplies and becomes a force that propels the story. In a context such as this, the story will always move in ways that discriminate against that character.[29]

As one of my students who read Naitō's introduction noted, "This is an unsettling and scary issue to ponder." She went on to ask, "If I watch the news like a movie, am I doing something wrong by seeing real war like a movie or something right by not trusting the story I'm seeing is real?" This question is one that Hoshino raises time and again in his fiction.

In keeping with the literary "incident-ism" and interest in "news" characteristic of his work, Hoshino takes the very title *Lonely Hearts Killer* (written in katakana to approximate the English pronunciation) from actual "incidents." Using "lonely hearts" personal columns to identify their victims, Martha Beck and Raymond Martinez Fernandez became the notorious "Lonely Hearts Killers" of the 1940s in the U.S. The novel also features a wide range of issues drawn from contemporary tabloid news (the lives of royalty and Internet suicide pacts) and right-wing punditry (anti-immigrant xenophobia and support for martial law), as well as incidents from Japan's present and past. Roughly two-thirds of the novel takes place in the mountain retreat (*sansō*), which, while introduced as a safe haven from the violence and chaos gripping the Island Country, evokes images of a real-life mountain retreat associated with one of the most "shocking" incidents of the 1970s: the Asama-Sansō incident (or the headquarters of the Aum Shinrikyo cult a few decades later). The image of a separatist (and, to some, dangerous) group of young adults holed up in a remote mountain retreat—no matter how fundamentally different that group might be—draws on televisual history of the moment when, as Setsu Shigematsu explains, a radical left appeared to turn on itself in a spectacle that was seen as signaling the end of certain revolutionary possibilities of the late 1960s and early 1970s in Japan.[30]

In February 1972, five members of the Japanese URA took over a lodge, holding a woman hostage, and the entire standoff was simulcast on Japan's national television network NHK. This televised "incident" is etched into the memories of Japanese people who were alive at the time. For example, the mother of a friend of mine recalled being pregnant at the time and worrying that the "stress" of watching the "terrifying" news would affect the health of her unborn child. The unforgettable image of 1970s leftist radicals in a mountain retreat (or fleeing to the mountains after blowing up police stations or killing politicians) often shows up in movies (such as Ogata Akira's film *Boy's Choir* [2000]), comics, and literature set in that period. A film in 2001 starring Yakusho Kōji depicts the standoff with "terrorists" from the police point of view.[31] The Asama-Sansō incident and NHK's coverage of it are also part of a much larger televisual and filmic history that is layered into *Lonely Hearts Killer*.

The individual chapter titles reflect the role and function of media in the "incident-ization" of death in the novel. The title of the first chapter is "The Sea of Tranquility," which refers not only to one young man's apocalyptic fantasy of a lunar landscape described in a document he released over the Internet before dying, but to the "art film" another character later makes to memorialize and express her relationship to that young man and the "incident" he perpetrates. This chapter title might also remind some readers of the title of Mishima's final tetralogy, *Hōjō no umi* (The Sea of Fertility), named after another "sea" on the moon and closely associated in the minds of many readers with Mishima's dramatic suicide. The second chapter, "The Love Suicide Era," is named after the news media's label for the fictional period of time covered in that chapter. The term "love suicide (*shinjū*)" itself evokes a long literary tradition for those familiar with works such as *Love Suicide at Amijima* of the eighteenth century and the life (and death) of the modern novelist Dazai Osamu. The third chapter and mountain pass where the retreat is located are named after Luis Buñuel's film *Subida al Cielo* (1951), which was released under the title *Mexican Bus Ride* in the U.S. but is better translated as "Ascent to Heaven." That film features an autonomous, somewhat communal village in the mountains of Mexico. Various media's reach into the story includes other references to films, such as *The Lady from Shanghai*, the Internet, cellular phones and text messaging, radio, and, of course, television. One central character (Mikoto) works at a television station while another (Inoue) runs an independent webcast site; one (Kisaragi) submits an op-ed piece to a newspaper while another (Mokuren) takes out an advertisement in a newspaper. The mother of yet another character (Iroha) is described as a "news junkie." Reporters (and the corporations and outlets for which they work) also drive much of the novel's plot and are involved in some of the most dramatic scenes.

We live with "infotainment" and news media that capitalize on "incidents," and many of us remember certain events (the Asama-Sansō siege, the O. J. Simpson freeway chase, the Columbine shootings) as they were shown on television. Yet as familiar as we all are with the conditions Hoshino integrates into his fiction, his works have been received as almost "foreign" by some prominent Japanese readers. In her commentary at the end of the paperback edition of *Mezameyo to ningyo wa utau* (The Mermaid Sings Wake Up; 2004), the novel that won Hoshino the Mishima Yukio Prize in 2000, the author (and translator of Madonna's children's books into Japanese) Kakuda Mitsuyo writes:

> Reading Hoshino's novels is like traveling to a strange land all by yourself. You touch down on an airfield in a foreign country, get your passport stamped, and leave the airport all nerves and anticipation. The area around an airport is more or less the same in any country. It is sterile and without character. There, you have no real sense of having come somewhere new. But then you take a deep breath and a smell you've never encountered enters your nose, a wind you've never felt brushes against your skin, and an unknown substance rains down upon your head.[32]

While Hoshino does create richly complex, compelling, and often surprising fictional worlds, Kakuda's airport analogy sidesteps the explicit political content of Hoshino's writing, which very directly engages topical debates, headlines, and lived realities of contemporary Japan. The impulse for some to read the familiar in Hoshino's writing as foreign, to distance themselves, and to separate is perhaps predictable given the unpleasant nature of the struggles Hoshino depicts.

Caravan Culture

Hoshino's fiction is simultaneously concerned with specific Japanese contexts and internationalist (and anti-nationalist) in scope. One sees this reflected in his life as a professional writer. For example, Hoshino has participated in several of what have come to be known as "writers' caravans." He has traveled and presented readings with writers from, for example, India and Taiwan. Operating outside traditional literary reading circuits and venues, these caravans bring together writers who otherwise might not have the opportunity to share concerns and ideas with one another. Caravan organizers provide makeshift translations and work with limited means to facilitate conversations and group readings. As a writer, Hoshino has allied himself not so much with the Japanese literary establishment, which has nonetheless recognized and celebrated some of his work with awards and accolades, as with his global peers. He has also lived in Mexico and traveled extensively in Latin America. It is perhaps not surprising, therefore, that his characters' experiences of Japan are not self-contained but, rather, always relating and related to other places.

Whether it is through the Japanese "juvenile criminals" living in exile in Peru in *The Treason Diaries*, the transnational "underground railroad" for immigrants in *Lonely Hearts Killer*, the reworking of the Urashima Tarō myth as immigrant saga in stories such as *Sand Planet*, the young Japanese man's search for guerrillas in "Chino," or the international romance in *The Tragedy of the Worussian Japanese*, movements and lives lived across borders figure prominently in his writing, as do other languages and places, particularly Spanish and Latin America.

The vocabularies and images of revolution, insurgency, and opposition to neoliberalism one finds represented in much of Hoshino's fiction are sometimes developed in Latin American contexts. Equally noticeable are references to Latin American cultural products throughout his oeuvre—Mexican beer in *Naburiai*; recordings of Andean flute music in *Sand Planet*; the Argentine tango great Ástor Piazzolla's *Live in Tokyo 1982* recording, which plays in the background as the characters Kenzo and Ivan watch a terrorist "incident" play out live on television in *The Tragedy of the Worussian Japanese*. Drawing together multiple cultures and places with slightly altered news stories is a hallmark of Hoshino's style, as is evident in the television-watching scene. Kenzo mutes the television's volume, and he and his daughter's boyfriend, Ivan, listen to Piazzolla's wildly intense music as "purple smoke billows out from inside" a famous skyscraper. As the tower collapses, Ivan says, "That's the work of George," implicating "his country's top man." Piazzolla's characteristically dissonant *nuevo tango*, a famous big city, and a president are thus layered into a private moment in an urban Japanese living room, much in the way that many of our private lives involve layers of mass-mediated and globalized "backdrops" and materially globalized relations.

When the presence of "the world" in Hoshino's fiction is discussed by Japanese literary critics, their focus is most often on Latin America. His reputation as an artist who engages Latin America is evident in the range of venues in which his opinion has been solicited—for example, in reviews of Spanish and Latin American films and in a featured conversation with Ōta Masakuni in a special issue of the journal *Gendai shisō* (Contemporary Thought) on Che Guevara.[33] However, it would be a mistake to characterize Hoshino's fiction or nonfiction as blithely celebrating Latin America, multiculturalism, the "foreign," or even the hybrid. Hybridity in his work is as much a site of crisis, where differential power operates both within and outside the hybrid space or body toward destructive ends, as it is an "equalizing" or egalitarian fantasy of infinite possibilities. Undoing the logic of the First World traveler who goes abroad to enjoy and maybe take home some "local flavor," Hoshino tackles the complicated and often ugly relationship of First World (primarily Japanese) subjects to the Third World. For example, in *The Treason Diaries*, we learn much less about why the fictionalized MRTA (Maruta) takes over the Japanese Embassy than how Yukinori experiences his involvement in the incident, and in the short story "Chino," the protagonist, Tomoyuki, travels to Central America in search of guerrillas (whom he hopes to join) and yet finds himself unable to divest himself of the yen (and its meanings) that make his very travels possible.[34]

Hoshino provokes in readers a discomfort or even revulsion toward some (or all) of his characters, which prompted one of my graduate students to confide, "I don't like Hoshino's characters, but I can't help getting caught up in his novels." Identification with Hoshino's often very flawed characters is surely complicated in different ways for different readers, but this student's response illustrates one of what I see as the signature features of Hoshino's work: No matter how repellent we may find a Hoshino character or situation, we can imagine ourselves into the worlds he creates—no matter how extreme, exaggerated, or fantastic they may at first glance seem. Therein lies the power of his fiction to provoke critical thinking. After all, if we can imagine ourselves into the apocalyptic, brutal, and painful spectacles he depicts, what does that say about how we understand and experience our own lived realities?

Critical turns or developments in Hoshino's plots often hinge on or respond to actual headlines, but equally important to his fictional worlds are the tellers, the newscasters, and the politics and processes of telling. The wages of telling on the teller are especially apparent in *Sand Planet*. Yoshinobu, the protagonist and unsuccessful journalist described earlier, appears to be so affected by the interpretations and extrapolations he creates out of "facts" that readers, as I explained, are left at a loss about how much of which story he tells is "real." Did a dramatic trauma trigger such a severe and ever escalating dissociative state that he cannot decipher fact from fiction? Is his memory of that trauma (or are his creepy reenactments of it) any more trustworthy than his tales of selective mute children in the woods or a folkloric immigrant saga involving homeless park dwellers? The unvoiced and unanswered question at the heart of the novella is: Is the entire story itself a dramatization of a breakdown "from the inside out"? One could say Hoshino's literary Molotov cocktails are also aimed at identity, both in its discrete, private form and in its broader articulations as a cultural or national signifier. In other words, if we are barely struggling to survive via Orphic functioning, can we even be sure who we are?

If nationality is a defining factor in identity, and the cultivation and unification of national identity is important in contemporary Japan, then Hoshino is surely a public dissident. In the spring of 2006, the popular baseball player Suzuki Ichirō left the Seattle Mariners to play for his home country of Japan in the World Baseball Classic, and he made comments prior to and after a game with South Korea that Hoshino found problematic, more so for how they would be received by the Japanese public than for how Ichirō (as he is known) may have intended them.[35] For example, Hoshino was concerned that by saying it would be "the greatest humiliation" of his baseball career to lose to South Korea, Ichirō made it seem acceptable to think less of Koreans. Of course, wanting to win (or not wanting to lose) is different from feeling "humiliated" to lose to someone. In an essay for the *Chūnichi Shimbun*, Hoshino contends that the word Ichirō used, "*kutsujoku*," connotes humiliation in the sense of being put in a position "beneath" oneself. This differential valuing, Hoshino observes, overrides any notion of rivalry or competition among equals (or "worthy" opponents) and can easily be translated into an amplification of anti—Korean sentiment in Japan. "No matter how you interpret it," he writes, "Ichirō's comments were discriminatory."[36] Hoshino has similarly written about expressions of nationalism (subtle and overt) in soccer and other sports. After Hoshino's essay about Ichirō appeared, right-wing criticisms of the writer, which had already been occurring, escalated. Internet publications such as *Police Japan* and discussion threads on the popular site 2channel featured threatening rants decrying him as a *han-nichi sakka* (anti—Japanese writer).[37]

One might thus be surprised that Hoshino's portrayal of two emperors in *Lonely Hearts Killer* is anything but vilifying and negative. They are relatively likeable and sympathetic characters who are not perfect but who seem earnest and thoughtful. In thinking about the sibling emperors and their story, it is important to note that Hoshino's fiction invariably calls attention to its embattled relationship to "Japaneseness" in critical but also sometimes playful ways. This playfulness is evident even at the level of word choice. In his novella *Zainichi woroshiyajin no higeki* (The Tragedy of the Worussian Japanese; 2005), the word *Nihon* (Japan) appears, as do the names of various places in Japan, but other proper nouns, such as *Anamerika* and *Worussia* are slightly altered to disarticulate them from their usual referents, a practice taken up by other writers, including Amiri Baraka (who has called Ronald Reagan "the Ray gun") and Ōba Minako (who has used creative "misspellings" to shake up the familiar in her fiction).[38] Although the proper noun *Nihon* is not used in *Lonely Hearts Killer* and the word *nihongo* (Japanese language) is used only once (when Iroha is badgered by a reporter), the story takes place in a nation referred to as the Island Country, and identifiably Japanese places such as Shinjuku and an Isetan department store are referred to by their usual names. Titles of famous Japanese newspapers, literary journals, and magazines are only slightly altered, often in very humorous ways. Like the anarchist protesters in Nagoya, Hoshino uses humor to provoke political questioning. The conventional words for China and Chinese (*chūgoku* and *chūgokugo*) are replaced with words based on the root word usually reserved for Chinese food and Chinatowns (*chūka*), such as *chūkago* (an invented word something akin to how "China-ese" might sound in English).

The emperors in *Lonely Hearts Killer* are referred to throughout as *okami*. The structure of the emperor system and the sense of a "continuous" and "uninterrupted" national and cultural identity it suggests have often been invoked to assert "Japaneseness." To some, nothing could be "more Japanese" than the emperor system, and critics of this system have been the targets of right wing nationalist violence on numerous occasions. The use of "okami" to refer to emperors is striking, particularly in the first chapter, where the word always appears in boldface. "Okami" means "emperor," the "imperial house," the "government," and "the powers that be," but also "proprietress" or female manager (of a restaurant, bar, etc.). While "*tennō*" may be a more common way to refer to the emperor in Japanese, "okami" lends itself to several themes that are pronounced in the novel. "Okami" is written phonetically in katakana throughout, which leaves available room to invest it with multiple meanings. If written as the term for an emperor in *kanji* (Chinese characters), the character for "above" or "top" would be used, underscoring political and social hierarchy and differential power (*jōge*, or "top-down" relations). The homonymous "proprietress" also proves significant, as one character notes, when the young emperor is succeeded by his sister.

We first encounter "okami" through the media, specifically through Inoue's characterizations of media accounts of the young okami's death in the first chapter. In these stories, as Inoue relates them, the young okami is distinguished from other recent okami by virtue of his youth, his sincerity, and the public's reaction to his unexpected death. For example, Inoue, who is the narrator of the first chapter, describes a public overcome with grief and notes, "It wasn't like this after the deaths of the previous **Okami**. And that must be further proof that the young **Okami** was different" (7). Evoking the beginning of the Heisei era in 1989, when the current emperor was in his fifties, and the public response to the political ascension of the affectedly youthful pentagenarian Koizumi Junichirō to the prime ministership in 2001, this passage establishes a plausible fictional alternative to the real present and sets up the island empire's saga that unfolds. The young okami makes an appeal at his succession ceremony that assures the Island Nation's citizens that they are special and important. His exhortation to cultivate the self and tolerate the Other is couched in the rhetoric of diversity but contributes to what Inoue refers to as self-serving interpretations. In the following passage, we are also subtly alerted to the potential for a sense of cultural superiority to hold sway over the island country's majority:

> The young **Okami** succeeded in mid-life and was like a breath of fresh air. He introduced an atmosphere of newness and made it feel as if we'd been unburdened of the collective death our aging society had shouldered and like our whole society was rejuvenated. He wanted to make a powerful statement at his succession ceremony and ended up stirring up a whirlpool of solidarity and inspiration with his ad-lib suggestion: "We must all live life in our own way and, instead of studying the face of another, hold ourselves to be precious and meet one another with respect in this Island Country. Isn't a 'big-as-life' society like that what we all should be building?" The content of his speech was good enough, but for many who heard him, it was the young **Okami**'s way of speaking that was truly as "big-as-life." More and more people, especially those in their thirties and forties, felt like they could trust the **Okami**, that he understood them all. Particularly since he was still single at that age and, moreover, didn't give off any marrying vibes, the growing sector of the population made up of middle-aged singles, divorcés, and even those who live as couples for appearance's sake felt a sense of connection that one could say was more than a bit self-serving. He took on a meaning different from the **Okami** before him. (8–9)

The popularity of the young emperor who captures so much of the public's imagination is quickly seized on by nationalists who recognize such a figure's potential to galvanize public sentiment in the service of their political goals.

Inoue tells us that the nationalist youth called for a "Restoration" (harking back to the Meiji Restoration) not long before the okami's death. Their plan (to restore the okami's right to hold political office and authority) is described this way:

Politicians today have fallen out of favor because they only work for a handful of vested interests, and those intellectuals and media moguls who could claim some charismatic popularity abused their power until they ended up destroying themselves. No politicians who have since emerged had enough support to take control of the government. At best, we are under crisis conditions in which the "sensibly nonpartisan" NGO types who move in and out of Parliament's revolving door have exposed their own incompetence. If we extend political rights to the **Okami** and He's elected, He could attract support that crosses party lines, and, in that case, without any barriers to Him taking charge of the government and without harming democracy in the least, our movement could give new life to the shell of this so-called democracy! (23)

After relating their plan, Inoue notes that heightened interest in the okami, along with hopes and expectations that he could in fact be a strong political leader, lent credibility to the otherwise "impossible proposition."

Inoue's own thoughts on both the okami and the political system are initially far more cynical. Yet the chapter he narrates (or writes) is the only one in which the word "okami" appears in boldface, and he is arguably the character most affected by okami:

For me, their sensational message smacked of mania mixed with a syrupy romance novel and just like the kind of fantasy the mass media loves. That could be because no one around me thought it would make a lick of difference whether the prime minister was the **Okami** or anybody else, for that matter. The media denounces political incompetence and corruption, but if the people around me or I were to tell it, the whole political scene is nothing more than groups of statesmen being moved around and played with by some unknown apparatus. Even if there weren't any politicians, society would keep running on autopilot. Or maybe like how the seasons change, governments are one of those things that spin around on their own. That's why even if a really strong leader appears, that person can't be more than what the machine dictates. We lack the optimistic energy to invest hope in or count on that sort of system. The only people who thought, without any basis, that society would change after the new **Okami**'s era began were relatively older. There probably aren't many people who can so much as imagine feeling connected to a government. (50)

Inoue, a twenty-something disaffected independent videographer who lives with his parents in a suburb of Tokyo, thus does not share the nationalist youth's excitement over the prospect of an emperor with political power. In the very first line of the novel, he claims that the emperor's death has not affected him significantly in any way. Inoue shows a political cynicism shared by many young adults in the First World. This cynicism, disillusionment, or apathy also appears in *Almanac of the Dead*: "The masses of people in Asia and Africa, and the Americas too, no longer believed in so-called 'elected' leaders; they were listening to strange voices inside themselves."[39] The voices to which Inoue listens are equally "strange." They lead him to see the real world around him as if it were a movie and eventually to believe that by killing his friend's boyfriend, Mikoto, and himself that a better world without any okami could be possible.

It is important to note that Mikoto's experience of the okami's death differs from Inoue's. The young emperor's death triggers a dissociative break in many young people, such as Mikoto, who shut down, almost catatonic, as if they suddenly sense something is terribly wrong or lose their will to live. Although, as we are told, individual youth "shut down" for various and specific reasons, the media labels them all "spirited away," and the phenomenon fascinates Inoue, who maintains he is utterly unaffected by other people in general. When his apathy comes into contact with the "spirited away" through his much anticipated introduction to Mikoto, the results are explosive, the Molotov cocktail that sets off the plot.

Apathy

While there is much to be said about Inoue's fascination with his best friend's boyfriend, Mikoto, and the events leading up to their deaths, where the two fit into social and political structures within the island nation and larger world are of particular significance to my reading of the novel. Inoue embodies a kind of privilege particular to the First World experience (which includes the affluent elite who enjoy First World status in the Third World). He never wants for food or shelter; he lives off his parents without the immediate need to work; he can pursue hobbies and entertainment; and he is quickly irritated and almost always self-absorbed. He carries the dis-ease, discomfort, and rage of First World consumerism, but the analysis he develops to explain these feelings (whether you call it nihilist, romantic, deluded, or something else) stops short of engaging political realities or the feelings and lives of others beyond the level of a morbid and melodramatic fantasy of an "other world."

Mikoto's life is in many ways the inverse of Inoue's, even though it is also decidedly First World. Inoue lives off his parents while Mikoto supports his.

Inoue describes his own parents as "liberal and genuinely invested in trying to be attentive to my life choices." Yet, he adds, "It's almost tragic how much they don't understand. Tragic to them—I don't give it much thought" (12). Inoue's descriptions of his parents are particularly unflattering when they raise questions related to his comfortable situation. Inoue's First World arrogance and sense of entitlement are most evident when he takes his experience as universal; when he, for example, dismisses the struggle anyone might encounter in working for a living because it "does not seem real" to him. It is not until Inoue introduces his resentment at being alive that we begin to see how this arrangement with his parents is not working for him:

> By assuming the debt to my family for room and board—and this is coming from the vantage point of someone who takes the meals they serve me for granted—I forfeited the right to choose starving to death from the get-go. Therein lies the cost of leeching off your parents. Among the average households of today, you'll find situations like mine everywhere. Parents allow themselves to be consumed while their kids sponge off them for years, and all the while both sides are thinking something isn't right. But since the circumstances are supposed to be part of a temporary and transitional phase, everyone defers the debt collection and hides any fears that they are losing their power to resist. Barring any major outbursts of conflict, year after year passes uneventfully. The upshot of all this being that the cost of staying alive is silence. (13–14)

While often the subject of jokes in popular culture, the figure of the adult child living with his parents in Lonely Hearts Killer is disturbing. Even Inoue wishes he had not "capitulated to the terms" of such a "silencing" arrangement. Yet prolonged dependence is not the only example of failed or inadequate parenting in the novel.

We learn about the differences in Inoue's and Mikoto's financial and familial situations from Inoue in the first chapter:

> I don't think about money when I'm filming. And at any rate, I'd given up on earning any. For someone who lives off others, nothing is more depressing than the thought of working in order to eat. People who go about their business as freelancers and say the same are a dime a dozen, but it's just an excuse. They are nothing more than words for fabricating an "authentic sense of being alive."

Mikoto might be a little different in that regard. He worked in the news department at a TV station. Even though he was young, he quickly was able to buy an apartment in Chiba, where he lived with his parents, whom he'd brought up from Daisen. According to Iroha, Mikoto's parents had no interest in getting by in the world, so the whole family had ended up in dire straits. Mikoto started supporting his family financially when he was still in high school. (28–29)

Mikoto's dramatic response to the young okami's death might be understood as a short-circuiting of his premature assumption of caretaker or provider responsibilities. Like the two okami who shoulder symbolic responsibility and might opt out under pressure in the end of Lonely Hearts Killer, Mikoto cracks under the pressure he endures as the "provider" for his "incorrect" family. In a society in which, Inoue tells us, adult children living off their parents constitute a normative situation, a family such as Mikoto's is aberrant.

In their first conversation, Mikoto tries to explain his experience after the okami's death to Inoue. He likens it to a kind of betrayal, of being confronted with a truth that had been obscured by what he had been socialized to believe (that, for example, there is meaning in life and death). He tells Inoue:

> "The breakdown caught me unaware, like a sneak attack. I don't remember clearly, but I thought something to the effect of this is nothing more than one person's death, and when one person dies, somewhere another is born, and it doesn't change anything. Then, I suddenly lost the will to do anything."
>
> "Because the same thing goes on for eternity?"
>
> "Up until that point, I'd been amazed by the concept of eternity. But this was different. What I felt was, first of all, that what I'd just thought had been a lie. The end of one life wasn't going to be replaced by the beginning of another. Because, at least in this Island Country, more people are dying than are being born. I can count the number of friends or superiors in my life who have kids. Inoue, I'll bet you've never even touched a child."
>
> "Now that you mention it, no, I never have." (56–57)

A young man who had assumed the role of parenting in his family and another who was in the midst of a prolonged state of dependence come to an understanding that something in their society is deeply wrong. The symptoms of that "wrongness" include a wide range of insufficient or destructive parenting, all of which are, in various ways, linked to the ultimate parent, the okami.

In the long second chapter, Iroha refers to the Island Country as a nation of children, drawing on the idea that the population as a whole has developed a dependence on the okami as symbolic parents. She reflects on Inoue's description of his family life and how he felt "being able to die" in a society such as theirs meant being able to exercise personal agency, to escape the embrace of the okami. Iroha muses:

> I wonder just how many mature, independent, self-sufficient, and responsible adults there are. Maybe those of us on these protruding islands are just a bunch of kids playing games like make-believe grownups and make-believe lovers, pretending to want to die and pretending to die. It's an island of children, where children just produce more children, and in a place like that, there can be no society in the true sense. Even though there are some kids passing as parents, there are no actual adult parents. In that sense, each and every one of us is an orphan. Where are our real adult parents? If they exist, who and where are they? (132)

In the final chapter, Mokuren suggests that by disappearing from public view, the new female okami, the sister of the *perhaps* deceased young okami, had *perhaps* decided not to serve as a proxy parent for all the "real" parents in the Island Country anymore—or decided it would be preferable to blend into the crowd and live as one of the many "children" herself.

Readers are left with the most questions in the case of Mokuren, whose story ends with such uncertainty as to preclude any facile interpretation, not only in terms of the nature of her transnational work as described earlier, but in terms of her attachments. She appears to have enjoyed better parenting than Inoue or Mikoto, but even that is somewhat ambiguous. Her parents seem to trust her to take on independent responsibilities (such as working in their business or buying a house in the mountains) and show up to support her (cooking meals, helping with projects around the house, and so on). They seem neither intrusive nor uninterested. Yet they are also the parents in the novel about whom we as readers know the least, and given the otherwise detailed attention to parenting in the novel, this lack of specificity surely is not accidental. We "meet" the parents of Inoue and Iroha, and we learn enough about Mikoto's parents and the okami to form our own opinions and interpretations as to the effectiveness or appropriateness of their (actual or symbolic) parenting. However, all we know of Mokuren's parents is that they help her get settled into the mountain lodge and have employed her. Readers are left with many layers of ambiguity in Mokuren's story, which allow us ample room to pose our own questions and make the interpretive claims that shape our understanding of the novel. Is she responding to social discrimination? Is she another one of the "parentless children" in the Island Country? Is she primarily interested in amassing wealth to have a good time? Is she a revolutionary? Might her parents be the only "good enough" parents in the novel?

These questions are critical to my reading of Lonely Hearts Killer because parents are implicated in the frustrations and rage of several key characters. Inoue, like so many others who struggle to make sense of why they are so angry (even when they might seem to have so much), implode in moments of desperation, hurting others in the process. His rage, as is the case for Yukinori in The Treason Diaries described in chapter 4, connects to his biological parents and to the emperor as parent. Because the modern project of nation building and the consolidation of national identity in Japan has often been expressed in terms of family relationships, it may be necessary to visit any analysis of parenting in Hoshino's fiction with the state and the emperor in mind. Hoshino's experiment in dismantling the imperial house in Lonely Hearts Killer can be seen as a crucial step in rethinking family fictions and their fallout in the lives of youth in Japan today. If the state, as parent, harms, how are individual parents, victims of poor parenting themselves, in any position to provide or create spaces in which their own children can thrive? In Lonely Hearts Killer, Hoshino suggests they cannot unless they create more radical and corrective opportunities for intersubjective connection.

A Case for Reparations

Look around you. Police roadblocks. Police searches without warrants. Politicians and their banker pals empty the U.S. Treasury
while police lock up the homeless and poor who beg for food. . . .
You breeders of child molesters, rapists, and mass murderers! We
are increasing quietly despite your bullets and germ warfare. You
destroyers can't figure out why you haven't wiped us out in five
hundred years of blasting, burning, and slaughter. You destroyers
can't figure out what's going wrong for you. . . . This is nothing!
This is only the beginning!

—Leslie Marmon Silko, *Almanac of the Dead*, 734

Official history, mutilated memory, is a long self-serving ceremony
for those give the orders in this world. Their spotlights illuminate
the heights and leave the grassroots in darkness. The always invisible are at best props on the stage of history, like Hollywood extras.
But they are the ones—the actors of real history, the denied, lied
about, hidden protagonists of past and present—who incarnate
the splendid spectrum of another possible reality.

—Eduardo Galeano, *Upside Down*, 325

Without a political analysis to support or even allow for a vision of
a better world, Inoue's solution in *Lonely Hearts Killer* (discussed in
chapter 6) can only be final—everyone must die; everything must
disappear. For him, "this world is the other world," filled with people already
dead. There is limited room for empathy or solidarity when one cannot hope.

Without hope, even the most understandable and righteous rage can corrode. As I have maintained throughout the second half of this book, it matters little how committed we may be in our disavowal of violence when we remain complicit in the conditions that engender violence. Violent resistance is already happening, and for this reason it warrants our critical attention, even if only for the most utilitarian and self-serving ends. This book also has addressed the desperate measures to which we, adults in the U.S. and Japan (as well as in other places), make our youth resort. We bombard them with mixed messages that aggravate and exacerbate alienation, oppression, exploitation, and abuse. Their ability to identify and respond to what actually grieves them is severely compromised because we blame them for their struggles and, simultaneously, limit their available means of expression. We then call their occasionally violent attempts to express *something* "inexplicable."

We do not prevent violence when we deny youth the opportunity to identify why they are angry and organize relevant strategies to challenge the conditions that fuel their anger; we only guarantee further rage and violence. We do not prevent violence when we tell youth they need to shape up and get *their* acts together. Yet it remains acceptable to blame youth for our own failings, to blame them when they, to borrow a metaphor Hoshino uses in *Lonely Hearts Killer*, poke holes in the screen on which we project a distorted picture of their lives and experiences. I have written this book because I believe it does not need to be this way and that we can, in fact, do better by our youth.

First, we must avoid viewing young people's grievances as isolated or located only in a past experience (of abuse or discrimination, for example). As is the case with other situations in which reparations are due, we must acknowledge that the problem is not *only* a historical one. The violations of the past and the finite periods we might associate with childhood or slavery, for example, are still with us, every day. The effects of child abuse and multigenerational slavery do not end with the emancipation of children or slaves, a reality that survivors and their children (who are also affected) have always been dying, often literally, to tell us. Their ability to communicate the lingering effects of violation has been hindered at every stage by the limited means of available expression, by the distractions and lies invoked to cover up or deny suffering, and by the shoulder-shrugging and hand-wringing conclusion that any complaint or violent "outburst" is "inexplicable."

Every now and then, there are moments of clarity when it comes to the subject of young people's rage. After the Sakakibara killings, the novelist Murakami Ryū was quoted in a special issue of *Aera* dedicated to the problem of "at-risk" youth as saying, "The idea if you go to a good school and get a job with a good company, you'll get ahead is a complete and utter lie. It's unfair for us not to be straight with kids by telling them we are full of shit."[1] Exposing the lies we tell and thinking creatively and expansively about reparations can offer means to acknowledge that past abuse impinges on a victim's ability to thrive in the present. Apologies, public acknowledgments of responsibility are important, and sometimes victims want nothing more than for us to admit to the harm we have caused. However, apologies do not address the material needs resulting from the harm we do. As Norma Field aptly explains in the case of Korean comfort women, "The recipient of an apology can't clothe herself in words."[2] We must also consider reparations as something other than a static tit-for-tat arrangement whereby a monetary amount paid erases culpability. Reparations do not and should not erase historical reality. Rather, they should serve to close the gap between perpetrator and victim or the oppressor and the oppressed and move us closer to societies in which the abuse of power is no longer so likely, so tempting, or so seemingly "natural." We cannot "repair" the past, but we can take reparative action to address the present.

When speaking of the reparations we, as adults, owe to abused, neglected, abandoned, and institutionalized youth, we have the opportunity to radically rethink our relationships and responsibilities to children. Perhaps no group is quicker to eliminate or assimilate itself into the dominant culture. Children are, after all, a temporary—if renewable—population. How, then, do we think about the payment and provision of reparations? It seems to me that a useful place to start would be to begin repairing that which currently engenders abuse and suffering and involving as many of us as possible in that project. By redirecting our resources to serve (and not further traumatize) abused, abandoned, and incarcerated youth, for example, we can work against the differential allocation of resources that very materially give some children access to substantially better opportunities than others. For me, starting the Youth Empowerment Academy (YEA!) at the University of Iowa was an attempt to develop a reparative (or different kind of "corrective") program for youth to whom I feel responsible.

My sense of responsibility had everything to do with unearned privilege from which I benefit due to my phenotypic profile. As a white woman in her forties who occasionally presents as "professional" in public, I am profiled as unthreatening and deserving of courtesy. For example, when I was leaving Japan after a recent trip, no one looked in my carry-on bag as I boarded the plane (even though the carry-on bags of others were searched), and when I arrived in the U.S., no one checked my bags or asked what I was bringing back with me. I was given the nod to move through as the Immigration and Customs Enforcement official smiled and took my customs form without reading it. The primary way in which my phenotypic profile gives me privilege in North America is through the disproportionate lack of contact I have had with the prison regime. To explain what this means in terms of opportunity and material privilege, I will compare my own circumstances to those of someone who has been profiled and punished very differently.

I am two years older than Eddy Zheng, who spent twenty years in prison and now, at the time of writing, faces deportation to China, a country he left at age twelve. In 1986, Eddy was sixteen and charged as an adult for robbery and kidnapping felonies. Since he was sent to prison, I have finished college, worked with youth, earned a doctorate, enjoyed a lengthy postdoctoral fellowship, and found gainful employment. I have been able to spend time with my loved ones. I have been able to eat what I want and sleep when I want. I have enjoyed a reasonable amount of privacy, along with a satisfying social life. I have been able to experience all that even though, like Eddy, I was involved in criminalized activity as a teenager. Although police were aware of my involvement, and the other youth who participated in the actions with me was sent to juvenile hall, I was never charged with any crime.

While much has changed since the 1980s, the reality of disproportionate incarceration has not. In the late 1990s, when my CASA kids (all youth of color) were caught smoking marijuana, punching a wall in frustration, or urinating in inappropriate locations, they were sent to juvenile hall. Much the same can be said of the youth of color with whom I have worked more recently. One eighth-grader was charged as an adult for a very minor act of arson on school property. In high school, I committed a more serious act of arson on school grounds, but no disciplinary action was taken against me whatsoever. This lack of punishment may be unthinkable in the age of "zero-tolerance" policies, but at the time I misunderstood the total lack of consequences as evidence that I was somehow too clever to get in real trouble and not that white women and girls are treated very differently by agents of the U.S. educational, policing, and prison regimes. Despite the high-profile (and extremely brief) incarcerations of celebrities such as Paris Hilton and Lindsay Lohan and the increasing population of white women in prisons, white women and girls are still likely to be seen as having been "led astray" or in need of psychiatric help for the same behavior for which men and boys, especially men and boys of color, are likely to be imprisoned. Of the more than 100,000 women in U.S. prisons today, more than half are women of color.[3] Women and girls of color, as well as transsexual and transgender people of any race, are also subjected to longer prison sentences than their white cissexual and cisgender counterparts.

It was with a deep awareness of how little I have been touched by the prison regime that I arrived at the University of Iowa in August 2005 as a new assistant professor. Shortly after my arrival, I was awarded a University of Iowa President's "Year of Public Engagement" grant for my proposal to develop YEA!, an educational program for so-called "at-risk" youth of color in Cedar Rapids and Iowa City. With the cooperation of a handful of very dedicated school counselors and teachers, the program was introduced to eighth-graders and ninth-graders who were encouraged to apply, and each youth who applied was accepted. The majority of the participants were African American, but a few African immigrant, Asian American, indigenous, and Latino youth also participated. While there were several programs in the area open to "all youth," such programs, as is often the case, do not effectively meet the needs and concerns of many youth of color. Even when such programs seem accessible, many youth of color will not attend. And everyone who worked with youth of color with whom I spoke indicated the need for much more support than was being offered.

The YEA! program consisted of biweekly, voluntary Saturday sessions on topics such as African Americans in the media, writing and performing autobiographies, the juvenile "justice" system, and filmmaking. Twenty-two youth participated, and seventeen had perfect attendance. Youth who had been identified as the most "at-risk" enthusiastically and regularly attended voluntary Saturday programs, asked to bring friends and siblings, and, when the program's funding ended, asked me, "When can we do it again?" They were highly engaged, creative, and willing to think critically. By the end of the program, most of the participants (many of whom had been failing multiple classes) also were beginning to show improvement in their grades at school. Four of the youth went on to earn scholarships to participate in the University of Iowa's Summer Journalism Workshops for high school students. The success of YEA! is not mysterious or simply a matter of luck, my personal skill with young people, or the wonderful volunteer instructors and assistants (all people of color) who shared their time and expertise. It has everything to do with the one message we made sure the youth took away from the program: "There is nothing wrong with you. There is something wrong with our society." It is far too easy for youth to think otherwise. By providing participant youth with opportunities to identify what is wrong with our society (from their perspective) and strategize ways to have the kinds of lives they want, given the realities of racial profiling, disproportionate incarceration, and the like, YEA! served as a space where the youth could develop analyses to explain why they were so angry and figure out ways to negotiate obstacles until we create a better society in which such efforts will no longer be necessary.

When we coach youth to think they are "the problem," we kill their spirits, to be sure, but we also may be killing them more literally. In the spring of 2006, shortly before a nationwide general strike in support of immigrants was to take place, a fourteen-year-old killed himself. Anthony Soltero had organized a walk-out at his school and participated in demonstrations against proposed anti-immigrant legislation. After the walk-out, on March 30, the vice-principal of De Anza Middle School in Ontario, California, called Anthony into the office. During that meeting, the vice-principal reportedly told Anthony, who had been suspended earlier that school year, that he now faced up to four years in prison for his role in the walk-out and that his parents would be fined. Anthony left the vice-principal's office, called his mother to tell her about the meeting, and then went home and shot himself. He died several days later.

If the vice-principal made the reported threats, they may have been baseless. He appears to have had neither the authority to make such threats nor the legal basis to justify them. Anthony's prior experience, however, most likely gave him few means of questioning what he was told. At fourteen, after having been "in trouble" at school, Anthony may have accepted that this white adult in a position of authority had the power to make real the punishment he described. I often wonder about what Anthony thought during those last hours of his life. Did he worry about the financial burden of the threatened fines on his parents, who already struggled to make ends meet? Did he regret his courageous stand with his classmates, his amazing ability to develop a political analysis and express his dissent? Was he thinking about prison? Was he overwhelmed by an anger that he only knew how to direct at himself? None of us can know, but it is incumbent on us to imagine nonetheless.

Empathic leaps require that we try to imagine what it feels like to be someone else. Even in an ideal situation, empathy takes effort and imagination. Without creative empathy, we might too easily accept certain stories (of "evildoers" or "criminals," for example) deployed to justify some people's suffering. The last moments in the life of any young person who commits suicide may be unbearably painful for us truly to imagine, but only by lingering for a while in even the most uncomfortable and awful speculations can we begin to identify the messages (about "personal responsibility," for example) we send that make some youth want to die. If we do imagine what their desperation might feel like, we can better appreciate the urgent need to let young people know that what ails them is not something unique to them or indicative of individual "badness." It is, rather, symptomatic of the societies in which we live, societies that all too often insist that certain victims author their own suffering or are too much like garbage to warrant our concern.

To refer back to the introduction to part 2 of this book, I think we can begin by daring to think, act, write, and even live "off-message." Anarchists are often very good at doing so, and it should not be surprising that anarchist communities can offer welcoming refuge to disaffected and angry youth. Narita Keisuke of the anarchist "infoshop" Irregular Rhythm Asylum in Tokyo provides a radical rereading of both social discrimination and youth violence in his editorial for the twelfth issue of the 'zine *Expansion of Life*.[4] Narita describes what it was like for him to watch television news coverage of the murder of a sixty-four year-old homeless man by two sixteen year-olds, and Narita recalls a news announcer describing how one boy reportedly said, "He was human scum (*kuzu*), so we figured it was OK if he died." The reporter decried these words and described the murder as inexplicable and terrible. Narita, who routinely makes common cause with homeless activists, explains that he initially agreed with the reporter's assessment. Yet he soon felt uncomfortable because, he writes, "The information and commercials [the media] habitually spew out send the kind of overall message that turns the homeless into 'scum.'" Narita shifts the focus away from where the camera was pointed (at the "deranged" boys) and back at the media that reinforces an unequal society's dictum.

It is very easy for me to love Anthony Soltero and grieve his death. It is much harder for me to love the two boys who killed the homeless man in Tokyo. But Narita's response to the latter reminds me that the desperate measures to which some youth resort are measures we make available to them.

The following are only some of the many groups and movements working in different ways to create better possibilities for youth.

The Alfie Roberts Institute
5871 Victoria, Suite 220
Montreal, Quebec H3W 2R7 Canada
http://www.ari-iar.org

Boston Youth Organizing Project
565 Boylston Street, 5th Floor
Boston, MA 02116 U.S.A.
http://www.byop.org

Critical Resistance
1904 Franklin Street, Suite 504
Oakland, CA 94612 U.S.A.
http://www.criticalresistance.org

Education not Incarceration
3280 Morcom Avenue
Oakland, CA 94619 U.S.A.
http://www.ednotinc.org

INCITE!
Women of Color against Violence
P.O. Box 226
Redmond, WA 98073 U.S.A.
http://www.incite-national.org

Irregular Rhythm Asylum
1–30–12–302 Shinjuku Shinjuku-ku
Tokyo 160–0022 Japan
http://a.sanpal.co.jp/irregular

One World Foundation
301 West 110th Street, Suite 3P
New York, NY 10026 U.S.A.
http://www.theoneworldfoundation
      .org

Seattle Young People's Project
2820 East Cherry Street
Seattle, WA 98122 U.S.A.
http://www.sypp.org

VietUnity
Attention: Hai Binh Nguyen
1432 3rd Avenue #4
Oakland, CA 94606 U.S.A.
http://www.vietunity.org

NOTES

Introduction

1. This and subsequent quotes come from telephone conversations between Alfredo Heredia and me that took place between 2002 and 2006.
2. "Shanking" is the act of stabbing someone with a makeshift knife or "shank."
3. The Bandung, or Asian-African, Conference of 1955 was held in Bandung, Indonesia, and attended by representatives of newly independent and other Asian and African countries (such as Algeria, China, Egypt, and India). Chief among the delegates' concerns were the struggle for self-determination and problems associated with imperialism and neocolonialism. For a detailed and informative discussion of the conference and its context, see Prashad, *The Darker Nations*.
4. Ibid., xv.
5. Ibid., xix.
6. For more about the San'ya day laborer community, see Fowler, *San'ya Blues*; Marr et al., "Day Laborers in Tokyo"; Oyama, *A Man with No Talents*; San'ya Welfare Center for Day Laborers website, available online at http://www.jca.apc.org/nojukusha/ san-ya. For information about the rights of the homeless and of day laborers and organizing in the Kamagasaki neighborhood of Osaka, see also Kamagasaki Patrol, website, available online at http://kamapat.seesaa.net or http://kamapat.seesaa.net/ category/164090-1.html.
7. Nakagami, "Amerika, Amerika, aoaza no Mongoroido to shite," 683–722.
8. Quoted in Tucker, "Yellow Panthers," 119.
9. Ibid., 114.
10. See Christian Caryl, "America's Unsinkable Fleet: Why the U.S. Is Pouring Forces into a Remote West Pacific Island," *Newsweek*, February 27, 2007; Eric Talmadge, "Standoff over U.S. Base Closure Sours U.S.-Japan Ties," Associated Press, December 29, 2009.
11. James Fujii made this claim in "The Rise of Local Currencies in Millennial Occupied Japan."
12. The U.S. military and the tourism industry dominate the economies of both Okinawa and Guam, and the large percentage of Guam's total land area occupied by

U.S. military bases (roughly 30 percent) appears likely to increase with recent U.S. Congress's approvals of increased funding ($193 million in 2007) for military construction in Guam and the proposed relocation of 8,000 U.S. Marines (and their family members) from Okinawa to Guam (more than half the costs of which are to be paid by the government of Japan). The details of the 2007 agreement are outlined in a press release posted on the official website of Madeleine Z. Bordallo, U.S. Congressional Delegate from Guam, available online at http://www.house.gov/bordallo/Press_Releases/2006/pro92906-1.html.

13. This encounter is documented in Tsuchiya Yutaka, dir. *Atarashii kamisama* [The New God], film, 1999.

14. Kenzaburō, "Japan's Dual Identity," 189–91.

15. Ibid., 190. Recent examples of the type of relations to which Ōe refers include the Japan Philippines Economic Partnership Agreement and the Japan Thailand Economic Partnership Agreement. For an archive of relevant articles and documents, see the website at http://www.bilaterals.org.

16. This statement is based on seventeen years of teaching experience at the University of Michigan; the University of California, Irvine; Stanford University; the University of Iowa; and McGill University.

17. See the Youth Empowerment Academy, University of Iowa, website, available online at http://yea.uiowa.edu.

18. Khadr, a Canadian citizen born in Toronto and raised in both Canada and Pakistan, was captured in Afghanistan in 2002 and taken to the U.S. "detention camp" at Guantánamo Bay, where he remains imprisoned at the time of this writing for alleged war crimes he committed in 2002 at fifteen.

19. Umezu, *Hyōryū Kyōshitsu*.

20. Ibid., 20–37.

21. Prashad, *The Darker Nations*, 12.

Part 1 Introduction

1. Janice Mirikitani, "In Remembrance," *Making Waves by Asian Women United of California*. Boston: Beacon Press, 1989. Copyright © 1989 by Asian Women United of California. Reprinted by permission of Beacon Press, Boston.

2. Nagata, *Legacy of Injustice*, xi.

3. Emiko Omori, dir., *Rabbit in the Moon: A Memoir/Documentary*, Point of View (POV) series, PBS, 1999.

4. Allison, *Skin*, 36.

5. Allison, "Forum III," 108.

6. Laub, "Truth and Testimony," 61.

7. Ibid., 63.

8. Grewal, *Circles of Sorrow, Lines of Struggle*, 15.

9. hooks, *Black Looks*, 176.

10. Silko, *Ceremony*, is about precisely this power of storytelling to make survival possible.

11. Etinger, "The Concentration Camp Syndrome and Its Late Sequelae," 127–62.

12. Alcoff and Gray, "Survivor Discourse."

13. Ibid., 265–66.

14. Proposition 209 passed with 54 percent of the votes and is now Section 31 of Article I in the California State Constitution. The ballot language did not indicate that the main goal of the proposition was to end affirmative action and gut sex-discrimination laws. Many have argued and sought to demonstrate that some of the voting public (mis)understood the proposition to be a reinforcement of existing civil-rights laws. The text in question reads: "Prohibits the state, local governments, districts, public universities, colleges, and schools, and other government instrumentalities from discriminating against or giving preferential treatment to any individual or group in public employment, public education, or public contracting on the basis of race, sex, color, ethnicity, or national origin."

    Affirmative action was understood or defined by the drafters of the legislation as "preferential" in nature (as opposed to reparative or corrective).

15. The list could be quite long, but two recent examples demonstrate this continuing pattern. In 2004, the conservative pundit Armstrong Williams accepted payment (of $240,000) from the Bush administration for promoting its "No Child Left Behind" policy. In June 2005, in New York City, a white man (Nicholas Minucci) brutally beat an African American man (Glenn Moore) while calling him a "nigger." Randall Kennedy, an African American professor at Harvard Law School, was called by Minucci's defense as an expert witness at trial, and Kennedy testified that Minucci's use of the word "has many meanings." For an interesting analysis on the Minucci case, see Margaret Kimberley, "Randall Kennedy Defends Racist Violence," *Black Commentator*, June 15, 2006, available online at: http://www.blackcommentator.com.

16. The California Civil Rights Initiative continues to be challenged due to its negative impact on access to education and employment opportunities.

17. According to the National Organization for Women (NOW), "White men and women have benefited more than racial and ethnic minorities in state hiring and under alternative admissions criteria to the Universities. White women are the largest beneficiaries, while white men have benefited as veterans, the disabled, and people over 40": "Position Paper: Affirmative Action," *Washington State* NOW *Activist*, January 1998, available online at: http://www.users.qwest.net/waffleck-asch/pp/affirma tive_action.html.

18. Abu-Jamal, who had become the minister of information for the Black Panther Party by age sixteen, went on to become a prominent radio journalist and supporter of John Africa's MOVE Movement. In 1981, Abu-Jamal was arrested for the murder of Police Officer Daniel Faulkner. Prosecutors cited Abu-Jamal's writings while with the Black Panther Party when arguing for a death sentence. For additional informa-

tion, see John Edginton, dir. *Mumia: A Case for Reasonable Doubt*, documentary, Otmoor Productions, 1996, which features interviews with many parties involved in the trial, including the judge and prosecuting attorneys. For more information, see the websites at http://www.freemumia.org and http://www.mumia.org.

19. Noelle Hanrahan's Prison Radio project is the most comprehensive source for Abu-Jamal's recordings: see the website at http://www.prisonradio.org.

20. Evidence that would have made clear that Pratt (also a veteran of the U.S. war in Vietnam and the godfather of Tupac Shakur) was in Oakland at the time of the murder in Santa Monica was actively suppressed during the trial, and Pratt was in prison until released in 1997, when he was granted a new trial and ultimately awarded damages by an Orange County judge. For information, see Olsen, *Last Man Standing*.

21. For a detailed study of COINTELPRO tactics and information on eavesdropping, disinformation and "Black Propaganda," fabrication of evidence, and assassinations, see Churchill and Vander Wall, *Agents of Repression*, esp. chap. 2.

22. hooks, *Black Looks*, 2.

23. Giroux, *Fugitive Cultures*, 62–64.

24. Kingsolver, *High Tide in Tucson*, 254–55.

25. An obvious example is the film *The Spook Who Sat by the Door* (1973), based on the novel by Sam Greenlee that depicts the first black CIA officer, who returns to the Chicago "projects" to organize black youth for a guerrilla war against the U.S. government.

26. See, e.g., Lloyd de Vries, "Letter May Back Yale Claim on Geronimo," Associated Press, May 9, 2006, and Margaret Kimberley, "Nazi Ties, Grave Robbing, and the Bush Family," *Black Commentator*, May 18, 2006.

27. See "Eddie Rickenbacker's: San Francisco Bar Celebrates Genocide and Abuse of Women," *San Francisco Bay Area Indymedia*, April 1, 2005, available online at http://www.indymedia.org/de/2005/04/114137.shtml.

CHAPTER ONE *Survivor Discourse*

1. For example, the jacket cover of Pelzer, *A Child Called "It,"* promotes the bestseller as an "inspirational story."

2. Create Media Project, *Nihon ichi minikui oya e no tegami*.

3. Miike Takashi, dir., *Katakuri-ke no kōfuku* [The Happiness of the Katakuris], Shōchiku Films, Tokyo, 2001.

4. Bruce Wallace, "In Japan, Crimes of 'Hate Beyond Reason,'" *Los Angeles Times*, May 27, 2007, available online at http://www.latimes.com.

5. Article 16 of the Universal Declaration of Human Rights includes the following phrase: "The family is the natural and fundamental group unit of society and is entitled to protection by society and the State." Article 26 includes the following:

"Parents have a prior right to choose the kind of education that shall be given to their children." See General Assembly Resolution 217A (III), United Nations doc. A/810 at 71 (1948), adopted December 10, 1948 (without dissent). A key reason both the U.S. and Somalia gave for refusing to ratify was the issue of military service for teenagers.

6. Chomsky, *The Umbrella of U.S. Power*, 50–51.

7. Jenkins, *The Children's Culture Reader*, 31.

8. Fanon, *Black Skin, White Masks*, 83–108. For an additional discussion of how "the more oppression increases, the more the colonizer needs justification," see Memmi, *The Colonizer and the Colonized*, 119–41.

9. This is also the analytic perspective informing my readings of the two novels (*Fazaa Fakkaa* and *Bastard out of Carolina*) discussed in chapters 2 and 3.

10. Ferenczi's understanding of Orpha is described in his clinical diaries, which have been translated by Balint and Zarday, *The Clinical Diary of Sándor Ferenczi*.

11. Guthrie, *Orpheus and Greek Religion*, 17.

12. Ibid., 39.

13. Ibid., 125.

14. Ferenczi, 25.

15. Ibid., 188.

16. Ibid., 185–86.

17. Ibid., 186. Ferenczi elaborates:

> Since making the discovery [that hysterics lie] Freud no longer loves his patients. He has returned to the love of his well-ordered and cultivated superego (a further proof of this being his antipathy toward and deprecating remarks about psychotics, perverts, and everything in general that is "too abnormal," so even against Indian mythology). Since this shock, this disillusionment, there is much less talk of trauma, the constitution now begins to play the principal role. Of course this involves a certain amount of fatalism. (Ibid., 93)

18. The correspondence between Ferenczi and Freud is cited in Judith Dupont's introduction *The Clinical Diary of Sándor Ferenczi*, xiii.

19. Ferenczi, 205.

20. Freud, "An Autobiographical Study," 34.

21. Ibid., 9.

22. Smith, "Orpha Reviving," 3.

23. Ibid., 26.

24. Ibid., 34.

25. It warrants mention that even stories told from the point of view of a survivor can be read as pornography.

26. Allison, *Bastard out of Carolina*, 124.

27. For detailed statistic and in-depth analyses, see Korbin, " 'Good Mothers,' 'Baby-killers,' and Fatal Child Maltreatment"; Males, *Framing Youth*.

28. Mike Cheung and Cynthia Furey, "DA Undecided on Baby's Death," *New University*, September 29, 2003, available online at: http://www.newuniversity.org/2003/09/news/da_undecided_on_babys121.

29. Associated Press, "Man Gets Jail in Daughter's Death," *Palo Alto Daily*, February 26, 2004, A16.

30. Mai Tran and Christine Hanley, "UCI Professor Avoids Charges," *Los Angeles Times*, October 4, 2003, available online at: http://www.latimes.com.

31. California Vehicle Code 15620.

32. At the time of writing, California Penal Code, Section 192, states:

> Manslaughter is the unlawful killing of a human being without malice. It is of three kinds:
>
> (a) Voluntary—upon a sudden quarrel or heat of passion.
>
> (b) Involuntary—in the commission of an unlawful act, not amounting to felony; or in the commission of a lawful act which might produce death, in an unlawful manner, or without due caution and circumspection. This subdivision shall not apply to acts committed in the driving of a vehicle.
>
> (c) Vehicular—
>
> (1) Except as provided in Section 191.5, driving a vehicle in the commission of an unlawful act, not amounting to felony, and with gross negligence; or driving a vehicle in the commission of a lawful act which might produce death, in an unlawful manner, and with gross negligence.
>
> (2) Except as provided in paragraph (3), driving a vehicle in the commission of an unlawful act, not amounting to felony, but without gross negligence; or driving a vehicle in the commission of a lawful act which might produce death, in an unlawful manner, but without gross negligence.
>
> (3) Driving a vehicle in violation of Section 23140, 23152, or 23153 of the Vehicle Code and in the commission of an unlawful act, not amounting to felony, but without gross negligence; or driving a vehicle in violation of Section 23140, 23152, or 23153 of the Vehicle Code and in the commission of a lawful act which might produce death, in an unlawful manner, but without gross negligence.
>
> (4) Driving a vehicle in connection with a violation of paragraph (3) of subdivision (a) of Section 550, where the vehicular collision or vehicular accident was knowingly caused for financial gain and proximately resulted in the death of any person. This provision shall not be construed to prevent prosecution of a defendant for the crime of murder.
>
> This section shall not be construed as making any homicide in the driving of a vehicle punishable which is not a proximate result of the commission of an unlawful act, not amounting to felony, or of the

commission of a lawful act which might produce death, in an unlawful manner.

"Gross negligence," as used in this section, shall not be construed as prohibiting or precluding a charge of murder under Section 188 upon facts exhibiting wantonness and a conscious disregard for life to support a finding of implied malice, or upon facts showing malice, consistent with the holding of the California Supreme Court in *People v. Watson*, 30 Cal. 3d 290.

33. Tran and Hanley, "UCI Professor Avoids Charges."
34. The public outrage fueled by sensationalized mass media reports of Judge Larry Manzanares's "theft" of a court laptop computer from one workplace site to another and claims that he used the laptop to view pornography are but one recent example of how in some cases professionals can be treated with suspicion. The case of Manzanares, a Latino former city attorney and district court judge in Denver, is particularly tragic in that the unrelenting media speculations related to his personal life led him to resign in February 2007 and kill himself four months later. The media attacks, significantly, came at a time when anti-Mexican and anti-immigrant sentiment in the State of Colorado was especially virulent and Congressman Tom Tancredo's hard-line "deport 'em all" rhetoric occupied space alongside newspaper stories about Manzanares's Internet use.
35. The journalist and essayist Yoshioka Shinobu discusses the case involving the father who beat his fourteen-year-old son to death with a baseball bat in an essay for *Bungei shunjū*, January 1998, 262–79. The lenient five-year sentence was reduced by the judge, who decided the father could be released after three years. According to Yoshioka, the boy had regularly had difficulty waking up in the morning. He had also often expressed suicidal ideations—telling his mother, for example, that he wished there was a big building he could jump off. Yoshioka's account claims that the mother responded by saying that it would be heartbreaking to have her child die before her. Yoshioka gives no indication of her having inquired as to why the boy wanted to die. The father was an elite Tokyo University graduate, and the family appeared, to most whom Yoshioka interviewed, to be "typical" and successful. Yoshioka also notes that the boy boasted about how "nice" his father was on many occasions. Such representations add to the image of the boy as having been to blame, because they reinforce images of the father as loving and appropriate. The father reportedly purchased books on "domestic violence" because the boy had been "acting out" violently at home. Some family members, according to Yoshioka, related incidents in which "everyone was involved in domestic violence." Questions arising from these kinds of media reports will be addressed at length in chapter 4.
36. Masami Ito, "The Diet Lowers Incarceration Age to 'about 12,'" *Japan Times*, May 26, 2007, available online at http://www.japantimes.co.jp.

37. Butler, *Conspiracy of Silence*, 11.
38. Ferenczi, 189–90.
39. Nishizawa, *Kodomo no torauma*, 53.
40. Ferenczi, 32.

CHAPTER TWO Shizuko, the Silent Girl

1. In Japanese bookstores, books considered "women's fiction" are often housed on separate shelves.
2. Naitō, "Re-organizing Gender and Nationalism." Shockey's translation of the talk is scheduled to appear in an upcoming issue of the journal *Mechademia* (*Mechademia* 5: *Fanthropologies*, Minneapolis: University of Minnesota Press). The New Nationalisms East Asia Writers' Symposium is documented on the Internet at http://newnatio nalisms.blogspot.com. *Otaku* generally refers to "subcultures" and the fans and "geeks" associated with them. Anime, manga, and videogame otaku are perhaps the most common examples in the popular imagination. Some liken otaku subcultures to *Star Trek* fan culture (so-called Trekkies).
3. Naitō, "Re-organizing Gender and Nationalism."
4. Ibid.
5. The U.S. State Department maintains lists of countries engaged in human trafficking, particularly as it pertains to trafficking of children. The "tiers" of violators listed in the 2006 "Trafficking in Persons Report" makes clear how even this seeming interest in childrens' (and adults') safety is overwhelmed by other political exigencies. For example, Japan is a "tier-two" nation (not horrible, but not "safe"), and the U.S. is not even listed. Countries at the "tier-four" (or worst) level include North Korea and Iran (representing the "Axis of Evil") and Cuba and Venezuela (representing the socialists): U.S. State Department, "Trafficking in Persons Report," available online at http://www.state.gov/g/tip/rls/tiprpt/2006/65985.htm.
6. See, e.g., the writings of Boye de Mente.
7. The biblical story of Lot (Genesis 19:30–38) includes the following passage after Lot's wife is turned into a pillar of salt and he retreats into the wilderness: "And the firstborn said unto the younger, Our father is old, and there is not a man in the earth to come in unto us after the manner of all earth: Come let us make our father drink wine, and we will lie with him, that we may preserve seed of our father. And they made their father drink wine that night; and the firstborn went in and lay with her father; and he perceived not when she lay down nor when she arose." In the following passages, the younger daughter is described as doing the same, and both daughters become pregnant, eventually giving birth to Moab and Ben-am'mi.
8. Herman, *Father-Daughter Incest*, 38–39.
9. Uchida, *Yarare onna no iibun*, 10.
10. Ibid., 10–11.

11. For excellent discussions of the *shishōsetsu* literary tradition, which does shape public reception in the case of *Father Fucker*, see Fowler, *The Rhetoric of Confession*; Suzuki, *Narrating the Self*.

12. Uchida, *Yarare onna no iibun*, 12–13.

13. Ibid., 195.

14. Staub, "The Use of Fiction in an Analysis," 12.

15. Felman, "Education and Crisis, or the Vicissitudes of Teaching," 55.

16. Uchida, *Fazaa Fakkaa*, 3. Subsequent references to this work within this chapter are in parentheses.

17. Uchida was born in 1959. According to the narrator, Shizuko left home at sixteen, cut off ties with her mother and sister at twenty-seven, and is telling her story at thirty-seven.

18. In the film version of the novel, the stepfather beats Shizuko and locks her inside an outhouse, one of many details changed by the filmmakers.

19. Van der Kolk and van der Hart, "The Intrusive Past," 176.

20. Lanzmann, "The Obscenity of Understanding," 204.

21. The film version of *Fazaa Fakkaa* was released by Fujisankei Pony Canyon Filmmakers.

22. Staub, "The Use of Fiction in an Analysis," 24.

23. Naitō, "Mikan to uragiri," 262.

24. In some works, such as Kōno Taeko's short story "Snow," the "ending" refuses to let us leave, forcing us to examine how the moment came to pass and what it could mean. "Snow" is the story of a young woman, Hayako, whose memories of child abuse are triggered by snow. Hayako decides to venture out into the snow, the source of migraines and a trigger for traumatic memories, and tells her fiancé to bury her in the snow. Then the story suddenly ends, compelling readers to wonder what happens next: Is Hayako, by flooding herself with pain and confronting the abuse, preparing to recover, or is this a moment of surrender? When I have used this text in the classroom, I have found students to be both disturbed and disappointed by the ending, and they frequently have responded to their feelings by creating endings. An excellent translation of this story (and some of Kōno's other works) by Lucy North is available in Kōno, *Toddler Hunting and Other Stories*.

25. Butler, *Conspiracy of Silence*, 119.

26. Brown, "Not Outside the Range," 106–7.

27. Scheper-Hughes and Sargent, *Small Wars*, 22.

28. Underreporting and misreporting of deaths resulting from fatal child maltreatment in both Japan and the United States renders all reported rates of such deaths only the most conservative estimates.

29. Korbin, " 'Good Mothers,' 'Baby-killers,' and Fatal Child Maltreatment," 253.

30. This term is borrowed from D. W. Winnicott and his concept of the "good enough mother": see Winnicott, *Home Is Where We Start From*.

31. Terr, "Childhood Trauma," 70.

32. Ibid., 72.

33. Van der Kolk and van der Hart, "The Intrusive Past," 158.

34. Ibid., 70.

35. Ibid., 159.

36. Ibid., 160.

37. Ibid., 164.

38. Terr, "Childhood Trauma," 73.

39. In the film version of *Father Fucker*, they take a taxi to Hiroki's home, and the mother is nervous, regretting not having worn a kimono. She also thinks they should pick up a cake or other gift to give Hiroki's parents, but the stepfather reminds her that they are not going to visit. Shortly after they begin discussing the pregnancy and the stepfather begins to show his anger, the mother apologizes to Hiroki's parents for bothering them and tries to get the stepfather to leave, but he violently lashes out at her and tells her to "shut up." His ensuing violence is very abbreviated compared with the other violence in the novel. In the film, the stepfather takes Shizuko home with them instead of leaving her at Hiroki's house, and the first scene depicting sexual assault follows closely after. The manner in which the sexual abuse escalates, therefore, is presented differently in the film.

40. While some may contend that sleepovers are not as common in Japan as they are in the U.S., it is very common for abused children in both countries to be isolated from peers. If we read the newness of the sleepover experience as normative, we risk downplaying the noteworthiness of this new experience for Shizuko. If this unfamiliar experience were indeed "normal" in Japan, it would not have required special mention here.

41. Herman, *Trauma and Recovery*, 100.

42. In this passage she calls him her *chichi* (dad), not her "stepfather."

43. Although it is not part of this study, the sequel is equally deserving of critical attention. See idem, *Atashi ga umi ni kaeru made*, esp. 52–76. In an unpublished manuscript, "Women Drawing the Boundaries of Sexual Representation and Practice," Setsu Shigematsu provides a cogent and compelling analysis of Shizuko's "struggle for economic autonomy" in the sequel.

44. Herman, *Father-Daughter Incest*, 71–73.

CHAPTER THREE Bastard out of Carolina

The title of this chapter is taken from the title of a Ruth Brown song mentioned in Allison, *Bastard out of Carolina*, 256. Subsequent references to this work within this chapter are in parentheses.

1. In her doctoral dissertation, Setsu Shigematsu documents and analyzes how some women's liberation activists in Japan made the exposure and indictment of First

World privilege central to their politics: see Shigematsu, "Tanaka Mitsu and the Women's Liberation Movement in Japan."

2. Stories of white women's suffering and redemption abound in U.S. literature and popular culture, from the seventeenth century captive narrative of Mary Rowlandson to the film *Girl Interrupted* (1999).

3. Katagiri, "Blurring the 'Color-Line'?," available online at http://www.49thparallel .bham.ac.uk/back/issue6/katagiri.htm.

4. Smith, *Conquest*, 1.

5. Ibid., 26.

6. Kevin Alexander Gray, " 'Segregation (and Hypocrisy) Forever': The Legacy of Strom Thurmond," *Counterpunch*, March 8, 2004, available online at http://www.counterpu nch.org/gray03082004.html.

7. Gray, "Segregation (and Hypocrisy) Forever."

8. Nicole Larisey Griffith, "Poor Raging Girl: Dorothy Allison's *Bastard out of Carolina*," review article, WomenWriters.net, August 20, 1999, available online at http://www .womenwriters.net/bookreviews/griffith2.htm. Griffith writes:

> Images of blackness are *more beautiful* than the dirty whiteness of the poor white family. And images of *pure whiteness* are utterly repellant. The hierarchy of racial beauty (and power) is thus upset. Allison renders American Indians and African Americans more beautiful than the disempowered and hated white trash community. Moreover, Allison paints socially accepted white people in the most grotesque light of all.
>
> Though the Boatwrights are *physically white*, they are *socially, biologically, and economically colored*. That is, they do not have access to the power which is usually the privilege of whiteness in this country. (Emphasis added)

9. Her Aunt Raylene says, "Don't think about it" (301).

10. In addition to explaining that she started *Father Fucker* to "figure out" why she was in so much pain, Uchida has written about how several scenes in the novel are based on her own memories: see esp. Uchida, *Anata mo ninpu shashin o torō*, 179.

11. Allison, *Two or Three Things I Know For Sure*, 43–44.

12. Ibid., 1–2.

13. Garbarino and Stott, *What Children Can Tell Us*, 9.

14. See "Pursued by Cries," in Sekimori, *Hibakusha*, 86–88.

15. Herman, *Trauma and Recovery*, 96.

16. It is worth noting, however, that Bone does attribute information regarding discomfort her mother experienced while pregnant with her to her mother on the first page. Here, again, we are easily reminded of Shizuko and her mother.

17. Herman, *Trauma and Recovery*, 96.

18. Ibid., 106.

19. Garbarino and Stott, *What Children Can Tell Us*, 80.

20. Megan, "Moving toward Truth," 76.

21. Winnicott, "Physical and Emotional Disturbances in an Adolescent Girl," 369–74.

22. Herman, *Trauma and Recovery*, 101.

23. Ibid., 105.

24. Garbarino and Stott, *What Children Can Tell Us*, 162.

25. Allison, *Skin*, 34.

26. Giroux, *Fugitive Cultures*, 9.

Part 2 Introduction

1. Mark Kitchell, dir., *Berkeley in the Sixties*, film, First Run Features, 1990.

2. For more information on this aspect of the Panthers' history, see Newton, *Revolutionary Suicide*; idem, *War against the Panthers*, the published version of Newton's doctoral dissertation for the University of California, Santa Cruz; Hilliard and Weise, *The Huey P. Newton Reader*, which includes a chapter on the "Panther Bill."

3. This is also the fear expressed by U.S. politicians and experts who feared a global uprising of people of color against the U.S. and Western Europe during the Pacific War. For example, in his essay "Frantic to Join . . . the Japanese Army," George Lipsitz observes, "As far back as the 1920s, the Department of Justice and agents from military intelligence had expressed fears of a Japanese-Black alliance. . . . Similar fears haunted policymakers during World War II." The essay is in Fujitani et al., *Perilous Memories*, 347–77, and Lipsitz, *The Possessive Investment in Whiteness*, 185–211.

4. Shortly after September 11, Saskia Sassen's essay "Governance Hotspots: Challenges We Must Face in the Post-September 11 World" circulated on the Internet and is now available on the Social Science Research Council Archive, available online at http://www.ssrc.org/sept11/essays/sassen.htm. Sassen describes her analysis as "one way of de-centering the discussion in that it is not exclusively centered in the suffering and losses experienced by the US." Ward Churchill is more direct in the opening of his article, "Some People Push Back: On the Justice of Roosting Chickens," September 12, 2001, available online at http://www.ratical.org/ratville/CAH/WC091201.html:

   When queried by reporters concerning his views on the assassination of John F. Kennedy in November 1963, Malcolm X famously—and quite charitably, all things considered—replied that it was merely a case of "chickens coming home to roost." On the morning of September 11, 2001, a few more chickens—along with some half-million dead Iraqi children—came home to roost in a very big way at the twin towers of New York's World Trade Center. Well, actually, a few of them seem to have nestled in at the Pentagon as well.

   Finally, Susan Sontag wrote, "Where is the acknowledgment that this was not a 'cowardly' attack on 'civilization' or 'liberty' or 'humanity' or 'the free world,' but an attack on the world's self-proclaimed superpower, undertaken as a consequence of specific American alliances and actions?": Susan Sontag, "Talk of the Town," *New Yorker*, September 24, 2001.

5. Amiri Baraka released this poem over the Internet, both on his website at http://www.amiribaraka.com and via e-mail. It has appeared widely on the Internet since then, as well as in chapbooks and newsletters. The House of Nehisi Press and Small Press Distribution have also released it in book form as *Somebody Blew up America and Other Poems* (2003 and 2004 editions).

6. Parts of this section are revisions of Hurley, "Abrogating Laurels in an Upside-Down World."

7. Dower, *War without Mercy*, 89.

8. Osayande, "The Backlash against Amiri Baraka and the Repression of the Black Moral Vanguard."

9. Ibid., 8.

10. Parts of this section are revisions of Hurley, "First They Came for Sherman Austin and the Anarchists of Color."

11. Ibid.

12. Fass, *Kidnapped*, 8–9.

13. Ellen Sorokin, "Summer of Fear: High-Profile Kidnappings Belie Trend," *Washington Times*, August 15, 2002, available online at http://www.washingtontimes.com.

14. For example, the San Mateo County Child Abuse Council regularly reports such information on its website, at http://www.smccapc.org.

15. "Explosion in Child Abuse Reported," *Japan Times*, July 24, 2002, available online at http://www.japantimes.co.jp. See also the web pages of the Child Abuse Prevention Center, http://www.ccap.or.jp; Kodomo Hiroba, http://www.geocities.co.jp/Never Land/1015; and Japan Child Abuse Prevention, http://www.jcap.org.

16. Sheryl WuDunn, "Japan Admitting, and Fighting, Child Abuse," *New York Times*, August 15, 1999, A1.

17. Ibid.

18. The publicly available statistics in this paragraph come from the FBI and the San Mateo County, California, Department of Justice in the U.S. and the Japanese government's Cabinet "white papers" on youth. None of the data on child abuse in either country can be considered completely reliable, because the vast majority of abuse cases are not reported.

19. Fass, *Kidnapped*, 8.

20. Ibid., 254.

21. Elaine Cassel, "The Lynne Stewart Case: When Representing an Accused Terrorist Can Mean the Lawyer Risks Jail, Too," *Counterpunch*, October 12, 2002, available online at http://www.counterpunch.org/cassel11012.html.

22. Ibid.

23. Cassel, "Stretching the Definition of 'Terrorism' to New Limits," *Counterpunch*, Feb-

ruary 14, 2005, available online at http://www.counterpunch.org/casse102142005
.html.

24. Steven Salaita, "Islamophobia and the American Presidency," *Pacific Free Press*, December 27, 2009, available online at http://www.pacificfreepress.com.

CHAPTER FOUR *Engendering First World Fears*

1. See Davis, *Are Prisons Obsolete?*

2. The case of Lionel Tate, who was sentenced to life in prison for killing a six-year-old in Florida, reflects how "juvenile justice" is inextricably linked to and affected by social anxieties over "youth violence." Tate was fourteen years old at the time of the killing, which occurred while he was reenacting behavior he had seen on a wrestling program. His competence to stand trial was effectively challenged; his sentence was reversed, and a new was trial ordered in 2003, despite widespread calls for him to be tried and treated as an adult.

3. Janet Knipe, quoted in Catherine Saillant, "Foster Teens Work to Improve the System that Raised Them," *Los Angeles Times*, June 25, 2001, available online at http://www.latimes.com.

4. Dyron Brewer was found dead in his cell in a California Youth Authority (CYA) facility on the morning of September 14, 2004. His was the fourth mysterious death in the CYA in 2004. Brewer had no history of health problems or drug abuse to explain his sudden and mysterious death. Groups such as the Ella Baker Center of Oakland (with its "Books Not Bars" program) have pushed for an open investigation of the CYA deaths.

5. For example, paragraph 4 of California Penal Code 186.22 is an enhancement clause:

   Any person who is convicted of a felony enumerated in this paragraph committed for the benefit of, at the direction of, or in association with any criminal street gang, with the specific intent to promote, further, or assist in any criminal conduct by gang members, shall, upon conviction of that felony, be sentenced to an indeterminate term of life imprisonment with a minimum term of the indeterminate sentence calculated as the greater of: (A) The term determined by the court pursuant to Section 1170 for the underlying conviction, including any enhancement applicable under Chapter 4.5 (commencing with Section 1170) of Title 7 of Part 2, or any period prescribed by Section 3046, if the felony is any of the offenses enumerated in subparagraphs (B) or (C) of this paragraph. (B) Imprisonment in the state prison for 15 years, if the felony is a home invasion robbery, in violation of subparagraph (A) of paragraph (1) of subdivision (a) of Section 213; carjacking, as defined in Section 215; a felony violation of Section 246; or a violation of Section 12022.55. (C) Imprisonment in the state prison for seven years, if the felony is extortion, as defined in Section 519; or threats to victims and witnesses, as defined in Section 136.1.

As is the case in terrorism and security enhancements, gang enhancements tack additional years onto existing sentences.

6. Leslie Neale, dir., *Juvies*, film, Chance Films, 2004.

7. This assertion is laughable according to Magdalano Rose-Avila, founder of Homies Unidos and executive director of the Northwest Immigrant Rights Project. He spoke with Amy Goodman of *Democracy Now!* on April 8, 2005. A transcript is available online at its website, http://www.democracynow.org:

> To think that al Qaeda would get the most identifiable group of immigrants and ask them to bring rocket launchers and weapons of mass destruction—I can just see a bunch of homies, you know, home boys and home girls, saying, "Hola rey! Do you have your rocket launcher? Let's bring it across the border," with their baggy pants, their tattoos, shaved heads. It is not happening. That is a shell game that they are doing. They arrested 103 gang members in this country to say they're doing something about terrorists.

8. The House of Representatives passed H.R. 1279 on May 11, 2005, and the Senate version, Feinstein's S.155, was referred to committee and is not law at the time I am writing.

9. Children's Rights Project, Human Rights Watch "High Country Lockup: Children in Confinement in Colorado," August 1997.

10. Ibid.

11. Bruce Dixon, "Ten Worst Places to Be Black," *Black Commentator*, July 14, 2005, available online at http://www.blackcommentator.com.

12. *Asahi Chūgakusei*, March 15, 1998, 4.

13. See Adrienne Hurley, "Stop the Violence; Kids Are Watching," *Los Angeles Times*, December 16, 2001, available online at: http://articles.latimes.com/2001/dec/16/local/me-15360.

14. Becker, "The Role of Sanctions in the Destruction of Yugoslavia," 108.

15. The following description is typical of the characterizations that the murder was "inexplicable":

> Brazill shot Grunow on May 26, 2000, the last day of classes for Lake Worth Community Middle School. A boy without any history of disciplinary problems, Brazill was suspended that day for throwing a water balloon.
>
> Upset that he would not be able to say goodbye to two friends for the summer, he returned to school with a gun and demanded that Grunow let him see the two girls, who were in his class. When the teacher refused, Brazill shot him between the eyes.
>
> The highly emotional trial featured the testimony of 23 students—including Brazill—and many more teachers and community figures. Several of the children broke down on the stand when recalling the shooting of a beloved teacher by the mild-mannered and well-liked boy.

Sam Handlin, "Brazill Convicted of Second-Degree Murder; Sentencing Looms," Court TV. The article is no longer available online since Court TV has become Tru TV.

16. See, e.g., Jo Best, "Japan: School Kids to be Tagged with RFID chips," CNET Asia, December 7, 2004.

17. Todd Lewan, "Chip Implants Linked to Animal Tumors," Associated Press, September 7, 2007.

18. Richard Stallman, statement entered into the transcripts for the RFID Town Hall Meeting, November 15, 2003, available online at http://www.rfidprivacy.org/2003/townhall.htm.

19. Of course, the use of RFID is not restricted to young populations. Liz McIntyre (http://www.spychips.com) and Annalee Newitz (http://www.techsploitation.com) have been following RFID in the corporate world, where it has been used to track the movements of employees (such as those who have certain security clearances), and the remote tracking of a range of consumer goods. CityWatcher, a video surveillance company in Ohio that contracts with police and the government, for example, implanted RFID chips in two of its employees, an event that was heralded as a first. Newitz went so far as to have an RFID chip implanted in her own arm as part of her ongoing investigation into the device. For more information, see "Ohio Company Implants Workers with ID Chips," *Democracy Now!*, February 24, 2006, available online at http://www.democracynow.org/2006/2/24/headlines.

20. John Solomon, "Government Concludes Some AIDS Drug Experiments on Foster Child Violated Rules," Associated Press, June 17, 2005.

21. Ibid.

22. Jamie Doran, dir., *Guinea Pig Kids*, BBC Two, November 30, 2004.

23. Ibid. See also "Guinea Pig Kids: How New York City Is Using Children to Test Experimental AIDS Drugs," *Democracy Now*, December 22, 2004. A transcript is available online at: http://www.democracynow.org.

24. Norimitsu Onishi, "Japanese Greet Freed Hostages not as Heroes but as Reckless Fools," *New York Times*, April 24, 2004, C1.

25. Naitō, "Literature in Japanese and the Emperor System," unpaginated.

26. Ibid.

27. Ibid.

28. Chie Matsumoto, "Bouncing Back: Former Iraq Hostage Continues Humanitarian Battle," *International Herald Tribune/Asahi Shimbun*, September 18, 2004, available online at http://www.japanfocus.org/-Matsumoto-Chie/1560.

29. Ibid.

30. Onishi, "Japanese Greet Freed Hostages not as Heroes but as Reckless Fools."

31. One glaring example is the case of Sherman Austin mentioned in the introduction to part 2.

32. Reuters, "Peru Rebels Were Executed, Report Suggests," *New York Times*, May 18, 2002, A5.

33. Miyuki Nakajima, "4. 2. 3.," released on *Watashi no kodomo ni Narinasai*, Pony Canyon Records, Tokyo, 1998.

34. Brian Bergstrom, a Ph.D. candidate in Japanese literature at the University of Chicago, has written an exquisite translation of this and several of Hoshino's other stories that are scheduled to be published by PM Press in the near future.

35. Hoshino, "Uragiri Nikki [The Treason Diaries]," 121. "Uragiri Nikki" was originally published in *Bungei* a year earlier.

36. See, e.g., Yoichi Clark Shimatsu's piece on the siege for Pacific News Network at http://www.pacificnews.org/jinn/stories/3.01/970103-red-army.html.

37. *Hajiku* can also be thought of as akin to "snapping" or "snapping off," which is germane to my discussion of the verb *kireru* in relation to youth violence in the next chapter. In his as yet unpublished, excellent translation of "Uragiri Nikki," Brian Bergstrom translates *hajikareta* as "broken." This is a fine choice for communicating the subtle violence Hoshino's use connotes, even though it lacks the "cast off" or "ricocheted" nuances I highlight in my reading. The *hajikareta* people and places are indeed "broken" by the social, economic, and political systems I see as the object of Hoshino's critique in this novella. In an e-mail sent to me on June 27, 2007, Hoshino explained that while he was not sure whether there was any connection between the words *kireru* and *hajiku*, he was hoping to convey a sense of rejection or exclusion (*tsumahajiki*) by using the latter.

38. See the website maintained by the Committee to Free Lori Berenson at http://www.freelori.org.

39. Naitō, "Literature in Japanese and the Emperor System."

40. Maya Jaggi, "Book Review of *In the Forest of the Soul*," *Guardian* (London), February 5, 2005, 20.

CHAPTER FIVE *"Killer Kids" and "Cutters"*

1. Strong, *A Bright Red Scream.*
2. Ibid., xix.
3. Herman, *Trauma and Recovery*, 103.
4. Ibid., 103.
5. See the report by Kjeld Duits entitled "A Murder Case that Could Spell Trouble for Foreigners," at http://www.ikjeld.com/japannews/00000273.php.
6. Okazaki, *Endo obu za warudo.*
7. Itō Yoshirō, "Shonen A no kokuhaku" [The Confessions of Youth A], *Josei Sebun*. In March 26, 1998, 222–23, part of a series about violent juvenile crime, addresses this incident. One of the four boys describes the home life of another boy involved in the rape and killing. He recalls that the other boy's mother was violently abusive. The boy once called the police after his mother had threatened to kill him, and when the police arrived, she asked them to take him away "because a child who tries to break

up this home is not my child." The most detailed accounts of the home lives and abuse histories of high-profile juvenile offenders, such as this one, appear in women's magazines such as *Josei Sebun*, but not in "serious" newsmagazines that target a predominantly male readership.

8. Mishima, *The Sailor Who Fell from Grace with the Sea*, 55.

9. Ibid., 61.

10. See, e.g., the discussion of this novel in relation to the "Sakakibara" incidents at http://members.at.infoseek.co.jp/postx/koube/gogonoeikou.html (in Japanese).

11. "17 sai no ochitsuku" [Self-soothing for 17-year-olds], pt. 2 *Asahi Shimbun*, May 8, 2000, O34.

12. After the series of butterfly-knife attacks that captured headlines in January and February 1998, the *Asahi Chūgakusei Weekly* [Middle School Student Weekly Newspaper] featured regular letters from students about knives at school.

13. Some youth hold very different theories—ranging from the date (April 20) as being a coded reference to "420" (a slang reference to marijuana) to the theory that Harris and Klebold were pawns in a conspiracy to further restrict kids' freedom at school.

14. As will become increasingly apparent in the discussion that follows, child abuse is very often not understood as such. Many adults do not perceive a difference between, for example, "strict discipline" and "abuse," or as is very often the case, abuse is understood to be "discipline" or "moral instruction." The very important distinction between setting appropriate limits and boundaries for children and the abuse of power in adult–child relations is thus frequently masked by conventional vocabularies of child rearing. Thus, any attempt to reveal the connections between childhood trauma and subsequent violent behavior is made more difficult.

15. Males, *Kids and Guns*, chap. 3.

16. Lisa Belkin, "Parents Blaming Parents," *New York Times Magazine*, October 31, 1999, section 6, page 61.

17. A brief chronology of the events prior to the boy's arrest may be useful for those who do not remember them. On March 16, 1997, two girls were attacked, and one was killed. On May 24, Jun Hase did not come home. On May 27, his severed head was discovered in front of the school gate. On June 4, a second letter arrived at the Kobe newspaper. On June 9, police described a suspect, a twenty- to forty-year-old man of approximately five feet, five inches tall. Soon after, people learned of an amateur rock band from nearby Osaka called Sakakibara (using the same characters the boy had used to create his pseudonym) who had put out an independent album with songs referring to people as vegetables and criminal acts with language that appeared in the boy's letters.

18. A news release by Amnesty International (no. 22/04/97, July 4, 1997), expressed concerns that "the suspect should not be '*compelled to give testimony or to confess guilt*' . . . and should have access to a legal advisor at all times '*throughout the proceedings.*'"

19. Copies of the original handwritten letter have appeared in countless publications. I

translated this from a copy that appeared in "Kodomo ga abunai" [At-risk youth; kids are dangerous], special issue, *Aera*, November 1997, 44.

20. The books written by the mother of Yamashita Ayaka, who was also killed by the "Sakakibara" boy, however, beg to be considered in more complex ways. Hase Jun's father has also written a book: see Hase, Jun; Yamashita, *Ayaka he.*

21. Otsuki Eiji, "Naifu to shonen" [Knives and youth], *Chūō koron*, April 1998), 268–79.

22. KTLA evening news, Los Angeles, April 22, 1999.

23. Nationally released video news interview by KUSA, Denver, April 21, 1999.

24. "Kodomo ga abunai," *Aera*, November 1997, 67.

25. Terawaki Ken, "*Gakkō ni ikanai jiyū mo aru*" [You Have the Freedom Not to Go to School, Too], *Shio*, April 4, 1998, 76–85.

26. "Kodomo ga abunai," *Aera*, November 1997, 14.

27. Kadono, *Sukuuru sekusharuharasumento.*

28. Ibid., 33.

29. Ibid., 56.

30. Ibid., 102–8.

31. Ibid., 130–33.

32. "Mō hitotsu no Seija no kōshin kyōgaku shinsō no subete" [All the shocking truth of another when the saints go marching in], *Shūkan Josei*, April 7, 1998, 38–39.

33. Ikeda, *Jidō gyakutai.*

34. Sasaya and Shiina, *Kōritsuita me; idem, Zoku Kōritsuita me.*

35. From a personal interview with Shiina, March 31, 1998.

36. Ibid.

CHAPTER SIX *Lonely Hearts Revolution*

Some sections in this chapter are adapted from my translator's introduction to Hoshino, *Lonely Hearts Killer*. The quotation in the second epigraph is from Hane, *Reflections on the Way to the Gallows*, 66.

1. Although perhaps a forgotten detail, among the initial stories to emerge on September 11, 2001, about who was responsible for the attacks on the Pentagon and World Trade Center was a report that an anonymous caller phoned the offices of a newspaper in Jordan to say that the Japanese Red Army claimed responsibility for the attacks.

2. At the time, according to Naitō Chizuko, "There was an incredible law regarding a 'High Treason Offense,' which ruled that it was a crime even to think about inflicting injury upon the Imperial Household, and the sole sentence was the death penalty. For such a High Treason Offense, the trials were all done in secrecy, and the defendant had the right to trial only once. Twenty-four out of the 26 were found guilty and sentenced to death. The following day, 12 of them were given a reduced sentence of life in prison as a special favor from the Emperor himself. The remaining 12 were

executed just one week later": Naitō, "Literature in Japanese and the Emperor System." For further analysis, see idem, "Monogatari to ansatsu."

3. Descriptions of "investiture" and other official duties can be seen on the official home page of the Imperial Household at http://www.kunaicho.go.jp/e04/ed04-03 .html.

4. In May 1910, Kanno told her interrogators, "Emperor Mutsuhito, compared with other emperors in history, seems to be popular with the people and is a good individual. Although I feel sorry for him personally, he is, as emperor, the chief person responsible for the exploitation of the people economically. Politically he is at the root of all the crimes being committed, and intellectually he is the fundamental cause of superstitious beliefs. A person in such a position, I concluded, must be killed": Hane, *Reflections on the Way to the Gallows*, 56.

5. It warrants mention that Kanno was perhaps one of only three anarchists who may have actually been engaged in some level of plotting an assassination attempt. The others, including the majority of those executed, are now understood to have been uninvolved in any such conspiracy. Of course, as Hélène Bowen Raddeker observes, Kanno was "not alone in painting a picture of life in late Meiji as an escalating fight against power": Raddeker, *Treacherous Women of Imperial Japan*, 189.

6. The closest Hoshino has come to indicating otherwise are a few vague words in the Spring 2006 issue of *Bungei* dedicated to his work, when Hoshino is asked by his fellow author Shimada Masahiko, "How many people do you wish would die?" Hoshino answers only, "Ōgon no hitori" (A golden one person): "Tokushū Hoshino Tomoyuki," *Bungei*, February 1, 2006, 26.

7. Hoshino, "I of the Ambiguous Identity."

8. Hoshino's Internet journal or blog (as well as his Twitter page and archives) can be accessed online here: http://www.hoshinot.jp.

9. Klein, *No Logo*, 311–12.

10. Precarity here refers to the social movements developing in response to actual precarious social and personal situations that are tied to precarious or unstable working situations. For example, the term is often used to refer to low-paying service sector jobs without benefits, long-term security, or possibilities for "advancement." In Japan, activists may carry signs with slogans such as "Hatarakette iuna" (Don't Tell Me to Work!) to draw attention to the actual conditions of temporary and precarious employment. More information is available at http://a.sanpal.co.jp/paff.

11. According to a report by the Mainichi News Service, the "no-sex strike" was organized by members of the Raelian Movement, a sex-positive religious or spiritual community (and not a political or social justice movement) that teaches human life was designed by extraterrestrials.

12. See http://www.insanereagan.com.

13. The following is from the *Mainichi Shimbun* report dated November 7, 2004 (in English):

Niiza, Saitama—Remnants of a homemade mortar were found here Sunday after explosions were heard, possibly set off by radicals to disrupt celebrations at a nearby Self-Defense Forces [SDF] base, police said.

Nobody was injured in the two blasts heard going off just before 9 A.M. about 1 kilometer away from the SDF's Asaka Base, where celebrations were being held to commemorate the 50th anniversary of the country's forces.

Radical guerrillas have been blamed for setting up the mortars, which were found in a forest and had been aimed at the Asaka Base, where Prime Minister Junichiro Koizumi attended a function. Small bomb remnants were found later at another location in a vacant lot. Extremist forces had picketed the celebrations and there was a demonstration held near the base.

A woman who had been hanging out her laundry at the time one of the blasts went off said it sounded like fireworks. She reported hearing at least two men talking and another blast going off some minutes later.

A Niiza resident reported the explosions to the police after hearing the blasts and spotting smoke rising from the area where the devices were later found.

14. " 'Suicide' Bid at Koizumi's Home," *Asahi Shimbun Evening Edition*, August 31, 2005, 023.
15. Naitō, *Teikoku to ansatsu*, 287.
16. Ibid., 303–9.
17. The interview can be read or watched online at http://www.democracynow.org/2003/ 11/17/nypd_attack_benefit_for_anarchist_group.
18. Eric Lichtblau, "FBI Scrutinizes Antiwar Rallies," *New York Times*, November 23, 2003, 1.
19. Molly Ivins, "Free Speech for Peace People," *Sacramento Bee*, November 27, 2003. The column is archived by Creators Syndicate on their website at http://www.creators .com/opinion/molly-ivins/molly-ivins-november-27.html.
20. Ibid.
21. See Churchill, *Pacifism as Pathology*.
22. Silko, *Almanac of the Dead*, 216.
23. Hoshino, *Ronrii Haatsu Kiraa*, 184–87. Subsequent references to page numbers for this work within this chapter are in parentheses.
24. Newton, *Revolutionary Suicide*, 5. (It warrants mention that *Revolutionary Suicide* was originally published by Harcourt Brace Javonovich in 1973.)
25. Ibid., 6–7.
26. Silko, *Almanac of the Dead*, 723.
27. Tomoyuki Hoshino, "Suna no Wakusei," in idem, *Fantasista*, 62.
28. Ibid., 75–76.
29. Naitō, *Teikoku to ansatsu*, 9–11.
30. Setsu Shigematsu is to be credited for this interpretive approach, which she has shared with me in conversations.

31. The film *Totsunyū seyo! Asama sansō jiken* (2001) is based on the memoirs of the police officer turned politician Sassa Atsuyuki.

32. See Mitsuyo Kakuda's afterword in the paperback edition of Hoshino, *Mezameyo to ningyo ha utau*, 144.

33. Masakuni Ōta and Tomoyuki Hoshino, "Gebara to wa dareka" [Who was Guevara?], *Gendai Shisō*, vol. 32-13, October 2004, 12–26.

34. Lucy Fraser's excellent translation of "Chino" at one time was available online on Hoshino's website and the J'Lit Project. Unfortunately, at the time of writing, it does not appear to be available.

35. Suzuki Ichirō plays for the Seattle Mariners in the U.S. and represented and played for Japan in the World Baseball Classic in 2006.

36. Tomoyuki Hoshino, "Sabetsu ha nakattaka? WBC ga matou kurai nashonaruri-zumu" [Wasn't There Discrimination? The WBC Wrapped in a Shadow of Nationalism], *Chūnichi Shimbun*, April 3, 2006.

37. See "Han-nichi sakka Hoshino Tomoyuki no mondai hatsugen" [The Troubling Remarks of Anti-Japanese Writer Hoshino Tomoyuki], available online at http://www.policejapan.com/syakai/20060414/index.html.

38. See, e.g., "Yureitachi no fukkatsusai [Ghosts' Easter]," *Chikuma gendai bungaku taikei*, vol. 91 (Tokyo: Chikuma, 1978). In the story, she writes about "Raten Ameriya" [Latin Ameriya] and "Anguro Ameriya" [Anglo Ameriya].

39. Silko, *Almanac of the Dead*, 513. "Lecha pointed out that the Indians had nothing to do with elections. Whatever happened among the political candidates did not matter to the millions and millions who were starving": ibid., 592.

Conclusion

1. Ryū Murakami, "Kodomo ni totte genki no deru koto ga nani mo nai" [There's nothing for kids to feel good about], "Kodomo ga abunai," *Aera*, November 1997, 14.

2. Field, *From My Grandmother's Bedside*, 156.

3. More information is available online at http://www.incite-national.org.

4. Published in 2005. On the 'zine, see the website at http://a.sanpal.co.jp/u-do-sha/eol/index.html. On Irregular Rhythm Asylum, see the websites at http://a.sanpal.co.jp/irregular and http://irregularrhythmasylum.blogspot.com.

BIBLIOGRAPHY

Alcoff, Linda, and Laura Gray. "Survivor Discourse: Transgression or Recuperation." *Signs* (Winter 1993): 260–90.

Allison, Dorothy. *Bastard out of Carolina*. New York: Plume, 1993.

———. "Forum III: Self-Revelation: The Art of Rewriting Personal History." *Critical Condition: Women on the Edge of Violence*, ed. Amy Scholder. San Francisco: City Lights, 1993.

———. *Skin*. Ithaca: Firebrand, 1994.

———. *Two or Three Things I Know for Sure*. New York: Dutton, 1995.

Becker, Richard. "The Role of Sanctions in the Destruction of Yugoslavia." *NATO in the Balkans*, ed. Ramsay Clark et al. New York: International Action Center, 1998.

Brown, Laura S. "Not Outside the Range: One Feminist Perspective on Psychic Trauma." *Trauma: Explorations in Memory*, ed. Cathy Caruth. Baltimore: John Hopkins University Press, 1995.

Butler, Sandra. *Conspiracy of Silence: The Trauma of Incest*. Volcano, Calif.: Volcano, 1978.

Chomsky, Noam. *The Umbrella of U.S. Power*. New York: Seven Stories, 1999.

Churchill, Ward. *Pacifism as Pathology: Reflections on the Role of Armed Struggle in North America*. Oakland: AK Press, 2007.

Churchill, Ward, and Jim Vander Wall. *Agents of Repression: The FBI's Secret Wars against the Black Panther Party and the American Indian Movement*. Cambridge: South End, 1998.

Create Media Project. *Nihon ichi minikui oya e no tegami* [Letters to Japan's Most Despicable Parents]. Tokyo: YWCA Mediaworks, 1997.

Davis, Angela Y. *Are Prisons Obsolete?* New York: Seven Stories, 2003.

Dower, John. *War without Mercy: Race and Power in the Pacific War*. New York: Pantheon, 1986.

Etinger, Leo. "The Concentration Camp Syndrome and Its Late Sequelae." *Survivors, Victims, and Perpetrators*, ed. J. E. Dimsdale. New York: Hemisphere, 1980.

Fanon, Frantz. *Black Skin, White Masks*, trans. Charles Lam Markmann. New York: Grove, 1967.

Fass, Paula S. *Kidnapped: Child Abduction in America*. Cambridge: Harvard University Press, 1997.

Felman, Shoshana. "Education and Crisis, or the Vicissitudes of Teaching." *Trauma: Explorations in Memory*, ed. Cathy Caruth. Baltimore: Johns Hopkins University Press, 1995.

Ferenczi, Sándor. *The Clinical Diary of Sándor Ferenczi*, Judith Dupont, ed., Michael Balint and Nicola Zarday, trans. Cambridge: Harvard University Press, 1988.

Field, Norma. *From My Grandmother's Bedside: Sketches of Postwar Tokyo*. Berkeley: University of California Press, 1997.

Fowler, Edward. *The Rhetoric of Confession: Shishōsetsu in Early Twentieth-Century Japanese Fiction*. Berkeley: University of California Press, 1992.

———. *San'ya Blues: Laboring Life in Contemporary Tokyo*. Ithaca: Cornell University Press, 1998.

Freud, Sigmund. *An Autobiographical Study*, trans. J. Strachey. New York: W. W. Norton and Company, 1952.

Fujii, James. "The Rise of Local Currencies in Millennial Occupied Japan." Paper presented at the Center for Asian and Pacific Studies, University of Iowa, Iowa City, April 27, 2007.

Fujitani, T., Geoffrey M. White, and Lisa Yoneyama, eds. *Perilous Memories: The Asia-Pacific War(s)*. Durham: Duke University Press, 2001.

Galeano, Eduardo. *Upside Down: A Primer for the Looking-Glass World*, trans. Mark Fried. New York: Picador, 1998.

Garbarino, James, and Frances M. Stott. *What Children Can Tell Us*. San Francisco: Jossey-Bass, 1992.

Giroux, Henry A. *Fugitive Cultures: Race, Violence, and Youth*. New York: Routledge, 1996.

Grewal, Gurleen. *Circles of Sorrow, Lines of Struggle: The Novels of Toni Morrison*. Baton Rouge: Louisiana State University Press, 1998.

Guthrie, W. K. C. *Orpheus and Greek Religion* (1952). Princeton: Princeton University Press, 1993.

Hane, Mikiso. *Reflections on the Way to the Gallows: Rebel Women in Prewar Japan*. Berkeley: University of California Press, 1998.

Hase, Mamoru. *Jun*. Tokyo: Shinchōsha, 1998.

Herman, Judith Lewis. *Father–Daughter Incest*. Cambridge: Harvard University Press, 1981.

———. *Trauma and Recovery: The Aftermath of Violence—from Domestic Abuse to Political Terror*. Cambridge: Harvard University Press, 1981.

Hilliard, David, and Donald Weise, eds. *The Huey P. Newton Reader*. New York: Seven Stories, 2002.

hooks, bell. *Black Looks: Race and Representation*. Boston: South End, 1992.

Hoshino, Tomoyuki. *Fantajisuta* [Fantasista]. Tokyo: Shūeisha, 2003.

———. "I of the Ambiguous Identity," trans. Adrienne Carey Hurley. Paper presented at New Nationalisms: An East Asia Writers' Symposium, University of Iowa, February 25, 2006.

———. *Lonely Hearts Killer*, trans. Adrienne Carey Hurley. Oakland: PM Press, 2009.

———. *Mezameyo to ningyo ha utau* [The Mermaid Sings Wake Up]. Tokyo: Shinchōsha, 2000.

———. *Ronrii Haatsu Kiraa* [Lonely Hearts Killer]. Tokyo: Chūōkōron, 2004.

———. *Uragiri Nikki* [The Treason Diaries]. *Naburiai*. Tokyo: Kawade, 1999.

Hurley, Adrienne Carey. "Abrogating Laurels in an Upside-Down World: The Anti-Baraka Campaign from New Jersey to Stanford." *Left Curve* 27 (2003): 10–15.

——. "First They Came for Sherman Austin and the Anarchists of Color: New Fronts in the War on Critical Thinking and the Criminalization of Youth." *Left Curve* 28 (2004): 100–109.

Ikeda, Yoshiko. *Jidō gyakutai* [Child Abuse]. Tokyo: Chūō kōronsha, 1987.

Jenkins, Henry, ed. *The Children's Culture Reader.* New York: New York University Press, 1998.

Kadono, Haruko, ed. *Sukuuru sekusharuharasumento* [School Sexual Harassment]. Tokyo: Gakuyō, 1990.

Kawai, Hayao. *Kodomo to aku* [Children and Evil]. Tokyo: Iwanami, 1997.

Kingsolver, Barbara. *High Tide in Tucson.* New York: Harper Collins, 1995.

Klein, Naomi. *No Logo.* New York: Picador, 1999.

Kōno, Taeko. *Toddler Hunting and Other Stories,* trans. Lucy North. New York: New Directions, 1996.

Korbin, Jill. " 'Good Mothers,' 'Baby-killers,' and Fatal Child Maltreatment." *Small Wars: The Cultural Politics of Childhood,* ed. Nancy Scheper-Hughes and Carolyn Sargent. Berkeley: University of California Press, 1998.

Lanzmann, Claude. "The Obscenity of Understanding: An Evening with Claude Lanzmann." *Trauma: Explorations in Memory,* ed. Cathy Caruth. Baltimore: Johns Hopkins University Press, 1995.

Laub, Dori. "Truth and Testimony: The Process and the Struggle." *Trauma: Explorations in Memory,* ed. Cathy Caruth. Baltimore: Johns Hopkins University Press, 1995.

Lipsitz, George. *The Possessive Investment in Whiteness: How White People Profit from Identity Politics.* Philadelphia: Temple University Press, 1998.

Malcolm X, "The Ballot or the Bullet." *Malcolm X Speaks,* ed. George Breitman. New York: Grove Press, 1965.

Males, Mike. *Framing Youth: Ten Myths about the Next Generation.* Monroe, Maine: Common Courage, 1999.

——. *"Kids and Guns": How Politicians, Experts, and the Press Fabricate Fear of Youth.* Monroe, Maine: Common Courage, 2000.

Marr, Matthew D., Abel Valenzuela, Janette Kawachi, and Takao Koike, eds. "Day Laborers in Tokyo: Preliminary Findings from the San'ya Day Labor Survey." Los Angeles: UCLA Working Papers, Center for the Study of Urban Poverty, June 2000.

Megan, Carolyn E. "Moving toward Truth: An Interview with Dorothy Allison." *Kenyon Review* 16, no. 4 (1994): 71–78.

Memmi, Albert. *The Colonizer and the Colonized,* trans. Howard Greenfield. New York: Beacon, 1965.

Mirikitani, Janice. "In Remembrance." *Making Waves: An Anthology of Writings by and about Asian American Women.* Boston: Beacon, 1989: 349–51.

Mishima, Yukio. *The Sailor Who Fell from Grace with the Sea,* trans. John Nathan. New York: Perigree, 1965.

Nagata, Donna K. *Legacy of Injustice: Exploring the Cross-Generational Impact of the Japanese American Internment.* New York: Plenum, 1993.

Naitō, Chizuko. "Literature in Japanese and the Emperor System," trans. Maiko Shiota. Paper presented at Representing Change Martin Luther King Week Symposium on the Arts and Social Justice Movements, Stanford University, Stanford, Calif., January 17, 2004.

——. "Mikan to uragiri" [Unfinished and Betrayed]. *Gendai Shisō* 27–28 (1999): 262.

——. "Monogatari to ansatsu: Binpi jiken kara taigyaku jiken wo tsuranuku kindai no seiri" [Tales and Assassinations: The Paradox of Modernity Penetrating through From the Binpi Incident to the Taigyaku Incident]. Ph.D. diss., University of Tokyo, 2004.

——. "Re-organizing Gender and Nationalism: Loliconized Japanese Society and Gender Bashing," trans. Nathan Shockey. Paper presented at the New Nationalisms East Asia Writers' Symposium, University of Iowa, Iowa City, February 26, 2006.

——. *Teikoku to ansatsu: Jendaa kara miru kindai nihon no media hensei* [Empires and Assassinations: A Gender Analysis of the Organization of Modern Japanese Media]. Tokyo: Shinyosha, 2005.

Nakagami, Kenji. "Amerika, Amerika, aoaza no mongoroido to shite" [America, America: As a Blue-Spotted Monogoloid]. *Nakagami Kenji zenshū*. Tokyo: Shūeisha, 1996: 683–722.

Newton, Huey P. *Revolutionary Suicide.* New York: Harcourt Brace Jovanovich, 1973.

——. *War against the Panthers: A Study of Repression in America.* New York: Harlem River, 1996.

Nishizawa, Satoru. *Kodomo no torauma* [Children's Trauma]. Tokyo: Kōdansha, 1997.

Ōe, Kenzaburō. "Japan's Dual Identity: A Writer's Dilemma." *Postmodernism and Japan*, ed. Masao Miyoshi and Harry Harootunian. Durham: Duke University Press, 1989.

Okazaki, Kyōko, *Endo obu za warudo* [End of the World]. Tokyo: Heibonsha, 1998.

Olsen, Jack. *Last Man Standing: The Tragedy and Triumph of Geronimo Pratt.* New York: Doubleday, 2000.

Osayande, Ewuare. "The Backlash against Amiri Baraka and the Repression of the Black Moral Vanguard." *Left Curve* 27 (2003): 5–9.

Oyama, Shiro. *A Man with No Talents: Memoirs of a Tokyo Day Laborer*, trans. Edward Fowler. Ithaca: Cornell University Press, 2005.

Pelzer, David. *A Child Called "It": One Child's Courage to Survive.* Deerfield Beach, Fla.: Health Communications, 1995.

Prashad, Vijay. *The Darker Nations: A People's History of the Third World.* New York: New Press, 2007.

Raddeker, Hélène Bowen. *Treacherous Women of Imperial Japan: Patriarchal Fictions, Patricidal Fantasies.* New York: Routledge, 1997.

Sapphire. *Push: A Novel.* New York: Vintage, 1997.

Sasaya, Nanae, and Atsuko Shiina. *Kōritsuita me* [Frozen Watchfulness]. Tokyo: Shūeisha, 1995.

——. *Zoku Kōritsuita me* [More Frozen Watchfulness]. Tokyo: Shūeisha, 1997.

Sekimori, Gaynor, trans. *Hibakusha: Survivors of Hiroshima and Nagasaki*. Tokyo: Kōsei, 1986.

Scheper-Hughes, Nancy, and Carolyn Sargent, eds. *Small Wars: The Cultural Politics of Childhood*. Berkeley: University of California Press, 1998.

Shigematsu, Setsu. "Tanaka Mitsu and the Women's Liberation Movement in Japan: Towards a Radical Feminist Ontology." Ph.D. diss., Cornell University, Ithaca, N.Y., 2003.

Silko, Leslie Marmon. *Almanac of the Dead*. New York: Penguin, 1991.

——. *Ceremony*. New York: Penguin, 1977.

Smith, Andrea. *Conquest: Sexual Violence and American Indian Genocide*. Cambridge: South End, 2005.

Smith, Nancy. "Orpha Reviving: 'Musing' about Sandor Ferenczi, Elizabeth Severn, and the Treatment of Trauma." Graduation paper, Institute for Contemporary Psychoanalysis, Los Angeles, 1999.

Staub, Dana Byron. "The Use of Fiction in an Analysis." Graduation paper, Institute for Contemporary Psychoanalysis, Los Angeles, 2000.

Strong, Marilee. *A Bright Red Scream: Self-Mutilation and the Language of Pain*. New York: Viking, 1998.

Suzuki, Tomi. *Narrating the Self: Fictions of Japanese Modernity*. Stanford: Stanford University Press, 1997.

Terr, Lenore. "Childhood Trauma: An Outline and Overview." *Essential Papers on Posttraumatic Stress Disorder*, ed. Mardi J. Horowitz. New York: New York University Press, 1999.

Tucker, William. "Yellow Panthers: Black Internationalism, Interracial Organizing, and Intercommunal Solidarity." Honors thesis in Africana studies, Brown University, Providence, R.I., 2004.

Uchida, Shungiku. *Anata mo ninpu shashin o torō* [You Should Take Pictures while Pregnant, Too]. Tokyo: PARCO, 1998.

——. *Atashi ga umi ni kaeru made* [Until I Go Back to the Sea]. Tokyo: Bungei shunjū, 1996.

——. *Fazaa Fakkaa* [Father Fucker]. Tokyo: Bungei shunjū, 1993.

——. *Yarare onna no iibun* [An Experienced Woman's Two Cents]. Tokyo: Bungei Shunjū, 1998.

Umezu, Kazuo. *Hyōryū Kyōshitsu* [Floating Classroom]. Tokyo: Shōgakkan, 1972.

Van der Kolk, Bessel A., and Onno van der Hart. "The Intrusive Past: The Flexibility of Memory and the Engraving of Trauma." *Trauma: Explorations in Memory*, ed. Cathy Caruth. Baltimore: Johns Hopkins University Press, 1995.

Winnicott, D. W. *Home Is Where We Start From: Essays by a Psychoanalyst*. New York: Norton, 1986.

——. "Physical and Emotional Disturbances in an Adolescent Girl." *Psycho-Analytic Explorations*, ed. Claire Winnicott, Ray Shepard, and Madeleine Davis. Cambridge: Harvard University Press, 1989.

Yamashita, Kyōko. *Ayaka he, "ikkiru chikara" o arigatou* [To Ayaka: Thank You for the "Strength to Live"]. Tokyo: Kawade, 1998.

INDEX

Abu-Jamal, Mumia (BPP), 26–27, 227–28
  n. 18, 228 n. 19
Administration of Children's Services
  (ACS), 132–33
admonition to repress, 23, 30–31, 89
adult-child relationship, 32–35, 61, 71,
  174, 242 n. 14
adult children (AC): definition of, 175; in
  Lonely Hearts Killer, 211–13
Alcoff, Linda, and Laura Gray, 25
Alexander, Roberta (BPP), 6–7
Allison, Dorothy: interview with, 97; *Skin*,
  100; on suffering, 22; *Two or Three Things
  I Know for Sure*, 76; Uchida and, 38, 48,
  82–87; on writing, 23; writing about,
  235 n. 8. See also *Bastard out of Carolina*
Almanac of the Dead (Silko), 191–94, 216;
  compared to *Lonely Hearts Killer*, 190,
  196, 210; electoral politics in, 246 n. 39;
  subjective violence in, 198. *See also*
  Silko, Leslie Marmon
Amamiya, Karin, 8
anarchism, 178–89; anti-authoritarianism
  and, 183; criminalization of, 116; in
  early twentieth century, 14; state repression vs., 117
Antiauthoritarian and Anarchist People of
  Color (APOC), 5, 188
apocalypse, 15–16, 94, 202–5
Asama-Sansō incident, 201–2, 245 n. 30,
  246 n. 31

Atarashii kamisama (The New God;
  Yotuka), 8, 226 n. 13
Aum Shinrikyo, 157, 178, 201
Austin, Sherman, 114–17
authoritarianism: anti-, 79, 178–89;
  Japan, United States, and, 4–5
autobiographical fiction, 12, 38, 46, 56,
  65, 75; parallel process and, 48–50,
  82–97. See also *Bastard out of Carolina*;
  Father Fucker

bad self. See self-blame
Bandung Conference, 4, 225 n. 3
Baraka, Amiri, 112–19, 206, 237 n. 5
Bastard out of Carolina (Allison): abuse in,
  38–39, 88–89, 91–92, 96–102; adult
  narrator in, 43–44; dissociation in, 43;
  double self in, 99–100; extended family
  in, 84–86; *Father Fucker* and, 12–13, 38,
  44, 73–74, 85–88, 103; mean sisters
  game in, 92–93, 97, 100; revivals in,
  93–95; storytelling and 13, 23, 82–83,
  87, 92–93; white supremacy and, 76–
  81. *See also* Allison, Dorothy
Bergstrom, Brian, 241 n. 34
Berkeley in the Sixties (Kitchell), 108–9
Black Panther Party (BPP): COINTELPRO
  and, 27; Japan and, 6–7; political theory of, 16, 194–95; self-defense and,
  108–9, 116, 189. *See also under names of
  individual members*

Bob Jones University, 75–79

bomb making: criminalization and, 114–15; in fiction and news media, 140, 161, 185, 244 n. 13

BPP. See Black Panther Party

Brazill, Nathaniel, 129, 239 n. 15

California: Black Panther Party and, 108–10; criminalized political thought in, 115–18, 220; Orange County, 9, 40–42; penal code of, 40, 230 n. 32, 238 n. 5; state politics in, 26, 125, 227 n. 14, 227 n. 16

capitalism, 2, 4, 7, 16, 73, 178–79; human experimentation and, 129–34; prisons and, 123; sexualization and, 47–50

child abuse, 11–12; culture of, data on, 118–19; discipline as euphemism for, 162, 174, 242 n. 14; liberation theory and, 34; oppression and, 39, 41, 61–63; prevalence of, 83, 154, 175–76; psychological impact of, 86, 216; repression and, 42–43; sexual, 56, 68–70, 82–84, 93–95, 101–2, 153, 172–73; social isolation and, 68, 89; the state and, 133, 163; youth violence and, 13, 32, 122–27, 152, 154. See also dissociation; neglect

Churchill, Ward, 110, 236 n. 4

close reading as advocacy, 44–45

COINTELPRO, 27, 228 n. 21

Columbine High School shooting incident, 14, 128–29, 160–62, 169, 198, 202. See also Harris, Eric; Klebold, Dylan

comfort women, 154, 217

Connerly, Ward, 26, 112

Court Appointed Special Advocate (CASA), 9, 44–45, 218

cutters, 151

Darker Nations, The (Prashad), 6, 16

depleted uranium, 8, 135

differential power and violence, 25–26, 109–10, 120–21, 180

direct action, 177–78, 184

dissociation: definitions of, 43–44; depictions of, 12, 56, 95, 140–42, 205, 210; incomplete, 151; mechanisms of, 65–71

Earle, Willie, 79–81

education system, 134, 164–66, 170–74

emperor system: critiques of, 14, 135, 178–87; emperor-lepsis and, 135–36; heteropatriarchy and, 62; top-down relations and, 207; violence and, 191–94

Empires and Assassinations (Naitō), 200–201

enforced terms of address, 64, 90

Etinger, Leo, 24–25

Expansion of Life, 221

False Memory Syndrome Foundation, 32

family fictions, 44, 54–55, 60–61, 103, 214

family values, 33, 39, 119, 152

Fanon, Frantz, 33–34

Father Fucker (Uchida), 12, 49–57, 66–72; adult narrator of, 65, 83; *Bastard out of Carolina* and, 13, 38, 44, 73–74, 85–87, 103; differential treatment of siblings in, 58–60; dissociation in, 43; film adaptation of, 39, 234 n. 39; knife scene in, 71–72, 109; oppression and, 61–63; Orpha and, 38, 88; sequel to, 234 n. 43; social isolation in, 234 n. 39; title of, 46–49

Fazaa Fakkaa (Uchida). See *Father Fucker*

Federal Bureau of Investigation (FBI), 118, 188–89

feeling states: communication of, 93; of fear and rage, 13, 110, 117; levels of, 78. See also *kireru*; *mukatsuku*

When the Saints Go Marching In, 155, 173–74
white supremacy, 76–81, 108–12; abolition of, 144, 190; instantiations of, 2–3,
26–29, 39, 127, 152, 191, 217–19; phenotype and, 120; violence of, 27–28,
194–95
Winnicott, D. W., 99–101, 233 n. 30
World Baseball Classic. See Hoshino,
Tomoyuki
Writers' Caravans. See Hoshino, Tomoyuki

Yamashita, Ayaka, 14, 243 n. 20
Yokota Air Base, 8

Yoshioka, Shinobu, 231 n. 35
Youth Empowerment Academy (YEA!), 9,
217–20
youth prisons, 3–4, 13, 76, 103, 126–29,
166, 218; abuse in, 3–4, 125; comparative analyses of, 122–23; deaths in, 125,
238 n. 4
Yū, Miri, 155–56

Zainichi woroshiyajin no higeki (The Tragedy
of the Worussian Japanese; Hoshino),
204–6
Zheng, Eddy, 218

Adrienne Carey Hurley is an assistant professor
of East Asian studies at McGill University.

Library of Congress Cataloging-in-Publication Data
Hurley, Adrienne Carey
Revolutionary suicide and other desperate measures :
narratives of youth and violence from Japan and the
United States / Adrienne Carey Hurley.
    p. cm.
Includes bibliographical references and index.
ISBN 978-0-8223-4942-6 (cloth : alk. paper)
ISBN 978-0-8223-4961-7 (pbk. : alk. paper)
1. Youth and violence—Japan. 2. Youth and violence—
United States. I. Title.
HQ799.2.V56H87 2011
303.60835—dc22   2010054507